Moral Issues in Psychology

Personalist Contributions to Selected Problems

Edited by

James M. DuBois

University Press of America, Inc.
Lanham • New York • London

Copyright © 1997 by
University Press of America,® Inc.
4720 Boston Way
Lanham, Maryland 20706

3 Henrietta Street
London, WC2E 8LU England

Library of Congress Cataloging-in-Publication Data

Moral issues in psychology : personalist contributions to selected
problems / edited by James M. Dubois.
p.   cm.
Includes bibliographical references.
1. Psychology--Moral and ethical aspects I. Dubois, James M.
BF76.4.M67 1996   174'.915--dc20   96-36306 CIP

ISBN 0-7618-0542-7 (cloth: alk. ppr.)
ISBN 0-7618-0543-5 (pbk: alk. ppr.)

Contents

Acknowledgements

This volume grew out of the second conference organized by the Institute for Personalist Psychology (IPP), held in October of 1995 at the University of Dallas in Irving, Texas. I would like to thank all those who helped to make this event possible, and all those who participated in the conference. Thanks to Glen Thurow and William Frank for inviting IPP to the University of Dallas, for arranging for some much-needed financial support, and for providing logistical support which helped to make things run smoothly. Thanks to Robert Kugelmann, chair of the psychology department at the University of Dallas, for helping with promotion and especially for securing continuing education units for those who attended. Thanks to Nick Healy at Franciscan University of Steubenville for again providing IPP with secretarial support in organizing the conference, and for making Franciscan University the first sustaining institution of IPP. Thanks to Michael Healy, Dean of Faculty at Franciscan University, for providing some of our speakers with faculty support grants which covered their travel expenses. Special thanks to the International Academy of Philosophy for covering the expense of two conference participants. Thanks to Consul William Dirk Warren for providing financial support for one of our speakers. Special thanks to an anonymous donor who helped to reduce debt incurred in organizing this event. I also want to thank Alan Schreck and Mary Kay Lacke for encouragement given during the period when IPP was hardly more than an idea. The entire IPP project has required not only financial, but moral support, and I thank all who have offered this. Special thanks to David and Justine Schmiesing for producing the camera-ready text, and to Jerzy Sokol for proofreading the galley proofs. Thanks to Kateryna Fedoryka for editing the editor's introduction. I am deeply grateful for the volunteer efforts of Andrew Hrezo and Michael Welker; they have helped with thousands of administrative details pertaining to the smooth operation of IPP, and I offer them many thanks. Thanks also to all the members of the IPP board of trustees and advisors for their commitment to the IPP project. Many thanks to all of the speakers at the conference, and hence authors of this volume. Your quality work made this project worth undertaking. Finally, I thank again the International Academy of Philosophy for providing IPP with a grant which helped to make the publication of this volume possible.

Introduction

James M. DuBois

The word *psychology* is used today to describe a number of very different fields of research and practice. However, they all share at least one thing in common: they cannot fulfill their tasks well without confronting and resolving certain moral issues.

The American Psychological Association (APA) has long recognized this fact, and accordingly has drafted ethical guidelines both for those working in clinical and experimental settings. Yet when the APA produced its *Ethical Principles of Psychologists and Code of Conduct* it chose to phrase its specific directives in the form "Psychologists do x" or "Psychologists do not do x." This way of phrasing things neatly avoids the use of ordinary moral language; it does not say that certain things *ought* to be done or *ought not* to be done, nor does it call certain behaviors *good* or *bad*, *right* or *wrong*. To have used such language in an authoritative document may well have opened the door to too many perplexing questions, questions that the APA may not have wanted to deal with. For example: What is an ought, and how does it differ from a statement of fact? Are ethical norms objective and discovered by us, or do they merely reflect judgments about subjective impressions or societal agreements? Does it fall within the scope of psychology to make pronouncements about moral norms, or is this rather the task of philosophers, sociologists or theologians? Do moral norms have anything to do with the flourishing of human nature or with mental well-being? Are there proper moral responses to common psychological phenomena such as hatred, pain and mental anguish? Can a secular psychology of the sort represented by the APA deal with all the moral issues which clinicians face when dealing with clients?

No doubt, one can do psychology without explicitly answering these questions. However, psychologists who consider these questions will find that they *act as though* the questions had been answered in a definite way. They either act as though moral norms were objective and discovered by us, or as though they were subjective or relative to the stipulative acts of society. They either act as though secular psychology can deal with all moral dilemmas, or as though it cannot. Thus,

1

it may be that most psychologists have already answered a lot of these questions tacitly. For the field of psychology as a whole, however, this is not enough. It would be a major theoretical shortcoming were psychologists to fail to investigate explicitly the nature and content of those norms which are so essential to the practice of psychology and of those more general norms that play a significant role in motivating or guiding an even wider range of human behaviors.

The present volume contains, in revised form, the invited papers which were delivered at the second conference organized by the Institute for Personalist Psychology (IPP), entitled "Moral Issues in Psychology." This conference served as a forum in which many different moral questions which concern psychologists, psychiatrists and counselors could be explicitly raised and investigated. A full half of the conference time was devoted to discussion, and naturally this cannot be captured in print. However, this volume should allow the reader to survey the problems which were investigated, and to consider some of the proposed answers. I suspect that it is impossible that any one person agree with all of the views put forth in these chapters (at least without falling into contradiction); but every piece will challenge the reader to consider critically new aspects of the relationship between psychology and morality or ethics.

The topics treated at the conference were diverse, but I think not wholly disparate. I have chosen to publish them under three broad headings, which I hope will serve to draw out the interconnections between papers: Section I— *Fundamental Issues in Moral Psychology and Education*; Section II—*Dealing with Hatred and Pain*; and Section III—*Morality and the Challenge of Naturalism*.

Section I begins with a piece by Marvin W. Berkowitz entitled "The Complete Moral Person: Anatomy and Formation." Berkowitz argues that contemporary approaches to modern moral education too often become polarized and competitive, whereas what is needed is precisely an integration, above all of the cognitive-developmental and the character formation approaches. But before this can happen, we need a comprehensive model of what a moral person is; that is, we need a *moral anatomy*. The moral anatomy offered by Berkowitz is one of the most complete available, and includes the following components: moral behavior, moral character, moral values, moral reason, moral emotion, and moral identity. After discussing each of these aspects, he moves on to consider *meta-moral* characteristics, that is, characteristics such as self-discipline and empathy, which are not moral *per se*, but which support the moral life. With the groundwork laid, he proceeds to ask how we might best educate the whole moral person. Logically enough, he tries to show how parents and school teachers might proceed using the concepts of modeling, just community, character education, dilemma discussion, and love of the good, in order to provide formation of each of the six components of the moral person listed above. Berkowitz does not pretend that he has produced an easy algorithm for producing morally good persons; but he does provide us with an intelligent "road map," guiding us through an immensely entangled network of concepts and models which are operative in the field of moral psychology. His concluding discussion of moral development, moreover, inspires the educator and theorist alike to overcome professional competitiveness in order to appreciate better what is valuable in a variety of systems, and ultimately, in order better to serve the children of today, a task whose importance he rightly insists on.

Chapter Two is entitled, "Moral Goodness and Mental Health." Josef Seifert opens up this piece with the claim that many phenomena in medicine and psychology can be known intuitively, and should be subjected to a rational, philosophical analysis. Among these issues he includes manifold relationships between, on the one hand, moral goodness and mental health, and on the other, moral evil and mental illness or "unhealth." He concedes readily that mental illness is not a moral fault, just as mental health is not a virtue. Further, he acknowledges that a certain degree of mental health is needed in order to be a moral agent. But he claims that the relationships between moral goodness and mental health do not stop at this. Among other things, he claims that mental health requires the ability to distinguish between good and evil, that moral evil can contribute to the destruction of the rationality which is an essential element of mental health, and that morally culpable acts of experimenting with dangerous drugs can lead to states of addiction which severely reduce our ability to be moral agents. This paper, which brings us into dialogue with contemporary philosophers of medicine such as Engelhardt and Roa, as well as many great philosophical personalities including Plato, Descartes, Nietzsche, and Scheler, will challenge many of us to rethink our understanding of mental health.

In Section Two, we turn to consider some concrete problems which arise in clinical practice and direct care. In Chapter Three Paul Vitz and Philip Mango discuss, "Hatred and Forgiveness: Major Moral Dilemmas in Secular Psychology." Vitz and Mango point out that hatred has the characteristics both of a defense mechanism and of something which is maintained volitionally. Hatred serves to protect us from pain, but—as with most defense mechanisms—at a high price. Hatred deprives the one who hates of peace and joy and can lead naturally to acts of hatred. Forgiveness is presented by Vitz and Mango as a healing act, and the proper response to hatred. It is, according to the authors, most often a process which involves stages resembling closely the stages of grieving discussed by Kubler-Ross. Each stage presents its own challenges, and the tendency towards false forgiveness, which can take on many forms, is ever-present. The refusal to forgive is seen by Vitz and Mango as a cause of splitting, a phenomenon discussed by Melanie Klein and others. In this case, the one who hates sees himself as all-good and the object of hate as all-bad—a neurotic illusion if it is true that all of us have done wrong, an illusion which is based on and fosters a victim mentality. The authors go on to note that as persons work through hatred, they almost inevitably must confront their own guilt. Although they have been victims of some wrong, they must face the fact that their hatred has led them to hurt others and to deprive themselves of peace and happiness. Vitz and Mango argue that this presents a dilemma for secular psychotherapy. Freud once wrote: "And now, just suppose I said to a patient: 'I, Professor Sigmund Freud, forgive thee thy sins.' What a fool I should make of myself." Neither the psychologist, nor the patient himself, can forgive the patient for the wrongs he has done. Vitz and Mango argue that at this crucial point "psychology must defer to religion, since psychology has no effective answer to the problem of genuine guilt, or to its correlate, the need for the forgiveness of one's self."

Robert Kugelmann provides us with a thought-provoking fourth chapter, entitled "Becoming Responsible for Pain: Contradictions in Pain Management." Kugelmann notes that psychology has always wrestled with an apparently unreconcilable conflict between freedom and determinism. This conflict and the contradictions which arise from it are manifested in a variety of ways, some of which can be witnessed in contemporary programs of chronic pain management. Pain management programs have increasingly required people who suffer pain to take responsibility for their pain and its treatment. Kugelmann sees this as partly arising as a reaction to a wide-spread gospel of irresponsibility, which encouraged people to assume the role of victims and to look to someone else as responsible for their suffering. Although these two responses to pain differ, they share in common the insistence on holding *someone* responsible for pain. Although the present model which rejects the victim mentality is appealing to many, Kugelmann finds that it makes responsibility a vice, for responsibility is no longer treated as an end in itself, but as a means of managing pain. Moreover, it is cruel in that it hold persons responsible for something they suffer, rather than do. But even more fundamentally problematic is the very the notion of responsibility which is operative here. According to Kugelmann, it is intimately connected to the notion of the "modern self" or autonomous individual. The language of pain management thus becomes one of holding *you* responsible for *your* pain. Kugelmann explores Levinas's analysis of personal existence in order to present a new model of the person, of responsibility and of suffering, one which in the end allows us to speak of "*my* responsibility *to you*."

Section Three, *Morality and the Challenge of Naturalism*, is perhaps the most diverse section, including two discussion sections, one on the source of the ethical norms which govern the practice of psychology, the other on the relationship of psychology to philosophy. The section concludes with a paper on the depth psychology of Carl Jung and Gnosticism.

Though they treat of very different themes, all of these papers in one way or another confront the challenge of naturalism. Naturalism could be defined as the view that everything around us can be understood in terms of laws which govern nature. Nature in this context can be understood more or less broadly. In most contemporary forms, naturalism goes hand in hand with materialism and the doctrine of evolution. But just as Freud allowed for a kind of determinism which was psychic rather than physical (while leaving open the possibility of a future reduction of the psychic to the physical), naturalism has at times recognized the psychic or the spiritual. What naturalism must leave out, however, is a personal God who has designed, who has created, and who governs nature. Moreover, naturalism does not recognize a kind of morality that arises from something other than nature in its present form. For naturalism, moral codes are typically seen as arising with the aim of simply preserving nature in existence, or allowing it to actualize all of its various potentials, including those potentials that are based in the instincts. Foreign to naturalism would be any notion of divine commandment, or of responding adequately to the intrinsic value of certain beings, e.g. the intrinsic value of persons. For naturalism, persons do not differ fundamentally from other animals, in the sense that they constitute a new kind of being with a higher and different kind of value than that of nonpersonal beings. Each of the contributions in Section III somehow deal with the challenge that naturalism poses to psychology.

Chapter Five has been entitled "Can Psychology Discover Moral Norms?" and it includes a two-part debate between Howard Kendler, who would label himself a natural science psychologist, and John Crosby, who might well be labeled a personalist philosopher. The debate begins with Kendler's piece on "Psychology, Ethics, and the Naturalistic Fallacy." The kind of psychology that Kendler represents is behaviorist and prescribes "an *objective (intersubjective)* observational base" for psychology. Kendler insists that we can gain *a sense of understanding* in a variety of ways that go beyond the methods of natural science psychology, but seems to question whether these other methods yield objective knowledge. Crosby, in contrast, believes that all sciences, including psychology, depend on assumptions which can be genuinely known using non-empirical methods, and moreover, he believes that the kind of psychology practiced by Viktor Frankl and others, which allows for the study of consciousness, meaning, and value constitutes a more authentic psychology than does natural science psychology.

Kendler and Crosby share the belief that there is a naturalistic fallacy, that one may not logically move from propositions that assert something *is* to prescriptions that it *ought* to be, or, one cannot move directly from a statement of natural fact to a statement of a moral ought. Therefore, they both agree that psychologists cannot move, for example, from a *descriptive statement* to the effect that abortion causes or does not cause depression in women who have had abortions to the *moral judgment* that abortion is morally good or morally evil. Where Kendler and Crosby disagree is whether there are non-empirical forms of cognition which might allow us to discover moral norms which are universal and objective. Kendler argues, both in this piece and in his reply to Crosby entitled, "Religion and Science," that there is no one moral code which is universally valid, and that this is witnessed in the empirical fact of disagreement about moral issues. Hence, he believes that human beings must design a moral code with the aim of producing a "morally effective society" in which people can "practice their own morality without impinging on the morality of others."

In contrast, Crosby believes that there is one moral order, binding universally on all human beings, and claims that a "moral norm is not called into question when people fail to live in accordance with it, any more than the laws of logic are

called into question when people reason illogically." Crosby further thinks that
natural science cannot operate in a value-free manner, that science itself requires
that the scientist appreciate, for example, the value of getting at the real facts and
of communicating truthfully. Moreover, he notes that there is little intersubjective
agreement within the field of psychology itself concerning the first principles of
the science, that these principles stand in the same boat as ethical principles. Finally, Crosby observes that Kendler has elsewhere mentioned his revulsion at the
idea of "mass rapes, gassing political opponents and shooting innocent bystanders" and asks what should hinder Kendler from "recognizing objective moral evil
in these things."

In his reply to Crosby, Kendler notes that he is equally morally outraged or
repulsed when a victim of rape is denied the opportunity to have an abortion, and
asks whether Crosby will encourage him to see objective evil in this, and if not,
how the disagreement about "what is really there in the moral world" should be
resolved. Kendler seems to acknowledge that there are two questions here, one
epistemological, concerning our (for him alleged) ability to know moral norms,
the other ontological, concerning whether there really is a moral world which contains moral truths which are waiting to be known by us. But, he demands that those
who claim there is such a moral world, capable of being known in an intersubjective
fashion, offer an account of moral disagreement, an account of those factors that
interfere with so-called "value perception" or moral intuition. This has been done
by some philosophers, including Scheler, von Hildebrand, Brink and Butchvarov,
but Crosby takes his reply in another direction, trying to point to inner contradictions in Kendler's position, and clarifying misunderstandings of his own view. The
debate ends, so to speak, with Kendler expressing his worry about the consequences
of an absolutist ethics, namely that it could lead to totalitarianism, and Crosby
expressing his worries about a subjectivistic or relativistic ethics, namely, that it
leaves a moral vacuum which could be filled by anything, including totalitarianism. The debate between Kendler and Crosby leaves many questions unanswered,
but it succeeds in touching on many important issues and in presenting two fundamentally different views of morality, thus allowing one to see how a personalist
and objectivist ethics might try to deal with the challenges posed by a pragmatic
and naturalist ethics.

The next discussion is between Richard Cross and John White, concerning
"Psychology and Philosophy: Points of Contact and Divergence." Cross opens the
discussion with a paper which asks "Is Psychology a Part of Philosophy?", sub-
titled, "The Problem of Induction in Empirical Research." Cross argues that there
are two kinds of psychology, one which is scientific, and one which is inherently
philosophical and a part of philosophy. Each has its own proper method: the scientific using inductive enumeration, the philosophical using natural induction. He
provides us with interesting reflections on the work of Roger Sperry in neuroscience and of Carl Rogers in therapy in order to illustrate the different methods.

In his reply to Cross, White tries to show that the two forms of knowledge discussed by Cross are fundamentally different, so much so that we might consider whether both ought to be seen as species of induction. He suggests that Cross's examples of philosophical induction really present us with instances of direct knowledge, or intuition. White goes on to try to sketch ways in which both approaches may be interpreted realistically (i.e. as having real objects corresponding to the respective forms of cognition). He suggests also some important ways in which philosophical methodology deviates from the naive attitude characteristic of everyday common sense experience, thus making it in its own way scientific. White concludes by proposing the need to consider ways in which scientific and philosophical psychology "complement and, to some extent, interpenetrate each other."

The significance of this latter point is easily seen if one relates this discussion to the debate between Kendler and Crosby. It is commonly recognized that the natural sciences operate using many philosophical assumptions concerning, e.g., the validity of certain rules of logic or the trustworthiness of the senses. But Crosby argued that psychology, and all other sciences, are also guided by certain value judgments which are not known empirically, e.g. concerning the value of truth and honesty. All this perhaps serves to suggest that a *rationally grounded* scientific psychology must be in constant dialogue with philosophy. Likewise, if we consider the body-soul problem which has perplexed philosophers throughout the ages, we see how naive it would be for philosophical psychologists to proceed while ignoring a wealth of scientific information that has been gained about the relationship of mental processes to brain processes. Philosophy often finds itself operating with material gained from the empirical sciences, and rightly so. Although it is important to respect the different objects and methods proper to natural science and philosophy, it is also right to insist on the interpenetration of the two, especially if we wish to develop a psychology of persons which aims to be as complete as possible in its description of human learning, motivation, and mental well-being, to name just a few items proper to psychology. In the end, one finds that the contributions of Cross and White mutually complement each other, in spite of, and partly due to, their differences.

Before discussing the closing chapter of the volume, I would like to cite an excerpt from a 1981 pronouncement of the National Academy of Science, one to which Kendler refers in his article:

> Religion and science are separate and mutually exclusive realms of human thought whose presentation in the same context leads to a misunderstanding of scientific theory and religious belief.

Within the philosophy of science, there have been increasingly many people who, following Feyerabend, have seen the tendency of science to become a world view, and no one could miss the religious character of the *Vienna Manifesto*, which boldly painted a positivist, scientific world view, according to which everything is in theory knowable, there is no mystery, and there would be no meaningful state-ments about things like minds, God, or love. Vitz, in his book *Psychology as Reli-gion* has argued cogently that psychology has become something of a secular reli-gion. However, elsewhere, he has noted another, more positive, way in which psy-chology *could* be related to religion: If all sciences must start with major assump-tions which are not proven within the science, why can't a psychologist build a model of personality using Christian assumptions? In my opinion, the only pos-sible argument against this could be that we prefer a system whose assumptions are nevertheless known to be true using natural reason, even if using non-empiri-cal, philosophical methods. But within a framework that denies the need for this, or the possibility of this (as most contemporary philosophies of science and psy-chology do), Vitz's suggested approach seems valid.

These reflections may help us to appreciate the framework in which Chapter Seven is set. Satinover presents us with a study on "The Gnostic Core of Jungian Psychology: Radiating Effects on the Moral Order." He begins by observing that a "distinctive danger of psychology is that it tends to establish itself not merely as a narrow discipline with access to but a part of the truth concerning man's nature, but as a total *Weltanschauung*, or worldview." Jungian psychology is certainly one such psychology. Moreover, it has been immensely well-received by persons of Christian faith, partly due to the fact that it considers a spiritual dimension, and partly because Jung occasionally refers approvingly to Christ. In this article Satinover is concerned with showing Christians that Jungianism actually finds its spiritual roots in the occult, more specifically in alchemy, and is fundamentally opposed to a Christian worldview and ethics. Jungian psychology contributes to a certain version of naturalistic ethics which encourages us to see good and evil as stemming from the same fabric, namely, nature, and encourages the worship of the instincts. He admits that the contemporary practice of Jungian psychology often proceeds in a way which appears more innocent than Jung's own way. Yet he ex-horts the reader to consider that the great monotheistic religions present us with an ethics of irreconcilable opposites, of objective good and evil, and that this requires us to make hard choices which are ultimately directed towards God. Seen against the background of the debate between Kendler and Crosby, Satinover offers a third view of ethics, a view according to which both natural science and philosophy are inadequate for the task of producing or discovering an ethics; for ethics is tied to the revealed commands of God. I shall not make any attempt to resolve this debate. But I do hope that it encourages honest and intelligent discussion among psy-chologists, philosophers and theologians of different persuasions, with the ulti-mate aim of better understanding the way things really are.

I. Fundamental Issues in Moral Psychology and Education

1

The Complete Moral Person: Anatomy and Formation

Marvin W. Berkowitz

One of the most fundamental and important problems of both psychology and philosophy is the nature of the moral person. This is so not only for theoretical reasons, but also for practical reasons of optimizing the moral formation of our youth. As we approach a new millennium, it may be worthwhile to look at some of the long-standing obstacles to understanding moral personhood and implementing effective moral education as well as to suggest a perspective that offers the potential to transcend those problems.[1] This paper represents such an attempt by presenting an integrative model of the moral person and then suggesting a comprehensive model of moral education based upon that integrative view. First, however, the problems that have subverted recent attempts at effective moral education[2] will be addressed.

I. The Blind Men and the Elephant

Robert Coles (1986) and Alasdair MacIntyre (1981) have argued that modern social science has little to offer in the consideration of moral personhood. Others (e.g., Damon, 1988) argue that social science offers a firm foundation for considering humanity's moral nature and for building community, family and school interventions. Whereas I tend to agree more strongly with the latter point of view, the picture is not as clear as either camp would have it. Typically, social scientists offer many competing theories, methods, and rationales concerning solutions to the problems of youth and, consequently, of society. Unfortunately, too much emphasis is placed on the "competing" aspect and not enough on the "solutions" aspect. Usually the pattern is for various schools of thought to coexist, each with its own set of advocates. The result is a discourse fraught with competition and even vitriolic wrangling over the guiding question: Which theory is correct? (e.g., Kohlberg & Mayer, 1972; Wynne, 1991).

So fundamental has this perspective become, that we lose sight of the fact that this is typically the wrong question. Rarely is it a simple choice between a correct and an incorrect theory. This dualistic perspective ignores the fundamental dialectical nature of science. It also ignores the basic multidimensional nature of human development. As a result we keep trying to explain and control human behavior with very narrow simplistic models, rather than embracing the complexity and richness of human functioning and searching for equivalently complex and rich solutions. As Ryan and Lickona (1987) argue, "current models of moral development and values education are not comprehensive enough to capture the full complexity of human character" (p. 18).[3]

We can identify diverse groups, most noticeably (1) the cognitive-developmentalists who advocate the fostering of universal stages of moral reasoning through discussion of moral dilemmas and democratic school governance models, (2) the character educators who advocate changing behavior by instilling habits through school advocacy, and (3) the "religious right," who propose reducing the separation of church and state in order to rely on religious teaching as the basis for moral education.[4] Within each of these camps, there is also great diversity. What we lack however is any ground swell of integration, synthesis, or unity. We have instead each perspective claiming to be the correct one and vigorously attempting to discredit the others. We continue to suffer the plight of the proverbial blind men and the elephant.

It should be noted that there are exceptions to this monomania. Conceptually we can turn to the work of Jacques Benninga (1988) who has offered a cogent argument for synthesis, to Power, Higgins, and Kohlberg's (1989b) attempt to bridge the cognitive-developmental and character approaches, to James Rest (1985) who offered one of the earliest frameworks for integrating models of moral development, and to Thomas Lickona (1991a) who has argued most consistently and effectively for an integrated approach to moral education (cf. Ryan & Lickona, 1987). Practically, there is the example of the Child Development Project (Watson, Solomon, Battisch, Schaps, & Solomon, 1989) which is a quite eclectic and effective moral education program. Editorially, there is a volume by Nucci (1989) trying to bring the two camps together, and organizationally, there is the Character Education Project which purports to aim for a synthesis of all approaches to moral education as a means of creating a national moral education agenda in the USA. These however are exceptions to the rule and have been fairly ineffective in influencing moral education thus far, perhaps with the exception of Lickona's work. Let us therefore turn to a second explanation of why moral education tends to remain so unidimensional.

II. Humpty-Dumpty

One of the most fundamental impediments to an integrated approach to moral education has been the virtual absence of a comprehensive model of the moral person in the social sciences. The moral person has been shattered into pieces and there are no guidelines for putting it together again.

What we need is a more complete examination of the nature of the moral person; i.e., a moral anatomy. Walker's (1995) critique of the tendency to rely purely upon Kohlberg's cognitive-developmental model could easily be applied to any of the other models we have mentioned.

> But it has become apparent that this pervasive influence has imparted a rather constricted view of moral functioning, which we must now strive to overcome. This constricted view of moral functioning arose from Kohlberg's a priori and consequently restricted notion of morality (following in the Platonic and Kantian traditions in moral philosophy which emphasize justice and individualism) and from his impoverished description of the moral agent. (p.1)

After this analysis of the problem, we will offer a preliminary model of an anatomy of the moral person, with the hopes that this attempt will generate a more concerted focus on the nature of moral personhood.

III. The Tower of Babel

One clear symptom of this disintegrated view of the moral person is a confusion of rhetoric. The literature is rife with terms such as *moral education, values education, social education, character education, democratic education*, etc. Lickona (1991a) titled his book *Educating for Character*, the first section in the book is "Educating for values and character," and, throughout, the terms "values," "character," "moral values," "moral education," "values education," "moral reasoning," etc. are used seemingly as synonyms and with little definition. Ryan and Lickona (1987), in the opening paragraph of Ryan and McLean's *Character development in schools and beyond*, used the following potpourri of terminology:

> Concern for the *values* and *morals* of the young is an enduring adult preoccupation. Down through recorded history, this worry about the *character* of the younger generation is evident. Concern, however, has never been enough to ensure that the young possess the type of *character* that can sustain the individual and society. Some societies have failed to transmit their *values* to the young. (p. 3, emphasis added)

Very few authors attempt to differentiate analytically such terms and few even attempt to explain how they are using them. More frequently they are chosen randomly or for their rhetorical impact.

One can clearly see the parallel to the blind men and the elephant parable. Each group sees morality as flourishing in a narrow realm, embraces models that directly address that realm, implements programs designed to affect that realm, and uses different criteria for choosing labels for their respective enterprises. The Tower of Babel is an apt metaphor.

To comprehend truly how morality develops, and therefore to be optimally able to educate for morality, a fuller understanding of this "moral agent" is a necessity. This is what we turn to next.

IV. A Moral Anatomy

If one were to dissect the moral person and categorize the different moral components that comprise human morality, what would be the constituent parts? I do not mean to suggest that the components to be described here represent the only psychological mapping of morality that is possible or even desirable. Nevertheless, it is necessary to begin somewhere, and these components seem to represent a taxonomy grounded in both psychology and common parlance. At the very least they should suffice to cover most of the terrain and serve as a basis for further discussion.

Moral behavior

Perhaps it is best to begin at the end; and the end of moral education is inevitably behavior. Kohlberg has been (inaccurately) criticized for educating solely for moral reasoning, which was understood to be unrelated to behavior. The point of the critique was that, even if Kohlberg was successful in promoting moral reasoning development, his was an exercise in futility because moral reasoning had nothing to do with how people actually behave.[5] Few would be comfortable with any moral education program that claimed not to affect how students behave. Indeed many opening rationales for moral education programs point directly to the woes of youth and/or society and imply the need to change such undesirable behaviors as youth crime, cheating, unsafe sexual behavior, suicide, drug use, and the like. The opening three pages of Lickona's (1983) "case for values education," the first three paragraphs of the preface to Damon's (1988) *The moral child*, the opening paragraph in Wynne (1991), the opening salvos in Ryan and Lickona's introductory chapter in Ryan and McLean's (1987) volume on character education, and the opening justification of Schulman and Mekler's (1985) *Bringing up a moral child* all focus on a chronicle of the modern ills of youth and society.

Clearly, one central aspect of the moral person is how the individual behaves. Whereas this may appear on the surface to be a simple matter, in actuality it is not quite so simple. One complication is the fundamental question of what counts as moral (or immoral) behavior. Part of this debate centers around whether any behavior can be judged morally. Aristotle (1987) for example argued that behaviors can be right or wrong in their own right. Kohlberg argued that a behavior can only be judged by considering the intentions of the actor. If I attempt to attack you to steal your money and inadvertently save you from a stray bullet that would have killed you, have I acted morally in saving your life? Piaget (1965) studied this issue in children and discovered that the consideration of intentions is a more mature moral stance than a simple reliance on the consequences of behavior.

Fortunately, we need not resolve this question to argue that behavior is a central aspect of being a moral person, for a reasonable argument would be that a person with good intentions who never acts on them is not fully a moral person. Furthermore, even if many acts are morally ambiguous without knowledge of the actor's intentions, many other acts are at least probabilistically morally clear. Sexually abusing a young child or mutilating a prisoner of war would be extraordinarily unlikely to have a morally sound justification, for example; i.e., one would have to envision a very bizarre and remarkably improbable circumstance to ever morally justify such an act.

Hence, the first component of moral personhood is acting morally. But merely engaging in right behavior, as central and important a component as it is, still is not adequate to define completely the moral person. It is hard to imagine a moral hero who does not think or feel, but merely acts according to some moral "program."

Moral Character

What else does it take to make a moral person? Perhaps this question is better understood in light of the first component, moral behavior. If moral behavior is our starting point in defining the moral person, what leads a person to act morally? That is, why do what is right?

The second element I will offer, moral character, is conceptually most closely related to behavior. "The roots of the word *character* are taken from the Greek 'to mark'. It suggests a focus on observable conduct" (Wynne, 1991, p. 139). For the purposes of this analysis, we will define character as personality, i.e. the unique and enduring tendency of an individual to act in certain ways and not in other ways. Lickona (1991b) defines it as "stable dispositions to respond to situations in moral ways—manifested in observable patterns (character traits) of kindness, honesty, responsibility, and a generalized respect for others" (p. 68). Ryan and Lickona (1987) define the character of the citizens of a society as "the extent to which a critical mass of its people hold, find their identity in and act upon a shared moral vision" (p. 3). The Character Education Partnership defines character as "knowing, caring about, and acting upon core ethical values" (p. 2).

It is necessary to digress for a moment and address the difference between moral character and other (i.e., nonmoral) aspects of character. This in itself is a critical and largely ignored issue for moral education and moral psychology. It seems inappropriate to call all of one's character a matter of morality.[6] We can be more or less distractible, or have a tendency toward sloppiness, or be more or less active, and not vary in our fundamental goodness. On the other hand tendencies toward honesty or cruelty could not be considered morally irrelevant in the same way. The difficulty in resolving this problem lies in two issues. First, what counts as a *moral* character trait? Different criteria have been offered and it is beyond the scope of this discussion to resolve this debate. Second, how should we deal with character traits that may aid in moral functioning but are not themselves issues of morality? It is clear that we can identify fundamentally moral character traits as well as traits that aid in moral functioning. (The latter category will be discussed in the section on "Meta-moral characteristics.") It is also clear that a systematic analysis of this categorization of character is needed.

In the past decade or so, character education has returned to popularity (e.g., Lickona, 1993; Ryan & McClean, 1987; Wynne & Ryan, 1993).[7] It relies in many instances on a model of virtue deriving from the work of Aristotle (Power et al., 1989b). The basic argument is that moral behavior must be learned, practiced and then will ultimately be internalized as character or virtue. Right behavior must be demonstrated and rewarded so it becomes a habit. It is the habitual acting coupled with reflection that result in the character trait. This creates an interesting circle with behavior: right behavior is modelled and shaped (by traditional learning methods) which leads to internalized tendencies which produce right behavior. Hence we can clearly see the relation between the first two elements in the moral anatomy: behavior and character.

Moral Values

The third element is perhaps the most ubiquitous, at least in rhetoric if not in fact: moral values. Before proceeding with our discussion it is necessary to continue our examination of moral vs. nonmoral elements. One of the criticisms of the Values Clarification model (Raths, Harmin, & Simon, 1966) is that it failed to differentiate between moral and other values. A teacher would be as likely to be instructed to lead an exercise about tastes in clothing as an exercise about life and death choices. Now while this is an exaggeration, it points to the need for such a conceptual and pedagogical distinction. An excellent analysis of this is offered by Turiel (1983). Turiel distinguished between three domains of social-knowledge: *moral, social-conventional,* and what ultimately became known as *personal* (cf. Berkowitz, Kahn, Mulry, & Piette, 1995; Nucci, 1981). The *moral* domain is distinguished by its universality, unalterability, prescriptivity, and intrinsic potential for harm. Social customs and norms, which are recognized to be particular to a given social context or group (non-universal) and changeable if the appropriate authority so chooses (alterability), are not issues of morality but issues of *social-convention.* Issues which are seen as non-legislatible, which rather are up to one's own tastes and desires, are considered to fall in the *personal* domain. Values clearly can be of any of these types. Moral education should be fundamentally concerned with moral values (Nucci, 1992); i.e., values that concern issues of intrinsic harm and universal prescriptivity. This distinction unfortunately is rarely made. Furthermore, when education concerns social conventions, it must recognize that different pedagogical techniques and claims are appropriate (Nucci, 1992); e.g., one cannot rely on the same justifications and authorities for legitimizing a moral claim (such as the right to control of one's own property) as for a social-conventional claim (such as adhering to one's school's dress code).

A further complication of this taxonomy is that it is both analytical and phenomenological. It is analytical in the sense that a given issue can be analyzed as best fitting one or the other of the domains of social knowledge (moral, conventional, or personal). It is also phenomenological in the sense that any individual may *treat* a given issue as falling in any of the domains, independent of its analytical nature. For example, Berkowitz, Kahn, Mulry, and Piette (1995) have argued that adolescents may phenomenologically experience matters of substance use quite differently than an ethical philosopher might. Numerous studies have demonstrated that adolescents tend not to perceive substance use as a matter of morality and instead view it as a matter of personal choice (e.g., Nucci, Guerra, & Lee, 1991; Power, Higgins, & Kohlberg, 1989a), whereas ethical philosophers frequently consider matters of self-harm as falling within the moral domain.

Despite this confusion, it is important to note that moral values are an important element in the anatomy of the moral person. But what exactly are moral values? Unfortunately this question is not easily answered, in large part because of the sloppiness in the use of the term *values*. Rokeach (1968, 1973) has done the most extensive work on values. He defines a value as an enduring preference for a particular behavior or end-state of being. This includes both a clear cognitive component (a belief) and an affective component (the valuing). Schwartz and Bilsky (1987), more recently, have offered a model of human values that defines values as "(a) concepts or beliefs, (b) about desirable end states or behaviors, (c) that transcend specific situations, (d) guide selection or evaluation of behavior and events, and (e) are ordered in relative importance" (p. 551). We can see that values and character traits are closely related with overlapping definitional features. Perhaps the clearest distinction is that a character trait is a *tendency to act* in certain ways and a value is a *tendency to believe* in the goodness or badness of an action or state of being. Values have more of a cognitive focus based in the belief aspect of the value.

It is also important to note that whereas Rokeach (1973) felt that values are few and central to our being, others use the term much more loosely to refer to anything we favor or disfavor. (For an excellent discussion of values, morality, and behavior, see Shields and Bredemeier, 1995).

From an alternative point of view, values may be thought of as internalized standards, e.g., as the content of the superego from a psychoanalytic point of view. These beliefs are internalized in different ways, depending on one's theoretical orientation. They may be internalized by a process of identification with one's same-gender parent or by simple imitation of significant role models.

Yet another view, although not specifically using the label *values*, comes from Kohlberg's model of the Just Community schools (Power et al., 1989a). Much of this model relies on the notion of norms. Such norms tend to be analyzed at the group level as well as at the individual level. Nevertheless, they closely resemble the notion of a value. Norms are affectively laden beliefs concerning how people or institutions ought to act.

The school, like the government, is an institution with a basic function of main-

taining and transmitting...the consensual values of society. The most fundamental are termed moral values. (Kohlberg, 1967, p. 165)

The "values" or norms that Kohlberg and his colleagues focused on most heavily
in the Just Community schools are caring, trust, collective responsibility, and participation. These norms fall close to those values identified by Schwartz and Bilsky
(1987) as serving not personal needs but relational motives or institutional demands. Perhaps of even more interest for this discussion is the fact that this approach adds some rather unusual aspects to the study of moral values. First, as
noted, they are concerned not only with the values that individuals hold, but also
with the values that communities of individuals hold. Second, they are concerned
with the development of such values as they move from an individual value to a
communal value. Third, they are interested in the justifications for values and how
they develop as well. Lastly, they focus attention on how an individual's stage of
moral reasoning (see next section) affects both whether and how a given value is
held by an individual.

As a matter of expediency, to extricate ourselves from the confusions and
disagreements in the field, we offer the following tentative definition of *moral
values*: Moral values are affectively laden beliefs concerning the rightness and
wrongness of behaviors or end states which are intrinsically potentially harmful
and are universal and unalterable in their prescriptivity.

Moral Reason

One might be tempted to end our moral anatomy at this point; i.e., with the
moral person consisting of behaviors, character, and values. However, to do so
would be to leave us also with the problem of a lack of a moral authority. By this
I mean that we have yet to invoke a basis for determining what is right or wrong
beyond the socialization that a particular individual has received. The question
"Whose values?" haunts the moral education field (Bennett, 1991; Etzioni,
Berkowitz, & Wilcox, 1994; Josephson, 1993). The same question can be applied
to character, although there we can in theory refer back to moral philosophy for a
justification of specific virtues, a recourse that is rarely invoked however (MacIntyre,
1981). Sooner or later, even the highly moral individual with clear and appropriate
moral values and moral character will confront a morally ambiguous, paradoxical,
or novel situation. She will need to determine which value to rely on, to generate
a new value, or choose between conflicting character traits (e.g., honesty vs. altru-
ism). Hence the need for the fourth element, moral reason, i.e., the ability to
reason about moral issues, reach moral conclusions, make moral decisions, etc.
We cannot anticipate all possible moral dilemmas and choices and correspond-
ingly "program" the individual for the values and virtues necessary to act morally
in each instance. A mature moral agent must be able to reflect on a moral problem
and make a rational moral judgment about it. Kohlberg's (1976) delineation of the
stages of moral reasoning development offers the best model for studying and

educating for the growth of moral reason.

It is worth noting that Kohlberg long lambasted the character education field for its "bag of virtues" approach, accusing them of somewhat arbitrarily choosing virtues from among a larger set. Somewhat ironically, Aristotle (1987) argued that the central virtue that provided coherence to the other virtues was practical reason, essentially the ability to reason well. It should be pointed out that, at the end of his life, Kohlberg and his colleagues did attempt a preliminary integration of the virtues model with his own (Power, Higgins, & Kohlberg, 1989b).

Additionally, as noted in the previous section on values, Kohlberg and his colleagues (Power et al., 1989a) focused much attention on the interaction of values and reason. In discussing how moral education (in the USA) is intended in part to promote the understanding of the United States Constitution, they argue that

> Kohlberg is not advocating a literal teaching of the Constitution. Rather, he sees the Constitution as representing the moral principle of justice and claims that it is by teaching "justice" that the schools can legitimately transmit "the consensual values of society." For justice, seen from the perspective of moral development theory, is not a given value, which can be concretely transmitted to or imposed on children, but it is the basic valuing process that underlies each person's capacity for moral judgment. (p. 15)

This analysis is closely related to the argument above that values (norms in Kohlberg's vernacular) are subject to interpretation through the stage of justice reasoning of the individual.

Moral reason is important not only for its relative level of maturity, but also for two other reasons. One may have developed mature moral reasoning capacities, but be unable to apply them in certain situations (Selman & Schultz, 1990). In that case, particular focus must be spent on learning to apply reasoning in those situations. One may also be making certain systematic cognitive errors that undermine the acceptable application of moral reasoning capacities in certain situations (Gibbs, Potter, & Goldstein, 1995).

Finally, as noted earlier, Kohlberg (Kohlberg & Candee, 1984) has long argued for the relation of moral reasoning to moral action. Many of his co-workers (Blasi, 1984; Kegan, 1982; Noam, 1985) have further explored the relation of moral reasoning to moral personality. We can therefore begin to see some of the connections among the first four elements of the moral anatomy.

Moral Emotion

This leads us to the fifth piece of the moral person: moral emotion. "Besides enumerating the *reasons for which* people act or should act, ethics must also call attention to the *energies through which* people are enabled to act for those reasons" (Samay, 1986, p. 71). Samay considers moral emotion to be the "root of the dynamism of moral life" (p. 72), "the general power supply of all behavior...the integrating force of all knowledge and valuation" (p. 73). Indeed, it is hard to imagine a moral person devoid of feeling. Psychoanalytic theory based much of its moral psychology on emotions such as guilt and shame. It is the sensitivity to others' distress that is at the heart of Hoffman's (1987) theory of moral socialization and serves as a major strand even in cognitive-developmentally derived models such as those of Gibbs (1991) and Selman (1980). Major cognitivists such as Piaget (1981) and Kohlberg (1976) acknowledged the central role of emotion in the development of reason. Clearly the degree of emphasis on emotion varies from one theory to another. Some, like Piaget, relegate it to the status of a source of energy but not of direction. Others (e.g., Caputo, 1986) argue that emotion ("moral sensibility") precedes and even controls moral reason. For example, Caputo takes the classically rational model of Kant and argues that Kantian logical principles emanate from a prior emotional sensitivity to others rather than the other way around.

There are typically two broad classes of moral emotion. The first class encompasses what may be called the self-critical emotions. These are emotions that are aversive and signal some form of self-censorship or negative self-evaluation in reaction to an undesirable thought or action. Here we refer to emotions such as guilt, shame, and regret. The second class of emotions are prosocial in nature. They represent some affective reaction to the plight of others. Here we refer to emotions such as empathy, compassion, and sympathy.

Whether moral emotions are understood to structure, fuel, or complement other moral processes such as reason, they are clearly fundamental to any complete anatomy of moral personhood. We have already demonstrated their essential role in the moral anatomy by noting that values are *affectively-laden* beliefs and that character entails knowing, *caring about*, and acting upon core ethical values.

Moral identity

Up to this point, we have endowed our moral person with five anatomical components: moral behavior, moral values, moral character, moral emotion, and moral reason. Once again we can recognize that we have done a fine job in constructing the core of a moral person. Someone who does the right thing, believes in and cares about goodness, consistently shows the personality traits of goodness, feels regret for transgressions and concern for others, and who can effectively figure out what is good or bad is certainly someone whom I would welcome to my world. Yet our anatomy is still incomplete. The sixth component, moral identity, is a bit different, however, from the five preceding components in three ways.

First, it has only recently been taken seriously by psychologists (Higgins-D'Alessandro, 1995), despite earlier statements about its importance by Erikson (1968). Erikson has long argued that the core of the adolescent's central developmental task of self-discovery is development of an ideology; and this ideology is what holds the self (the "identity") together. Second, and related, this component may be the only one that does not develop until relatively late in the formative years; i.e., it may be dependent upon, as just noted, a developmental task of adolescence. It requires, at least for its fullest manifestation, powers of self-reflection which do not develop fully and are certainly not manifested fully until adolescence at the earliest. Third, most recent mentions of moral identity come from the literature described earlier on moral exemplars (Colby & Damon, 1992; Walker, et al., 1995). That is, moral identity seems to be a salient character-istic of the most highly developed moral individuals. That is not to say it is not existent in others, merely that it seems *necessary* for moral excellence.

Colby and Damon (1992) suggest that the notion of moral identity they have observed in moral exemplars is a sense of self as centrally a moral being. "Moral identity is the condition of the self when moral values, principles and perspectives are essential to one's self-definition" (Higgins-D'Alessandro, 1995, p. 1). Moral exemplars, when they think of themselves, think of a self that strives to be moral and for whom being moral is critical to their sense of self. For some people beauty, or intelligence, or athletic acumen, or wealth may be critical to the way they see themselves, but to the moral exemplar being good is at the core of their sense of self. Now we can see from the data collected by Walker et al. (1995) that this characteristic of the moral person is not salient to most people. By asking adults to nominate a moral exemplar and then to indicate what led to their nomination, 568 characteristics of moral exemplars were cited by their subjects. Of these 568, only 6 may be construed as representative of the concept of moral identity (5 citations of being "self-reflective," 1 citation of being "self-righteous"), and these are only tangentially related at best.

We can clearly see that one's self-concept is related to one's behavior; indeed Aronson (1969) based his model of cognitive dissonance on the assumption that we all try to be consistent with our self-concepts and that we generally have self-concepts that suggest we are "good" people. Nisan (1985) argues that we want to think of ourselves as good people and are more willing to forgive our-selves our transgressions if we have been particularly good lately. The more spe-cific notion of moral identity has been elaborated by Blasi (1984) and Davidson and Youniss (1991) as an independent process of personal growth based on experi-ences of mutual egalitarian social coordinations. Blasi argues that

> Morality is more a characteristic of the agent than of either action or thinking; the ultimate source of goodness lies in good will, and good will is at the core of what a person is. (p. 130)

What is most troubling for these authors is how to relate moral identity to moral reason, a problem that we cannot hope to resolve here, but a problem that once again underscores the complexity of the relations among the components of the moral person. The model offered by Higgins-D'Alessandro (1995) comes closest to solving this problem and acknowledging the complexity of moral identity.

Meta-moral characteristics

Earlier we noted that many of the characteristics offered as examples of moral character are in actuality not matters of morality per se. For example, Etzioni, Berkowitz, and Wilcox (1994) offer self-discipline and empathy as the foundation of moral character, yet both may serve nefarious as well as moral ends. Grim, Kohlberg, and White (1968) empirically demonstrated the mediating role of attention in controlling cheating behavior, yet attention was shown to serve both resistance to temptation *and* attempts at cheating. Samay's (1986) concept of moral emotion and many of the characteristics of moral exemplars observed by Colby and Damon (1992) may also fit this category of characteristics that are not intrinsically moral but may *serve* moral ends. Indeed, Aristotle (1987) argued that practical reason, while not being clearly a moral character trait in itself, was the character trait that made the virtues possible.

By meta-moral characteristics we mean to denote those characteristics of the moral person that are not moral in themselves but serve to aid in moral functioning. It is difficult to imagine a person acting consistently morally without self-discipline, but it should be obvious that self-discipline is not intrinsically moral. Successful criminals and hedonists need self-discipline as well. It should be noted that we do not include in this category characteristics that a school or family may deem important but that is neither moral nor an aid to moral functioning; e.g., neatness. These are social-conventions that may have ample justification for inclusion in education or parenting emphases, but those justifications are not moral justifications.

When Wynne and Ryan (1993) assert that moral education should focus on "such long-honoured educational concerns as teaching character, academics, and discipline" (p. v), they are mixing moral and meta-moral characteristics. By character they tend to refer to moral character. But in academics and discipline, they are referring to aspects of the person that can serve morality but can also serve nefarious ends as well, i.e., meta-moral characteristics. We have thus identified six fundamentally moral components of the moral person, but have pointed out that we ought not ignore those aspects of the person that are not intrinsically moral but that nonetheless aid in moral functioning. More than morality is required to function morally (Rest, 1985).

Our moral person then has seven central elements: behavior, character, values, reason, emotion, identity, and meta-moral characteristics. It should be clear from the preceding discussion that these elements are not merely independent additive dimensions. They intimately interact and even overlap. To be a moral person is to have all of these elements and to have them in balance and harmony, working together.

V. The Moral Education of the Entire Moral Person

Even if one is still with me up to this point, i.e., in accepting that moral theorists are too fractionated and parochial and that we need an adequate model of the moral person, and even if one finds no major flaws in the proposed moral anatomy, it is at this juncture that agreement typically falls apart. How do we go about educating the moral person? Most theorists and practitioners entrench at this point, either because they are willing to *theoretically* accept an integrated model but not to practically implement it or because they remain blind and never really see more than the part of the elephant they are holding.

Parenting for morality

In discussing a comprehensive view of moral education, I am including extramural education as well. Clearly, the family is the predominant player in this aspect of moral formation. Let us begin there. There are two ways that we can approach preschool moral education: socialization of the preschool infant and training of parents. I will cover these topics only superficially, because my primary goal is to address moral education in schools.

To raise a child with the foundations for morality in the preschool years, one needs to address (1) the quality of the child's relationships, especially to the most significant others in the child's life (Magid & McKelvey, 1987), (2) the teaching of behavior patterns, including discipline and guidance, (3) the modeled behavior that the child is exposed to, and (4) the decision-making procedures and communication patterns of the family (Berkowitz, 1992). Clearly these are overlapping domains. We know that children develop healthier personalities and the tendency to develop appropriate healthy relationships with others if their caretakers are loving, consistent, responsive, appropriate, and sensitive to the child's signals. We also know that teaching of behavior is most effective when based on reward for desired behavior and not on punishment for undesired behavior. Furthermore, explaining one's responses to the child's behaviors, especially by highlighting consequences and affective responses, is critical to healthy child development. As regards role models, children are more likely to do as you do than as you say. Hence, it is very important for significant others to behave in the ways they advocate and the ways they want children to behave. Finally, it is clear as well that families that rely on authoritarian power assertion, strict unidirectional hierarchical decision-making, and a clear oppressive class structure produce less healthy and less moral children.

In contrast, families need to rely on open communication, group democratic decision-making, and general respect for children and their contributions to family issues. Clearly this latter suggestion becomes more operative as children reach school age, but it needs to begin earlier if it is to become a habit in the Aristotelian sense (Lickona, 1983). How to get parents to adopt this prescription is ultimately the challenge for family-based moral education. Parent training is clearly a key to this project. Some authors go so far as to suggest that no one should be allowed to raise a child without appropriate training (Westman, 1994), whereas most simply suggest good parenting techniques (Damon, 1988; Lickona, 1983; Schulman & Mekler, 1985). Regardless of whether or not one adopts a legal mandate perspective, it is clear that training parents to raise children is a critical component in a comprehensive approach to moral education.

Educating for morality
What then becomes the role of the school in the moral formation of the child? It can be seen in two ways: facilitation or remediation. Moral education in the school is facilitative if it complements the positive effects of the family on moral formation. It is remediative if it replaces or corrects for the absent or negative influences of the family. This difference is often embodied in debates over "Whose fault?" or "Whose responsibility?" in moral education, the family or the school. For the purposes of this discussion, however, it is not necessary to dwell on this difference.

Let us then turn to the moral anatomy and examine how the schools can optimally impact on the development of selected components. To discuss all seven components would be beyond the scope of this discussion. Furthermore, many of these components (e.g., moral identity) are not typically discussed in educational models. Hence, only moral values, character, reasoning, and emotion will be discussed here. It is important nonetheless to recognize the interrelatedness of all of the components.

Educating for values
Recall that values refer to the beliefs that children hold as to what is or isn't important, in a moral sense. Historically, there have been three general approaches to educating for values: values clarification, values inculcation, and the Just Community. These three approaches roughly parallel the trichotomy that Kohlberg applied to moral education (Kohlberg & Mayer, 1972). Values clarification holds that each person must generate his or her own set of moral values and education should merely provide the means for self-exploration and self-knowledge. Values inculcation, on the other hand contends that it is the school's role to educate children toward a values consensus. The Just Community considers values (norms) to be a product of the life of the school, most notably its moral atmosphere and governance structure. We will leave the values clarification approach aside, given its demise due to legitimate procedural and theoretical criticisms during the past decade or two.

Values inculcation typically involves messages about the value of selected behavior patterns; e.g., the desirability of loyalty or courage or honesty. How these messages are communicated can vary; e.g., poster campaigns, literature readings, electronic media presentations, lectures, etc. In any case, students are typically exposed to a variety of sorts of messages that convey the importance of the value in question. These may be followed with a variety of student activities aimed at reinforcing and elaborating the value, e.g., classroom discussion, written essay assignments, the creation of posters for the school, biographical reports on moral exemplars, etc. Many schools or classrooms will declare a "Value of the day/ week/month" and concentrate on that value until the next value becomes operative. Clearly, schools that rely purely on the advocacy of values miss many of the sources of values development. Perhaps the most glaring is the way values are lived in the school. This includes the hidden curriculum and the modeling by authorities. Values must not only be espoused but must be acted upon (Argyris & Schon, 1989).

We must remember that values come from a variety of sources. They can be derived from teaching, that is from explicit verbal advocacy. They can be learned from modeling, that is from the behavior of others. They can be learned both from individuals and from institutions. They can be learned from traditional authorities (e.g., teachers) and from peers. Hence schools must be concerned with many mechanisms and sources of values education. That indeed is the power of discovering the "hidden curriculum" of a school.

What then should be the source of values selected for inculcation via the curriculum (broadly defined)? Generally, two approaches are taken. One is to search for a universal set of values (Josephson, 1993). The other is to allow local generation of a set of values. The locality can vary from the nation, state, or region, to the local community, school district, school, or even classroom. In some cases, governments include a list of values to be taught in their education legislation (Arizona Department of Education, 1990). In other cases, such as the Sweet Home Central School District in New York, schools are encouraged to choose their own value lists, although with guidance and the suggestion that they focus on "the kind of human values that can be taught in public schools with literally no objection. These are values that are nonreligious, civic, democratic, human values that we often refer to as 'core values'" (Sweet Home Central School District, 1991).

How should this quandary be resolved? Not easily, I am afraid. Nevertheless, we can gain some insight by addressing the question of justification. First of all, we must return to the distinction between moral and other values. Those values that are not moral in nature require a different sort of justification than required by those that are moral. Personal values can be justified merely by an individual's choice; e.g., the preference for wool or cotton socks is purely a matter of personal choice. Social-conventional values are justified, on the other hand, by social agreement. Here the community can legitimately exercise authority over values; e.g., whether it is better to wear a uniform to school or not. Finally, moral values require yet a different sort of justification. They are not open to local or individual tastes. The justification for moral values lies intrinsically in the nature of the behavior in question. Theft of property derives others of their rightful property regardless of local opinions. Battery produces physical distress regardless of personal tastes. These are universal intrinsic characteristics of the actions themselves.

Hence their valuing cannot be questioned.[8] Clearly localities may select for emphasis different subsets of moral values from among the entire set. What they may *not* choose to do, however, is teach values that contradict universal values; e.g., it would not be permissible to teach "finders keepers, losers weepers" or "might makes right." Such values are ethically unjustifiable. Often, our democratic system is invoked as a justification for local determination of moral values. This can be appropriate in matters of moral ambiguity, but democracy was never intended to make morality a matter of public taste.

Therefore, selecting values for one's moral education program is legitimate, as long as the values selected are either (1) nonmoral or (2) morally justifiable. Local tastes are not adequate rationales for generating or justifying moral values.

If indeed values are beliefs, then we can learn much from the social science literature on attitude change. A vast body of literature has examined how best to manage changing attitudes. There is however a very important caution here. The technology of attitude change is not always ethically justifiable. Brainwashing for example is a form of attitude change. Indeed, some totalitarian regimes have devised forms of values education that are immoral. This points to an important lesson: one cannot advocate forms of moral education that are not in themselves morally justifiable and still retain legitimacy as a moral educator.

This brings us back once again to the notion that values can come from a variety of sources. The Just Community schools rely upon both the advocacy of authorities (e.g., teachers) and the power of the peer group in identifying and instilling values. This approach also relies on the power of the democratic process, the valuing process of justice, and the attachment of the students to the community they have formed in their school setting. Resulting values therefore will likely be just, communal, and strongly held (Power et al., 1989b).

There is no reason why moral values education can not rely on a hybrid of these two approaches: inculcation of a set of justifiable moral values and democratic communal self-regulation of the values agenda.

Educating for character

The flourishing character education movement is largely compatible with the values education issues discussed above. However, there is one significant difference. Character should produce personality development whereas value education should alter beliefs. Character education therefore needs to move beyond simple advocacy of desired behavioral tendencies. Character education can and should include a focus on the inculcation of beliefs, but must extend beyond that. Its primary goal is the development of moral habits, behavioral tendencies, that will hopefully themselves blossom into character traits or virtues. In Benninga's (1991) words "The school programs' emphases are on establishing early good habits in a controlled setting so that when their young students mature, those habits will be ingrained and generalize" (p. 129). Lickona (1991b) for example describes a classroom practice whereby a fifth grade teacher regularly schedules "appreciation time," a time for students to publicly acknowledge how others have helped them. This generates the habit of affirming others, which is assumed to potentially develop into a character trait of respect.[9] One interesting example of how character education is both compatible with and confused with values education is the use of literature to promote character development. Bennett (1991) has argued for literature to be used to promote "moral literacy" and has produced three anthologies of readings, including the highly popular *Book of virtues* (1993), which are intended to help parents foster character in their children. Ryan (1987) has developed a literature-based curriculum for promoting character around issues of sexual responsibility. Kilpatrick (1992) has argued repeatedly for the reliance upon stories as the central feature of character education. It is rather unlikely, from our moral anatomy, to think that reading literature will have much impact on the development of personality (i.e., character). As Carr (1991) has noted, modeling by educators is likely to be a more appropriate and effective means of affecting student character.

On the other hand, literature-based approaches certainly can have an impact on shaping attitudes and beliefs (i.e., values). This is not to say that teaching values should not be part of character education; indeed it must, for a reflection on what one values is a critical aspect of transforming habits into character. Yet to reduce character education to teaching about values is also quite inappropriate. Ironically, Bennett (1991) in the passage quoted above rejects the terminology of "teaching values" but creates a volume purported to promote character that is really a values anthology.

This character education emphasis on promoting "the dispositions to take certain kinds of actions in certain situations" (Wynne, 1991, p. 143) tends to focus on the processes of adult modeling of desired behaviors, school espoused valuing of those behaviors, and explicit teaching of the behaviors through contingencies (rewards and punishments) for behavior. Approaches such as Kohlberg's Just Community and other collectivist models also focus on the sanctions of the peer group, including disapproval, expulsion, and other forms of punishment as ways of highlighting and enforcing desired character traits such as caring for other members of the community and participating in community activities.

A further approach focuses on codes of behavior or ethics. For example, the military academies in the United States tend to center their character education approaches on such codes. The Cadet Honor Code at the US Military Academy at West Point states that "a cadet will not lie, cheat, or steal, nor tolerate those who do." The culture at the Academy strongly reinforces the Code and sanctions are clear and enforced.

Providing opportunities for students to act in virtuous ways is also an important aspect of character education. The proliferation of service learning components in high schools and universities reflects this emphasis.

Moral Issues in Psychology

Educating for moral reasoning
This may be where we are on our strongest empirically-grounded footing. There is a vast educational and psychological literature examining how to promote moral reason (e.g., Berkowitz, 1985; Power, Higgins, & Kohlberg, 1989a; Rest, 1979). There are two central forms of educating for moral reasoning: peer moral dilemma discussion and the Just Community.

The more practical and therefore more widely implemented technique is peer moral dilemma discussion (PMDD). Appropriate moral dilemmas are selected from anthologies, current events, history, literature, or the curriculum or are created by the teacher. Classes (or other student groups) are then guided through a critical but respectful discussion of the dilemma with the explicit aim of trying to figure out what the best moral solution is. As demonstrated by Berkowitz and Gibbs (1983), discussions in which peers focus analytically on each others' reasoning promote the most development. The role of the teacher is to facilitate an active consideration of the reasoning of one's co-discussants (Berkowitz, 1985).

The Just Community is a much more ambitious project but has been successfully carried out in a variety of contexts including schools (Power et al., 1989a), residential treatment centers (Blakeney & Blakeney, 1990), prisons (Hickey & Scharf, 1980), and workplaces (Higgins & Gordon, 1985). The core of the Just Community approach is democratic self-governance tied to promotion of justice and a sense of community. Decisions are made by a direct democracy and parliamentarian procedure, but with an explicit focus on maximizing justice in decisions and attempting to create and affirm a sense of the communal identity of the group.

Educating for moral affect
In some senses, moral affect is the most difficult part of the moral anatomy to account for in education. There are several reasons for this. First and foremost, most psychological accounts of moral emotions suggest they develop prior to the entrance to formal schooling (e.g., Dunn, 1987; Emde, Johnson & Easterbrooks, 1987; Hoffman, 1987; Kagan, 1981). Second, there is little research on educating for moral emotion in the schools. Third, much of the literature on moral affect concerns remediation and the lack of a typical emotional life (e.g., Magid & McKelvey, 1987). Nevertheless, we can offer some guidelines concerning educating for moral emotions.

Let us begin with the preschool experience. It is clear that emotions, including moral emotions, emerge in the first and second years of life (Emde et al., 1987). One of the most frequently cited affective components of moral development is empathy (Emde et al., 1987; Gibbs, 1991; Hoffman, 1987). Typically empathy is understood to be natural and to have a biological base as well as to be a source of moral reason and more mature moral affect. It is also assumed by many to have origins in the early attachment bonding of infant to caretaker (Kaye, 1982). Hence children should enter school with empathic capacities. Otherwise, we are in the realm of remediation, which is beyond the scope of this discussion.

Clearly, other moral emotions should also be present when the child enters schooling; emotions such as guilt, shame, hurt feelings, pride, etc. (Emde, et al., 1987; Gilligan, 1976). What then can the school provide beyond remediation? Perhaps this is best answered by turning to the notion of moral sensibility offered by Caputo (1986) but having its roots in classical Greek ethical philosophy as well as in other prominent ethical theories such as utilitarianism. The notion is that one must "love the good" as well as simply know it. Affect is infused in moral knowing. Hoffman (1991) argues that moral principles are "hot cognitions" because they are bound to moral affect. The question then becomes one of guiding the moral sensibilities through education. That is, the role of the school is to direct the child to care for the good and abhor the bad; e.g., empathize with victims and despise injustice.

Unfortunately, it is quite unclear how this is done. The literature on moral education pays little attention to this issue. Some argue (along the lines of John Stuart Mill, 1979) that humans have a natural tendency to desire the good; exposure is sufficient. Others argue that such moral "tastes" must be cultivated. For example, Bennett (1991) argues for promoting "moral literacy" in our children as a means of teaching them what the good is. From this perspective schools should teach children about moral virtues, about moral heroes, about great moral acts, and should expose children to great moral literature.

There is also a need to help children identify their moral emotions. Often they do not have verbal labels for what they feel or do not know which labels apply in a given instance. Talking about moral feelings and labeling them not only reduces a child's confusion about her feelings, but also can serve to legitimize them. The child who is torn between empathy for an outcast child and a fear of ostracizing by the peer group that is engaging in the bullying may feel that his empathic feelings are signs of weakness or wrong in some other way. Discussing and labeling them may serve to reduce the child's doubts about the value of his own feelings.

There is also a need in schools to allow children the opportunity to express their feelings. Schools tend to strive to avoid affective displays by children. They are messy and disruptive. A more appropriate approach is to redirect emotions in more acceptable ways. Ginott (1976) often reminded us that we should express our emotions but be sure they are verbalized in appropriate ways. Teachers of preschool children often tell them to "use your words, not your hands" when angry or frustrated.

So schools must teach about moral emotions, must model moral emotions, and must help children express, label and manage their moral emotions.

VI. The Problem of Development

As has been intimated throughout this discussion, moral educators (indeed, any educators) must be sensitive to developmental differences and changes. Nevertheless, this discussion has not taken adequate account of this issue, nor will it.

To do so would be to plan a progression of educational interventions each tailored to the developmental features of specific age/stage groups. For example, Peters (1966) adapts Aristotle's virtue education model by suggesting that young children must first learn correct behavior and then only later can reflect on values and character. Forms of early childhood family-based moral education (Berkowitz, 1992; Lickona, 1983) must differ from and precede later school-based moral education due to the developmental differences between preschool and primary school children. As noted, moral emotion education should precede formal schooling, whereas educating for moral identity would likely be more appropriate in secondary education.

This treatment does not have the luxury of dwelling on that level of analysis of moral education. Nonetheless, it is critical to point out that optimal moral education should not merely, as we have been arguing, be sensitive to the different aspects of the moral person, but must also be sensitive to the developmental differences and changes through which the moral person evolves. With that caveat in mind, let us summarize the preceding discussion with an overview of comprehensive moral education.

VII. The Comprehensive Approach to Moral Education

Moral education must start by answering two fundamental and interrelated questions: What are the grounding ethical principles that justify right and wrong? and What kind of moral person are we trying to form? As already argued, neither of these are arbitrary choices. There is certainly room for disagreement in the answers to these questions, but the disagreement is among a limited and time-tested set of options. After all, despite the fact that ethical theory had spent nearly two and one half millennia without achieving consensus on the grounding principles, the millennia have produced a very limited set of grounding principles about which ethical philosophers debate.

I have offered a model of the moral person, although it is clearly open to debate and incomplete as well. Whatever model one chooses, it must be consistent both with the grounding principles and empirical evidence about human nature (Aristotle, 1987; Kohlberg, 1971). Once these questions are answered satisfactorily, then the details of the comprehensive model of moral education can be addressed.

As an example, our model will rely upon the principles of justice (Power, Higgins, & Kohlberg, 1989a), respect for persons (Lickona, 1991a), and beneficence (Gilligan, 1982; Kohlberg, Boyd, & Levine, 1986). Our moral anatomy spells out the kind of moral person we are aiming to form through our comprehensive approach to moral education.

How should a school proceed to nurture the development of a mature moral agent who adheres to the principles of justice, respect, and beneficence and who embodies the psychological characteristics of moral character, moral reason, moral valuing, moral affect, moral identity, and moral behavior, as well as meta-moral characteristics? To demonstrate, we will address a subset of the educational components.

First, the school must explicitly address the question of which values and character traits are to be the focus of their educational efforts. These values and character traits must be consistent with (derivative of) the grounding principles. They must also be consistent with the characteristics of the social context, although this is a second order requirement that is superceded by the first order (grounding principle) requirement; e.g., in the USA it is acceptable for the derivative values to avoid religious issues and in Saudi Arabia for them to be explicitly based on religious criteria, but not in either case for the values to contradict universal principles of ethics.

The selected grounding principles and derivative values and character traits should be made an explicit part of the educational environment and agenda. They should be openly described and advocated. But there are two further steps that are necessary. One, they must be manifested in the behavior of the school's authorities (teachers, administrators, etc.). It is not enough merely to espouse them; they must be modeled for the students. Two, the governance structure of the school must be consistent with the grounding principles so that there is no undermining contradictory hidden curriculum.

> Even if the values of justice were discussed in classes, if the students perceive that getting along in school runs by a quite different set of norms, they will tend to perceive the latter as the real rules of the game and the former as nice talk one engages in with teachers. (Power et al., 1989a, p. 21)

As Kohlberg and his colleagues further suggest, this is best achieved by "opening up" the governance structure; i.e., "opening up that process and dealing with the ways everyday rules of behavior are made and enforced" (p. 23). The justification for this is twofold: (1) to preclude the undermining effects of the hidden curriculum; and (2) to create a moral atmosphere that is consistent with the grounding principles upon which the moral education program is based. The Just Community is the most extreme method for opening up the governance process, but others suggest other forms of democratic governance (e.g., Mosher, Kenny, & Garrod, 1994).

As noted above, merely valuing and knowing how to justify moral behavior is not sufficient to be a fully moral person. Thus the advocacy and modeling of the moral characteristics must be supplemented with some means of forming the rest of moral agency. There must also be educational components that (1) promote moral behavior and (2) foster mature moral reasoning, for example. For the former, clear behavioral expectations and contingencies are necessary. Once again, they must be consistent with the grounding principles, derivative values, and governance structure of the school. The last requirement suggests that the expectations and contingencies be open to scrutiny through a process that is just and democratic. Now here is where the "developmental problem" discussed above is particularly important. With younger children, this scrutiny is by necessity much more limited in scope and the good judgment and authority of the teachers is more central, whereas with secondary school students, the reverse is true.

Fostering moral reasoning development is best achieved through both curricular classroom discussions of moral issues and participation in the democratic governance of the school. The key elements for success here are a focus on active peer discussion of moral issues, a fair and considerate atmosphere and set of guidelines for such discussion, and an explicit orientation toward trying to discover the most just, respectful, and beneficent solution to a moral issue (rather than simply sampling individual moral "tastes").

The school, its personnel, and its curriculum must be infused with moral issues. They must be explicitly espoused, they must be modeled, they must be embodied in the life of the school. They must be part of the classroom curriculum (literature, projects, etc.). Furthermore, they must be monitored and enforced. As the literature on parenting suggests, good parents must not only set standards, they must also set high but attainable standards, monitor if those standards are met, enforce contingencies for adherence and deviance, and offer supports to help their children meet their standards. Again, all of these criteria are applicable to school-based moral education; but, as for families, they must be applied in ways that are fair, caring and respectful and which include the students as valued participants in the formation and maintenance of the education process.

To rely on part of this recipe, e.g., merely on authority-enforced behavior codes or merely on classroom discussions of moral dilemmas, is to educate for an incomplete moral person. Surely we do not want a society of individuals who are morally incomplete; i.e., who can reason well but do not act accordingly, or who act robotically but cannot reason when confronted with moral novelty. If that is so, then we need to devise moral education programs designed to foster the development of complete moral persons, with moral character, reason, values, emotion, and behavior. To do this we need to open our eyes and behold the entire elephant and to renounce our professional competitiveness and parochialisms and join together to learn from each approach what works and what is consistent with the grounding principles of ethical theory. Then and only then will we be educating for the entire moral person.

NOTES

1.　Clearly this project has been recently attempted by Alasdair MacIntyre (1982), but in his case he attempted to resolve the problems by resurrecting (in an adapted form) a single model, that of virtue ethics, rather than trying to integrate models as is done here. Nonetheless, it may be argued that virtue ethics, at least in the full Aristotelian form, may encompass most of the components to be proposed here.

2.　We use the term "moral education" here in a broad sense. It encompasses not only formal education, but parenting and community education as well. The question of terminology will be addressed in more detail below.

3.　I fear that the authors were unwittingly profound and insightful in this quotation. They were attempting to summarize the grounds of consensus among the chapter authors of Ryan and McLean's (1987) *Character development in schools and beyond*, and this quote was likely a partisan shot at the cognitive-developmental approach to moral education (e.g., Power, Higgins & Kohlberg, 1989a) and values clarification (Raths, Harmin & Simon, 1966).

4.　The values clarification movement largely died out after the 1970s due to prevalent critiques from all three of these groups.

5.　Whereas this argument has been, and continues to be, frequently asserted, it is patently inaccurate. Blasi (1980), Kohlberg and Candee (1984), Rest (1979), and others have offered extensive evidence for the significant relation of moral reasoning to behavior. Perhaps at the heart of this miscommunication is the inaccurate assumption that such a relation would require a near isomorphism between judgment and action. Unfortunately, as addressed in our moral anatomy, the moral person is complex and multifaceted. Hence moral behavior is multivariate. Clearly moral reasoning does significantly predict moral behavior, but it is only one of many factors that do so.

6.　Clearly this is a matter of terminology. If one, as many do, prefers to limit the domain identified by the term character to those aspects of personality that are moral (Lickona, 1991b), then indeed the qualifier "moral" in the term "moral character" is superfluous and redundant. Many others, however, include in "character" those aspects of personality that support moral behavior but are not moral in and of themselves (Wynne & Ryan, 1993). (These aspects will be discussed in a later section of this paper.) Finally, still others use the term "character" to refer only to these nonmoral aspects (Etzioni, Berkowitz, & Wilcox, 1994). As noted, in this paper, "character" will be used to indicate personality in a generic sense and "moral character" to refer to those aspects of character that are intrinsically moral or immoral.

7. Character education was highly popular in the first third of this century, but declined precipitously after the early 1930s due to research by Hartshorne and May (1928-30) suggesting that stable character traits did not exist. It virtually disappeared from the education literature after the middle 1950s (Power, Higgins, & Kohlberg, 1989b).

8. There is certainly the legitimate consideration of context and extenuating circumstances. Burglary may be the only means of surviving in an oppressive situation. Battery may be the only means of preventing murder or rape. This does not negate the point being made, however. It merely points to the need for a hierarchy of values, such that any given value may be judged universally right or wrong, unless it is superseded by a higher value. This point is all the more relevant when it is recognized that schools rarely address the interrelations of values and their relative positions in a hierarchy of values.

9. It is worth noting that this activity is simultaneously promoting self-esteem in those students being appreciated. Furthermore, it is publicly advocating the value of helping and rewarding helping behavior. This is an excellent example of how the components and processes of moral education are frequently linked together.

REFERENCES

Argyris, C., & Schon, D.A. (1989). *Theory in practice: Increasing professional effectiveness.* San Francisco: Jossey-Bass.

Aristotle (1987). *The Nichomachean ethics* (J.E. Weldon, Trans.). Albuquerque, NM: American Classical College Press.

Arizona Department of Education (1990). *Teaching values in the Arizona schools: The report of the Task Force on Values in Education for the State of Arizona.* Arizona Department of Education.

Bennett, W.J. (1991). Moral literacy and the formation of character. In J.S. Benninga (Ed.), *Moral, character, and civic education in the elementary school* (pp. 131-138). New York: Teachers College Press.

Bennett, W.J. (1993). *Book of virtues.* Bellevue, WA: S & S Trade.

Benninga, J.S. (1991). Moral and character education in the elementary school: An introduction. In J.S. Benninga (Ed.), *Moral, character, and civic education in the elementary school* (pp. 3-20). New York: Teachers College Press.

Berkowitz, M.W. (1985). The role of discussion in moral education. In M.W. Berkowitz & F. Oser (Eds.), *Moral education: Theory and application* (pp. 197-218). Hillsdale, NJ: L. Erlbaum.

Berkowitz, M.W. (1992). La interaccion familiar como educacion moral (Family interaction as moral education). *Communicacion, Lenguaje Y Educacion, 15,* 39-45.

Berkowitz, M.W., & Gibbs, J.C. (1983). Measuring the developmental features of moral discussion. *Merrill-Palmer Quarterly, 29,* 399-410.

Berkowitz, M.W., Kahn, J.P., Mulry, G., Piette, J. (1995). Psychological and philosophical considerations of prudence and morality. In M. Killen & D. Hart (Eds.), *Morality in everyday life: Developmental perspectives* (pp. 201-224). New York: Cambridge University Press.

Blakeney, C., & Blakeney, R. (1990). Reforming moral misbehaviour. *Journal of Moral Education, 19,* 101-113.

Blasi, A. (1980). Bridging moral cognition and moral action: A critical review of the literature. *Psychological Bulletin, 88,* 1-45.

Blasi, A. (1984). Moral identity: Its role in moral functioning. In W. Kurtines & J. Gewirtz (Eds.), *Morality, moral behavior, and moral development* (pp. 128-139). New York: Wiley.

Caputo, J. (1986). A phenomenology of moral sensibility. In G.F. McLean, F.E. Ellrod, D.L. Schindler, & J.A. Mann (Eds.), *Act and agent: Philosophical foundations for moral education and character development* (pp. 199-222). New York: University Press of America.

Carr, D. (1991). *Educating the virtues: An essay on the philosophical psychology of moral development and education.* London: Routledge.

Character Education Partnership. *Character education: Questions and answers.* Alexandria, VA: Character Education Partnership.

Coles, R. (1986). *The moral life of children.* Boston: The Atlantic Monthly Press.

Damon, W. (1988). *The moral child: Nurturing children's natural moral growth.* New York: The Free Press.

Dunn, J. (1987). The beginnings of moral understanding: Development in the second year. In J. Kagan & S. Lamb (Eds.), *The emergence of morality in young children* (pp. 91-112). Chicago: University of Chicago Press.

Emde, R., Johnson, W.F., & Easterbrooks, M.A. (1987). The Do's and Don'ts of early moral development: Psychoanalytic tradition and current research. In J. Kagan & S. Lamb (Eds.), *The emergence of morality in young children* (pp. 245-276). Chicago: University of Chicago Press.

Etzioni, A., Berkowitz, M.W., & Wilcox, W.B. (1994). *Character building for a democratic, civil society.* Position paper of the Communitarian Network, Washington, D.C.

Gibbs, J.C. (1991). Toward an integration of Kohlberg's and Hoffman's theories of morality. In W.M. Kurtines & J.L. Gewirtz (Eds.), *Handbook of moral behavior and development. Volume 1: Theory* (pp. 183-222).

Gibbs, J.C., Potter, G.B., & Goldstein, A.P. (1995). *The EQUIP program: Teaching youth to think and act responsibly through a peer-helping approach.* Champaign, IL: Research Press.

Gilligan, C. (1982). *In a different voice: Psychological theory and women's development.* Cambridge, MA: Harvard University Press.

Gilligan, J. (1976). Guilt and shame. In T. Lickona (Ed.), *Moral development and behavior: Theory, research and social issues.* New York: Holt Rinehart & Winston.

Ginott, H.G. (1976). *Between teacher and child.* New York: Avon Press.

Grim, P.F., Kohlberg, L., & White, S.H. (1968). Some relationships between conscience and attentional processes. *Journal of Personality and Social Psychology, 8,* 239-252.

Hartshorne, H., & May, M.A. (1928-1930). *Studies in the nature of character (Vols. 1-3).* New York: Macmillan.

Hickey, J. & Scharf, P. (1980). *Toward a just correctional system.* San Francisco: Jossey-Bass.

Higgins, A., & Gordon, F. (1985). Work climate and socio-moral development in two worker-owned companies. In M.W. Berkowitz & F. Oser (Eds.), *Moral education: Theory and application* (pp. 241-268). Hillsdale, NJ: L. Erlbaum and Associates.

Higgins-D'Alessandro, A. (1995). *The development of moral identity: Using a triarchic model of moral self to understand the emergence of moral identity.* Paper read at the 25th annual conference of the Association for Moral Education, New York City.

Hoffman, M.L. (1987). The contribution of empathy to justice and moral judgment. In N. Eisenberg & J. Strayer (Eds.), *Empathy and its development.* New York: Cambridge University Press.

Hoffman, M.L. (1991). Empathy, social cognition, and moral action. In W.M. Kurtines & J.L. Gewirtz (Eds.), *Handbook of moral behavior and development. Volume 1: Theory* (pp. 275-301). Hillsdale, NJ: L. Erlbaum.

Josephson, M. (1993). *The six pillars of character.* Marina del Rey, CA: Josephson Institute of Ethics.

Kagan, J. (1981). *The second year.* Cambridge, MA: Harvard University Press.

Kaye, K. (1982). *The mental and social life of babies: How parents create persons.* Chicago: University of Chicago Press.

Kegan, R. (1982). *The evolving self.* Cambridge, MA: Harvard University Press.

Kilpatrick, W.K. (1992). Moral character: Story-telling and virtue. In R.T. Knowles & G.F. McLean (Eds.), *Psychological foundations of moral education and character development: An integrated theory of moral development* (pp. 169-183). Washington, D.C.: The Council for Research in Values and Philosophy.

Kohlberg, L. (1967). Moral and religious education and the public schools: A developmental view. In T. Sizer (Ed.), *Religion and public education.* Boston: Houghton-Mifflin.

Kohlberg, L. (1971). From *is* to *ought*: How to commit the naturalistic fallacy and get away with it in the study of moral development. In T.Mischel (Ed.), *Cognitive development and epistemology.* New York: Academic Press.

Kohlberg, L. (1976). Moral stages and moralization: The cognitive-developmental approach. In T. Lickona (Ed.), *Moral development and behavior: Theory, research and social issues* (pp. 31-53). New York: Holt Rinehart and Winston.

Kohlberg, L., Boyd, D., & Levine, C. (1986). The return of stage 6: Its principle and moral point of view. In W. Edelstein & G. Nunner-Winkler (Eds.), *Zur Bestimmung der moral-philosophische und sozialwissenschafliche Beitraege zur Moralforschung.* Frankfurt: Suhrkamp-Verlag.

Kohlberg, L., & Candee, D. (1984). The relation of moral judgment to moral action. In W.M. Kurtines & J.L Gewirtz (Eds.), *Morality, moral behavior, and moral development.* New York: Wiley.

Kohlberg, L., & Mayer, R. (1972). Development as the aim of education. *Harvard Educational Review, 42,* 449-496.

Lickona, T. (1983). *Raising good children.* New York: Bantam Books.

Lickona, T. (1991a). *Educating for character: How our schools can teach respect and responsibility.* New York: Bantam.

Lickona, T. (1991b). An integrated approach to character development. In J.S. Benninga (Ed.), *Moral, character, and civic education in the elementary school* (pp. 67-83). New York: Teachers College Press.

Lickona, T. (1993, November). The return of character education. *Educational Leadership,* pp. 6-11.

MacIntyre, A. (1981). *After virtue.* Notre Dame, IN: University of Notre Dame Press.

Magid, K., & McKelvey, C.A. (1987). *High risk: Children without conscience.* New York: Bantam Books.

Mill, J.S. (1979). *Utilitarianism* (G.Sher, Ed.). Indianapolis, IN: Hackett Publishers.

Mosher, R., Kenny Jr., R.A., & Garrod, A. (1994). *Preparing for citizenship: Teaching youth to live democratically.* Westport, CT: Praeger.

Noam, G.G. (1985). Stage, phase, and style: The developmental dynamics of the self. In M.W. Berkowitz & F. Oser (Eds.), *Moral education: Theory and application* (pp. 321-346). Hillsdale, NJ: L. Erlbaum and Associates.

Nucci, L. (1981). Conceptions of personal issues: A domain distinct from moral or societal concepts. *Child Development, 52,* 114-121.

Nucci, L. (1982). Conceptual development in the moral and conventional domains: Implications for values education. *Review of Educational Research, 52,* 93-122.

Nucci, L. (Ed.). (1989). *Moral development and character education: A dialogue.* Berkeley, CA: McCutchan.

Nucci, L., Guerra, N., & Lee, J. (1991). Adolescent judgments of the personal, prudential, and normative aspects of drug usage. *Developmental Psychology, 27,* 841-848.

Piaget, J. (1965). *The moral judgment of the child.* (C.M. Gabain, Trans.), New York: Free Press. (First published in 1932).

Piaget, J. (1981). *Intelligence and affectivity: Their relationship during child development* (T.A. Brown & C.E.Kaeg, Trans.). Palo Alto, CA: Annual Reviews.

Power, F.C., Higgins, A., & Kohlberg, L. (1989a). *Lawrence Kohlberg's approach to moral education.* New York: Columbia University Press.

Power, F.C., Higgins, A., & Kohlberg, L. (1989b). The habit of the common life: Building character through democratic community schools. In L. Nucci (Ed.), *Moral development and character education: A dialogue* (pp. 125-143). Berkeley, CA: McCutchan.

Raths, L.E., Harmin, M., & Simon, S.B. (1966). *Values and teaching.* Columbus, OH: Charles E. Merrill.

Rest, J.R. (1979). *Development in judging moral issues.* Minneapolis, MN: University of Minnesota Press.

Rokeach, M. (1968). *Beliefs, attitudes, and values.* San Francisco: Jossey-Bass.

Rokeach, M. (1973). *The nature of human values.* New York: Free Press.

Ryan, K. (1987). The moral education of teachers. In K. Ryan & G.F. McLean (Eds.), *Character development in the schools and beyond* (pp. 358-379). New York: Praeger.

Ryan, K., & Lickona, T. (1987). Character development: The challenge and the model. In Ryan, K., & McLean, G.F. (Eds.), *Character development in schools and beyond* (pp. 3-35). New York: Praeger.

Ryan, K., & McLean, G.F. (Eds.) (1987). *Character development in schools and beyond.* New York: Praeger.

Samay, S.A. (1986). Affectivity: The power base of moral behavior. In G.F. McLean, F.E. Ellrod, D.L. Schindler, & J.A. Mann (Eds.), *Act and agent: Philosophical foundations for moral education and character development* (pp. 71-114). New York: University Press of America.

Schulman, M. & Mekler, E. (1985). *Bringing up a moral child: A new approach for teaching your child to be kind, just, and responsible.* Reading, MA: Addison-Wesley.

Schwartz, S.H., & Bilsky, W. (1987). Toward a universal psychological structure of human values. *Journal of Personality and Social Psychology, 53,* 550-562.

Selman, R. (1980). *The growth of interpersonal understanding.* New York: Academic Press.

Selman, R., & Schultz, L.H. (1990). *Making a friend in youth: Developmental theory and pair therapy.* Chicago: University of Chicago Press.

Shields, D.L.L., & Bredemeier, B.J.L. (1995). *Character development and physical activity.* Champaign, IL: Human Kinetics Press.

Sweet Home Central School District (1991). *Values education handbook.* Amherst, NY: Sweet Home Central School District.

Turiel, E. (1983). *The development of social knowledge: Morality and convention.* New York: Cambridge University Press.

Walker, L.J. (1995). Whither moral psychology? *Moral Education Forum, 20,* 1-8.

Walker, L.J., Pitts, R.C., Hennig, K.H., & Matsuba, M.K. (1995). Reasoning about morality and real-life moral problems. In M. Killen & D. Hart (Eds.), *Morality in everyday life: Developmental perspectives* (371-407). New York: Cambridge University Press.

Watson, M., Solomon, D., Battisch, V., Schaps, E., & Solomon, J. (1989). The Child Development Project: Combining traditional and developmental approaches to values education. In L.Nucci (Ed.), *Moral development and character education: A dialogue* (pp. 51-91). Berkeley, CA: McCutchan.

Westman, J.C. (1994). *Licensing parents: Can we prevent child abuse and neglect?* New York: Insight Books.

Wynne, E.A. (1991). Character and academics in the elementary school. In J.S. Benninga (Ed.), *Moral, character, and civic education in the elementary school* (pp. 139-155). New York: Teachers College Press.

Wynne, E.A., & Ryan, K. (1993). *Reclaiming our schools: A handbook on teaching character, academics, and discipline.* New York: Merrill.

2

Moral Goodness and Mental Health

Josef Seifert[1]

I. Introductory Remarks on the Problem of the Relationship Between Mental Health and Morality

That a philosopher speaks about moral goodness is common but what right does he have to speak about "mental health"? After all, mental health seems to be the exclusive domain of the empirical sciences of psychology and psychiatry. Well aware of the limits of a philosopher's justification to deal with such an issue, I base my treating it on a theoretical account, expounded elsewhere in detail,[2] and on the fact that many issues of medicine and psychology envelop highly intelligible essences and states of affairs that are open to specifically philosophical rational intuition and analysis. This applies also to the nature of mental health and unhealth.[3]

We agree with the eminent Chilean psychiatrist, Roa, who has recently declared that the nature of mental health and illness is accessible primarily through "an intuitive grasp of a cluster of manifestations that would justify the designation that this is a mentally ill rather than a delinquent or somatically sick patient."[4] According to him, ordinary persons frequently have a better grasp of what psychological health is than do learned theorists.[5] That the intuition of the ordinary person into what mental health is, is often better than the mixture of intuitions and opinions found in theories about mental health becomes particularly evident when one considers psychiatrists who even reject the very notion of mental health and declare it to be a mere invention.[6]

Without such a rational intuitive understanding of the nature of mental health we could not distinguish mental illness and psychotic maladaptation to society from the abominable political abuse of the term 'mental health' by Nazi-German and Communist psychiatrists who declared people mentally ill simply because they disagreed with the reigning ideology or stood fast in their moral convictions, rather than conforming to the demands of the political regime. It is not, as many psychiatrists and writers in this field hold today, the concept of mental health itself that is the cause of potential political abuse. Rather, the authentic intuition into what mental health and unhealth are, and their clear distinction from other phenomena, are the very condition for rejecting such political abuses and for distinguishing criminal deviation from the social order from the deviation of the mentally ill.[7]

Using in the following the term "mental health," I understand it in the broad sense of "psychological health," within which one could again differentiate between psychic health that is affected more by emotional and related disorders and mental health in a more restricted sense of the intactness of the cognitive faculties and intelligence. Mental illness as related to this latter dimension of mental health would strike primarily the rational, cognitive, and volitional spheres of consciousness and the imagination. I shall refer to phenomena situated within both of these groups of mental disorders. We could also distinguish different opposites to mental health: forms of retardation, mental illnesses (as the states suffered by the patient) and mental diseases as the underlying roots of mental disorders.[8] These would again differ from mere deficiencies and injuries that lead to mental incapacitation, etc. The notion of "mental health" which we are going to use in the following corresponds primarily to the opposites of mental illness and mental disease rather than to mental retardation and incapacitation.

Given the fundamental and primary character of the datum of health in general, and of mental health in particular, we cannot really define the content of "mental health" by reference to other things.[9] Nevertheless, the nature of mental health, which also has its foundation in the more primary data of life, mind, and person, can be analyzed and characterized in many ways.

Quite generally, it can be described as the actual or at least potential uninhibited flourishing and presence of the mental and rational life of finite[10] and specifically of embodied human persons.

Mental health involves a certain actualization of conscious and personal life suitable for an individual's stage of development, and even more the potential to live this life unimpeded. More specifically, it could be characterized as involving the following six marks.

1) The intactness of all the fundamental mental capacities of conscious life, including a conscious living of one's own body as one's own in a way appropriate to persons, unimpaired perception, cognition, will, and emotions.

2) The ability to make fundamental distinctions, especially of the real from the irreal and merely imagined, of other ontological modalities (as the possible and impossible, probable and improbable), and of good from evil. This also includes a "proper perception of reality, including the 'objective' sensibility towards the feelings of others." [11]

3) Having at one's free disposal the different perceptual, imaginative, intellectual, volitional and affective powers of personal life, as opposed to having one's consciousness invaded by strange images, hallucinations, irrational ideas, or irresistible compulsions. The psychic health of human affective life stands in contrast also to the crippling of the emotional life by the inability to feel, by affective

frigidity and by other emotional disorders.[12]

4) The possession of a fundamental self-consciousness, the acceptance of the 'I'[13] and the consciousness of the world and of other persons.

5) A certain ability to retain the identity of one's personality, convictions, ways of feeling, etc., in different situations and environments, and at the same time as an openness to change where objective factors require it.

6) A certain fundamental structural rationality of one's intellectual, volitional, and emotional acts. This rationality is not yet the higher rationality found in adequate knowledge of reality or in moral goodness—which includes much more than mental health—but a rationality which prevents one from holding totally absurd errors, from failing to make the most elementary distinctions, or from willing impossible or completely neutral things with great intensity. This rationality of mental health excludes for example the fear of entirely harmless things such as forks on a table, strong hatred of completely innocuous animals or humans, intense anger toward wholly innocent persons, and other forms of a fundamental structural irrationality of intentional acts.

Although these six characteristics of mental health do not constitute a strict definition, they serve to identify sufficiently well what I mean when I refer to mental health. I would like to turn now to the main question of this paper, namely: what is the relationship between morality and mental health? Is there any connection between moral goodness and mental health? Or between moral evil and mental illness? Should moral virtue in some way be equated with mental health, and moral evil with mental illness? While we find a partial equation of moral goodness and evil with mental health and illness in certain thinkers from the Greeks to Freud, their complete equation would be astonishing indeed. Will not all of us reject any identification of moral evil with mental illness, when we realize that precisely mental *health* is a condition of moral evil and even of legal responsibility? If one can demonstrate that a criminal was not in possession of his mental capacities, the charges against him will be dropped because evidently a certain measure of mental health is a condition of freedom and thus of moral and legal responsibility.

Recognizing this fact, Manuel Lavados has recently proposed that mental health, and indeed human health in general, is precisely a well-being that is on the one hand clearly distinct from the moral actions and virtues that proceed from freedom, and on the other hand is characterizable as a condition of freedom.[14] His attempt to understand health, both mental and physical, has the double merit of drawing, on the one hand, a clear line between the well-being of health and other higher goods for the person, especially moral goodness, a necessary line which the WHO-definition of health has not drawn, defining health since 1946 in terms more applicable to perfect goodness and happiness than to health.[15] On the other hand, his assertion throws light on a significant relation between morality and mental health: mental health is a condition of moral good or evil.

But is it perhaps also true that the inverse relation exists and that a certain measure of moral goodness is a condition of mental health? What exactly are the differences and relationships between moral goodness and mental health, and between moral evil and mental illness? This is the question I will primarily address in the following.

II. Essential Differences Between Health and Morality

We must grant to H. Tristram Engelhardt, Jr. that health (including mental health) is not a moral value, just as unhealth is not a moral fault.[16] We cannot blame someone for being unhealthy nor praise him for being healthy.

Some forms of mental health and unhealth do not require any knowledge on the part of the mentally ill; morality in all its forms, however, necessarily presupposes knowledge in the moral agent. It is strictly evident that without some understanding of the nature and object of our acts, we cannot perform morally good or evil acts. Mental health and unhealth do not have any necessary connection with freedom; they can be due to certain brain conditions, brain lesions or other causes that are completely outside the range of our freedom.[17] Moral values, on the other hand, could not exist at all without being rooted in free acts. If nature, our brain, or even an omnipotent God were to determine our acts from without, and if we could not act otherwise through our own free wills, there could be absolutely no moral good or evil in us.

Moral good and evil exist therefore only in persons—precisely because only persons can know in the strict sense and are free. Neither plants nor material things nor abstract ideas can be morally good or evil. This essential and inseparable bond between moral values and knowledge, as well as that between personhood, freedom, and morality, is an *a priori* and an eternal truth that can be easily seen although it has often been denied by those who believe that we can both be sinners and be completely determined by a divine predestination which would cause both good and evil in our wills, as Luther and still more clearly Calvin taught. Yet is it not evident to you as it is to me that, if our free spontaneous power to self-determination and to free acts would be an illusion, moral good and evil would be illusions as well? There is an absolute bond between morality and freedom.

In contrast, health can also exist in non-personal living beings such as in plants and animals. And although *mental health*—at least in its strict sense, prescinding from "psychic disorders" that can also afflict animals—can be found only in persons, because they alone have rational minds, it is not as deeply rooted in personhood as moral values because it is for the most part not grounded in freedom at all, and it is never as profoundly rooted in freedom as moral values are.

Accordingly, while mental health and unhealth do not have to be connected with our responsibility, moral values are necessarily linked to responsibility. Health and its opposites are not joined to merit and guilt if we fail to possess them without fault of our own, whereas moral good and evil are necessarily and essentially connected with merit and guilt. They deserve praise and blame, reward and punishment, in a way in which mental health and unhealth do not.

Thus moral evil and mental illness are clearly distinct from each other. This difference reveals itself also in many other marks of morality that are lacking in mental health, for example in the necessary connection between the moral good and evil in ourselves and our moral conscience which warns us against committing moral evil. The voice of conscience does not reproach us for lacking mental health but for acting wrongly, nor does it create any disharmony in our souls when we fall ill, but only when we do evil. Of course, our conscience can reproach us for *not having taken care of* our health, but then it refers precisely to free acts regarding health, never to mental or physical unhealth as such.

In light of the preceding reflections it seems that, apart from mental health being a condition for moral values or disvalues, a complete separation and chasm between mental health and morality is opening up. Inasmuch as something is morally good, it appears to be clearly beyond health; insofar as something is morally evil, it does not appear to involve mental illness but rather to presuppose mental health.

In reality, however, the relationship between morality and mental health is far more complex than has been suggested so far. Let us then examine more carefully the manifold relationships between morality and mental health. Such a study will lead us to develop a personalistic concept of mental health and to make several significant distinctions.

III. Various Relationships Between Mental Health and Morality

A. Some share of mental health is a condition of moral acts

As noted already, a significant part of the totality of states which we call mental health, at least those which are required for conscious and intelligent life and for the free rule over our acts, is a *condition of good or evil acts.* Mental unhealth can, of course, not only cause obstacles to freedom but also to many other aspects of mental life and health, particularly 1) to the central distinction between the real and the irreal or only imagined, 2) to freely disposing over the field of consciousness as opposed to being invaded by strange ideas, unpleasant moods without reasonable motivation, obsessive compulsions or anxieties. If health is a flourishing of life and of all the operations and potentialities of a living organism of a certain nature, then it is clear that mental unhealth can not only impede freedom, but likewise the ability to speak, to remember, to think logically, to imagine, to perceive, to feel one's body, etc.[18]

On the other hand, mental health is not always and absolutely a condition of moral good and evil because moral good and evil can obviously also exist in many mentally ill persons. Perhaps it exists even in any mentally ill person, as long as he is conscious and possesses a certain minimal human intelligence. We bring to mind here Scheler's and Frankl's thesis that mental unhealth cannot affect the deepest levels of the spirit and of morality, at least not the fundamental moral tenor or *Ur-intention (Gesinnung)*. In fact, it is one of the central theses of Max Scheler and of the logotherapy of Viktor Frankl inspired by Scheler's thought that—while the psyche can be ill, the spirit—and here especially the center of morally good and evil acts—cannot become ill and therefore the road to finding some meaning is always open to persons.[19]

Regardless of whether we agree with the full strength of Scheler's and Frankl's radical assertion, it seems clear that only very few forms of mental unhealth exclude *any* free act. Many forms of lack of mental health leave the moral agent and his freedom intact, at least to some extent. For obviously, lightly mentally retarded persons, but also persons with serious mental conditions such as schizophrenia or manic depression, can still act freely in many ways. They can, just like physically sick persons, be either noble or mean, either fall into despair or show saintly virtues of hope and of resistance to committing the suicide to which manic depressions may strongly dispose them, thus controlling their actions vis-à-vis such uncontrollable temptations that arise from their mental problems. And certainly, if a responsible psychiatrist sees that his patient is very seriously mentally ill, he will not conclude therefrom that his patient is unable to perform any morally good or evil acts.

Only if physical or mental health is so utterly destroyed that conscious and free acts have become unrealizable, or if the sick inclinations of a mind are so strong and absolutely domineering that their compulsory character (for example, in the obsessive neurotic or psychotic patient) suspends entirely the free power of the person to act, will free acts be wholly impeded by mental unhealth or by the mental effects of certain kinds of brain damage. Therefore, in some cases of severe depression, some psychiatrists believe that crude methods such as electro-shock and others, have to be applied precisely because any appeal to reason or freedom appear to be futile.

Many forms of mental unhealth (for example, paranoiac fears or irresistible irrational depressions, or strong urges to commit suicide, and others) do not even necessarily reduce freedom in its deepest moral sense. Of course, irresistible depressions, etc. may restrict our freedom in many ways and cause unfree symptoms such as the inability of a person in severe depression to make himself eat, or to feel a friendly disposition towards others, etc. But this does not involve necessarily a reduction of the deepest moral core of human freedom. This is particularly manifest on a moral-religious level of life and of moral drama. Regarding those relationships to freedom which are relevant for us here, this dimension of the drama of freedom concerning mental or other disorders which affect psychic experience may also be understood by persons without any religious faith or who reject the religious dimensions of the following examples. Some very serious forms of neuroses or depression which many great Saints suffered, either for spiritual or for immanent reasons of mental unhealth, or the demonic possession from which some Saints have not been spared, may even provide special occasions for heroic free acts.

To summarize our essential point: Any mental condition of unhealth that in any way has left some of our freedom intact, has left the person the capacity to be a moral agent.

B. Mental health requires the ability to distinguish between good and evil

Armando Roa has suggested that the *ability to distinguish good and evil,* even if not moral goodness itself, is part of mental health.[20] This relation between morality and mental health is clearly distinct from the role of physical and mental health as a *condition* of moral acts. For here a certain dimension of ethical value-perception and of the ability to take cognizance of moral values is judged to be part of mental health.

We might call such ability a cognitive condition of mental health and thus reckon some basic ethical knowledge among the conditions of mental health. This relation between morality and mental health is similar to many other (intellectual, rational or perceptual) cognitive elements of mental health: among them, for example, the ability to distinguish different things and persons, forms, numbers, faces, etc.

Perhaps we should include, however, in the notion of mental health only the original capacity of distinguishing good and evil so as to exclude that those forms of total or partial moral value blindness which result from different forms of pride and concupiscence be reckoned among forms of mental unhealth, although moral value-blindness in its radical forms might itself become pathological, as we shall see.[21]

C. Mental health as a morally relevant good and as an occasion for morally good acts

We said above that moral good and evil are utterly distinct from mental health. But is it not obvious that mental health and health in general are morally significant? Do we not consider it a crime committed in the Nazi-camp Ravensbruck that the female inmates there were objects of medical experiments that inflicted great damage on their health?[22] And would we not launch an even more poignant reproach if someone were to induce mental illness in a patient by operating on his brain or by injecting chemicals into it?

The answer lies open before all of us, but to understand its truth, we must introduce the crucial distinction between what is *morally good* and what is a *morally relevant good.*[23]

Moral values are characterized by the above mentioned characteristics (stemming from free action, being praise- or blameworthy, etc.). Health, also mental health, is never *per se* a moral value whose possession as such makes someone morally praiseworthy.

Morally relevant goods, such as human life, are those which are not necessarily morally good in themselves but which issue moral imperatives to the person. Nobody is morally good because he lives; nevertheless, human life is one of the most significant morally relevant goods. Likewise, we may say that health is unmistakably a morally relevant good.

There are three meanings or connotations of the term "morally relevant good," and we are dealing here with the first of them. Morally relevant good can indicate those goods that are precisely *not* morally good but impose moral imperatives on us and make our interest in them morally good. Then the accent lies on the difference between morally relevant and moral goods and evils. Morally relevant goods can secondly indicate those goods that issue moral calls and obligations in contradistinction to those which do not. Thirdly, morally relevant goods can mean simply all goods that stand over against our free acts, while the adequate response to them bestows a moral quality on our acts. In this third sense also all moral values are morally relevant.[24]

Now, acts of genuine interest in morally relevant goods such as mental health "bear on their back," as Scheler puts it, moral values.[25] He uses this expression because the object of concern here is not the moral value of our own action but the morally relevant good on the object-side.

Preserving our health or helping a patient to regain his mental health are morally good acts if they are properly motivated. Inasmuch as the realization of health and the cure from disease is within our free power, health and disease are eminently morally relevant and to this extent we can be morally blamed for not taking care of our health, neglecting or destroying it instead.

However, the moral relevance of health, and in particular of mental health, is not restricted to the sphere of external actions of preserving it or healing but touches more often inner responses which we can give to states of mental unhealth or to their origins. The inner stances which we freely take towards potentially or really pathogenic conditions—for example, a deep gratitude for the goods we receive in spite of our depressions, an inner acceptance of our sufferings in a spirit of penance. Such an acceptance can take many forms, for example that of Epictetus' Stoic acceptance of whatever lies outside of our free control. The Stoic acceptance itself can still be differently motivated. It may be even an expression of pure pride as Max Scheler interprets it in his essay on humility in *Rehabilitierung der Tugend*,[26] and then would be of no moral value. However, the Stoic attitude could also spring from an acceptance of God's will and from a gratitude towards God as it is expressed beautifully by Epictetus in his *Diatribes*.[27] Regardless of how we interpret the Stoic philosophy of *atharaxia* (of an indifference), the acceptance of sufferings can certainly also spring from a deep acceptance of God's will, as in an inner *fiat*.[28] While this is a profoundly good stance taken towards suffering, we can respond to crosses and sufferings also in a spirit of ingratitude, of contempt for others and of rebellion against our fate or against God. Only because health and sickness are in many ways morally relevant, can the stances we take vis-à-vis them be good or evil in many ways. And as Professor Vitz explained so well in his paper to this conference,[29] certain morally negative attitudes, like hatred and anger, can degenerate into pathological conditions, whereas positive responses, such as forgiveness, can become sources of healing. We shall return to this point.

D. Moral evil as cause and root of mental unhealth through mediation of chemical or physical agents

Moral good and evil can have still another relation to mental health: good or evil acts can destroy health or restore it. This can be seen most easily when mental unhealth or the restoration of health are caused by physical or chemical causes, but in a way that depends on our freedom.

We may certainly call drug-addiction a form of mental unhealth, one which also brings about bad effects on the physical health of the drug-addict. A drug-addict is devoured by a craving for a drug; he is not even in full possession of the free control of his actions. Consumed by his addiction, he becomes unable to foster family life and love; he is sick. This sickness will affect his volitions, his actions, his imagination, as well as his affections.

While the whole cluster of phenomena which constitute drug-addiction might lead to a point where they render freedom and moral evil in the sick individual inactualizable, thus excusing a drug-addicted criminal inasmuch as he is a patient more than a wrongdoer, the addiction itself might nevertheless have its root in moral evil. The person may, for example, have been free at the beginning when he chose to use drugs, knowing more or less clearly their devastating effects. The same is true about many other addictions, for example, alcoholism. Likewise, in spite of being in a state of partial loss of freedom, the drug-addict may still be free to submit to a cure or program of rehabilitation, and to this extent again moral factors appear. And thus also his free actions which lead to the restoration of his health are indirect causes of health by the mediation of other more direct causes, including physical ones (for example, certain medicines) which restore the drug-addict's health.

E. The healthiness of moral goodness and the destruction by moral evil of the rationality that is the most significant element of mental health

Moral evil can involve an irrationality similar to that of mental unhealth. Even if both are distinct inasmuch as neither states of mental illness nor the underlying mental diseases are within our direct power, while a consuming hatred is purely morally evil and not clinically called a mental disease, both have a decisive point in common: namely a profound irrationality. We do not mean here irrationality in the sense of unintelligibility. For the marks, structures, and causes of hatred as well as of mental diseases can be understood. Rather, we mean by irrationality a lack of meaningfulness of the relationship between conscious intentional acts and their objects. Here we come to see that mental illness contains two elements. Firstly, it is not within our free power. In this respect the irrationality, blindness and absurdity of certain forms of moral evil are distinct and opposed to mental unhealth because they are fully responsible. But a second and an even more essential element of mental unhealth is what Freud called the essence of neurosis, namely, a loss of the sense of reality, or a special type of irrational disproportion between the true nature of things and our response to them. In this respect, the madness of evil can be much madder than the harmless form of schizophrenic "mental unhealth" of the nice chap in the movie *Arsenic and Old Lace* who believes he is George Washington. And the innocent megalomaniac who believes himself to be a greater mind than Aristotle may be less foolish than the stupidly proud man whose megalomania is not an illness in the clinical sense, but whose conviction is indistinguishably similar in content and possibly even more in contrast with reality. Or the foolishness of the diabolical pride of a person who aspires to be like God and to dethrone God is—with respect to its degree of irrationality—much madder than any innocent madness. Alfred Adler also held this view.[30] Many Renaissance writings of great humanists such as Erasmus of Rotterdam on the foolishness of mankind and on the "fool's boat" (the *Narrenschiff*) and paintings (such as Breughel's *"Carneval and Lent")* made a similar point.

We may think also of certain combinations of sadism and cruelty. Here the kind of moral evil is linked to such a dark and irrational note that we could call it sick. Of course, the sickness here is essentially different from the one which is independent from any free response on the part of the free person. It is not in the same sense sickness, but it gives to the immoral acts of a certain kind a "sick" and shockingly irrational quality which, for example, the moral evil of Don Giovanni's adventures with women does not possess. This is not to exclude that also in Don Giovanni's behavior we find a deep irrationality which all forms of moral evil possess and which in his case contradicts the true nature of love, of commitment, of the value of sex as expression of faithful mutual love, etc. But this irrationality could be called the irrationality of evil as such, while the irrationality of other kinds of moral evil also shows a structural irrationality which is more akin to madness and mental illness than the pure irrationality of evil as such. Even lesser moral evils, such as the erotic phantasies of a transsexual or of one suffering from fetishism, may be much sicker than the graver sins of adultery of an Anna Karenina, for example. The pride of a man who tyranically and arrogantly treats his subjects and those of lesser intelligence is not as sick as the morally less evil but mad pride of a poorly gifted person who thinks himself to be the most brilliant mind on earth.

F. The inner logic of certain moral evils giving rise to states of actual mental disease which lie outside the scope of our freedom

I will argue here for a further and more direct relationship between morality and mental health. There also exists some *inner* link between mental health and morality such that certain dimensions of mental health are the fruit or even a dimension of moral goodness just as certain aspects of mental illness, far from rendering freely perpetrated moral evil impossible, are much rather the direct consequences and accompanying aspects of freely perpetrated moral evils.

We do not speak here yet of a higher and archetypical sense of health, in which moral goodness itself may be called health and moral evil disease. In this way Plato uses the term when he says of the souls of evil persons who will have to appear after death before the throne of the Judge of all souls, that "nothing healthy is in them."[31] Here health is equated with moral goodness, and disease with moral evil, which makes good sense if we consider the deepest essence of health as the flourishing and actualization of life and see that a *person's life in the deepest sense is inseparable from the moral good.* From this it follows that also *health* in the deepest sense is inseparable from moral goodness, for only in the morally good person can life flourish in the deepest and fullest sense. Nevertheless, mental health in a narrower and less metaphysical-moral sense, while it envelops many relationships to the moral sphere besides that of being a condition for moral goodness, is yet distinct from moral goodness itself. Contemporary authors such as Roa refer to this classical Greek identification of morality with mental health.[32] However, we will not use this term of mental health in the following.

There is a dimension of mental health in the literal sense, though, that is far more closely connected with moral good and evil than being a condition of moral acts or being morally relevant, or involving a fundamental ability to distinguish good and evil.

Certain types of immorality, such as the senseless cruelty of soldiers against women and children in the Balkan-war, and the effects these actions have on the whole mental life of the persons who commit them, may involve an irrationality that can properly be called pathological and a mental disease. In any event, the mental harmony of the soul can only be restored in such cases by a moral conversion. I found a beautiful confirmation of this point in Professor Vitz's paper on "Hatred and Forgiveness in Psychotherapy."

The connection between such moral evils and mental unhealth does not only concern a similar element of irrationality common to both forms of evil and of madness, nor just a comparatively "accidental" causation of mental disease by moral evil, as in the case in which a person is responsible for using drugs which then cause some mental illness. (This causation is called here "comparatively accidental" because the mental disease does not flow from the very essence of the moral evil itself but is caused by chemical and physiological agents which are extrinsic to the evil acts themselves.) In the case of the more direct causation of mental diseases by moral evils we are confronted with an inner logic which leads the habitual liar to entirely lose his sense of reality, a logic which leads the excessively proud man, possessed by a certain kind of pride that seeks superiority to others, to become a megalomaniac, or a certain type of hate-filled person to fall into the pathological "splitting" described by Vitz,[33] in which he sees himself as all-good and his hated opponent as all-evil. In fact, the connection between morality and mental health here is so close that I believe that it is not possible that a very humble person, a saint, would become a megalomaniac. Empirical investigations would have to be done to confirm this point, however. But whatever their outcome, it seems to be beyond any doubt—as all great poets know[34]—that a terrible pride, unresolved feelings of guilt, tormenting ambitions, passions of jealousy and hatred, etc., can have a truly maddening effect, and that they can destroy even the most noble mind in such a way that he becomes truly mentally ill in a clinical sense. Think also of the increasingly well explored "post-abortion-syndrome" in which many neurotic symptoms proceed clearly from unresolved feelings of guilt after abortions. Moral evil here gives rise, in a highly intelligible way, to true mental illness.

In other words, there are abysses of moral evil which are also abysses of spiritual and mental disease because in them the moral evil reaches such a degree of madness that the person loses his mind. Perhaps in this perspective it is quite legitimate that the psychiatrist Roa includes certain moral virtues as parts of mental health,[35] although it is possibly not their character of virtue as such which makes them parts of health but rather a certain additional rationality they possess and a power to counteract the described dimensions of "sick moral evils."

By way of example, it seems to me that Friedrich Nietzsche reached this stage of a merge between moral evil and mental unhealth when he wrote his *Antichrist,* even if the complete nervous breakdown which he experienced later when he embraced the horse that was cruelly beaten by its owner may not have had its origin in this type of madness.

Or as another example, consider the "sickness unto death," despair, which Soren Kierkegaard analyzes in his *Sickness unto Death.*[36] Despair not only affects mental health in many ways, according to Kierkegaard, but it is itself the ultimate sickness of the spirit, and at the same time a sickness of the soul which affects countless spheres of human consciousness and mental experience, which can lead to suicide, depressions, an abysmal sense of abjection, etc. At this point, the utter irrationality and consequent inability to relate adequately to the world and to God, as well as to other persons, constitute not only mental unhealth in the previously mentioned *purely moral* and *metaphysical* senses but also in a purely psychological sense. Yet this psychic or mental sickness flows intelligibly from the moral evil of despair.

G. Mental illness as consequence of "witnessing" horrendous moral evil of other persons or being a victim of it

In an analogously intelligible way, being hit by horrible fates also can give rise to mental diseases.[37] In some of these cases we encounter another highly intelligible relation between moral evil and mental disease: the moral evil perceived in *other persons,* especially when this moral evil is directed against us, can give rise to mental disease. Think of the origin of King Lear's madness (in Shakespeare's *King Lear*). His madness, while it may well have certain roots also in his own character and pride, originates clearly in the horrible treatment he receives from his two evil daughters Regan and Goneril. Lear would not have gone mad if he had only lost his 100 servants by death or disease rather than by the ingratitude of his daughters and their breaking the clear promise they had given him. He would not have gone mad even if he had suffered much greater evils by an externally caused poverty of his children. He would not have fallen mentally ill if his faithful servant Kent had had an accident and had been caught in a trap set up in the forest by hunters rather than having been put into the block by his daughters who wanted to dishonor him, their own father.

And Lear and Gloucester would not have lost their minds if, during a hunt, they had been exposed to the elements and to torrents of rain, rather than having been sent out into the tempest by their own children. It was precisely Lear's becoming victim of the utter ingratitude and heartless actions of his daughters and of his being informed about their fiendish cruelty against Gloucester which drove him into madness.

Many examples taken from real life could be cited as evidence of this relation between mental illness and immorality. Think of the many reports of mental disturbances among witnesses of Nazi-crimes in concentration camps or of crimes committed during the Balkan-war or in the Soviet Gulags. Or think of the famous case of the couple West in England in November 1995, whose story went through the world press on November 23 and who were accused of having sexually abused and murdered at least eight different girls. Mrs. West was found guilty of having murdered in a horrendous way several of these girls, including her own oldest daughter. The sadistic details of these murders were so atrocious that the Court decided to pay for psychiatric help for the members of the Jury, some of whom had been gravely traumatized and showed severe clinical symptoms of mental disease following their hearing and seeing the evidences of this famous case in recent British criminal history.

Thus there is also an intelligibly (although not necessarily) 'maddening effect' of certain types of moral evils committed by *other persons,* when these are witnessed or known by us, particularly when these moral evils reach a certain inhuman degree of moral monstrosity and cruelty and when we stand in special relationships to the persons who commit those evils, being their fathers, spouses, friends, benefactors or children.

A further source of this maddening effect of moral evils committed by others lies in not just witnessing those moral evils but in being their victim, or seeing a person we love become their victim, such as when a father or mother witnesses the cruel murder of their children. There are countless examples from real life which demonstrate such a maddening effect of the moral evils that inflict harm and sufferings on us. Think of all the reports of the psychic effects of the victims of child abuse, rape, etc. These provide a thousandfold empirical confirmation of this connection between moral evils and mental illnesses. The relation itself, however, is intelligible philosophically prior to all empirical case-studies. If we consider the conviction that the most perfect knowledge of such evils (for example, divine knowledge) does not lead to mental insanity, we realize that the mental insanity that proceeds from witnessing horrendous crimes has further conditions besides this knowledge and a certain degree of sensibility. Contingency and some measure of imperfection is here and in all other cases found in the subject of mental insanity and is a condition of any mental illness.

*H. Moral goods which are parts of mental health and moral evils which are simul-
taneously part of mental diseases*

Still another and even closer relationship between morality and mental health
is found in those cases in which morally good acts and attitudes are themselves
part of mental health and morally evil ones are part of mental illness. Here the
moral good does not merely promote mental health but is part thereof and the
moral evil does not only tend to give rise to mental unhealth but involves necessarily a dimension of mental unhealth.[38]

Think of a certain fundamental trust which can take the form of a trust in some
Divine goodness or also the form of a trust in other human beings flowing from a
sense of fundamental *human solidarity* which is ready to trust other human persons as long as no special reason for distrust is given. These attitudes, I argue, are
both morally good and part of mental health. Without being able to show here in
detail why these two dimensions of the fundamental trust are morally good, I might
mention a few reasons that support this claim. But let us first see what is easier to
recognize: namely, that some explicit or implicit trust in the ultimate metaphysical
origin of the world (or in God) and some basic trust in other human beings is a
necessary requirement for mental health. This can be seen immediately when we
consider their total absence. Imagine a man or a woman who chooses to doubt
every belief which is not absolutely certain and indubitable and who therefore
does not take one step in trust as long as he or she is not certain of its outcome and
who distrusts utterly other human persons because he or she can never know with
indubitable certainty their secret intentions and thoughts. Their fundamental distrust of other people may have its root in their disbelief in a good God or in their
assumption of a cruel God who may always be out to destroy them, disappoint
them, or deceive them.

If such an attitude, which is at times suggested by Descartes' radical doubt,
when it is not taken as a mere methodic but as a real doubt, is pushed to its extreme, it makes any social and interhuman relations impossible because it is always possible that our wife is unfaithful in her thoughts or actions when we do not
observe her, that our friends think secretly badly of us, etc. The same is true of all
the innumerable factors in our lives over which we have no control. The Stoics,
who recognized this fact, recommended that we just care for those things which
are given into our power. But this is impossible without some belief in divine
providence (which Epictetus and other Stoic philosophers had) because many things
which are not within our free power still are decisive for human happiness. If we
therefore were to distrust consciously and naively or unconsciously, that the whole
of being is in some "good hands," we would always have to be distrustful and
diffident and be afraid of the ultimate cause and power of the universe being either
neutral and merciless or an evil world-will that wants to destroy us. But then no
hope and no peace would be possible or justified. Our whole human and social life
rests on a certain human, social, and ultimately metaphysical fundamental trust in
our senses, in the continuation of the laws of nature, in the good intentions of some

people, and in the last analysis in the good will of the personal being on whom our whole existence and future depends.

There are different levels of such a fundamental trust. One is social and refers to interpersonal relationships, especially to those persons who are closest to us. If—as in Ferdinand Raimund's brilliant comedy *Alpenkönig und Menschenfeind*—this basic trust entirely breaks down so that the misanthropist in this play distrusts his wife, assumes that the knife in the hand of his cook was destined for murdering him, and so forth, any human relationship becomes impossible and a specific madness of the extreme misanthropist sets in.

If a person refuses to trust in any way that there will be some meaning and goodness in his future, and thus becomes anxious and afraid of any step he takes and refuses not only to take big steps such as getting married (out of fear of all calamities that could hit his marriage) but even any small step which involves some fundamental trust, such as crossing a street or walking home, he will fall into some mad depression or inability to trust. But a person who refuses all trust that goes beyond his strict evidence or that puts confidence into the good will of other persons without which a genuinely human life is impossible will fall into a madness that even surpasses that of Raimund's misanthropist who shows at least some traces of human trust. Thus a person who *refuses all trust* in other persons cannot remain mentally healthy. And if he seriously disbelieves in any solidarity and goodwill of other persons, on whom he depends in so many ways, and even in God, then he cannot possess any ultimate reason to remain mentally healthy. Nietzsche may have said for this reason in the *Gay Science,* where he describes all consequences of radical atheism, that no man had ever yet the strength to live in accordance with it.[39] Seen in this perspective, a radical and wholly logical atheist, who draws all existential consequences from his atheism, could not stay mentally healthy, at least if he does not substitute the trust in God by other immoral attitudes of which we shall still speak. Thus the radical refusal of this trust in God and in other human beings which leads to a total distrust of anybody and everything makes human life and the most normal human actions impossible, destroys any human and social relationship, work-relationship, and makes it even impossible to entrust one's life to an airplane, a car, etc.

Such an attitude both violates a certain moral goodness and a certain commonsensical reasonability of the audacity of trusting other human beings. If we can know with our reason that the absolute being must be infinitely good and possess the pure perfections of justice and goodness of will,[40] it is evident that we ought to put a fundamental trust in divine providence. Moreover, the available evidence that at least some human persons showed kindness towards us and are genuinely interested in our good, is sufficient evidence that they *deserve* some trust on our part, even if this trust goes beyond what is strictly speaking absolutely evident. Perhaps there are some children who were so cruelly abused that they have "good reason" to distrust all human beings. But the situation changes when a child or a person at least once experienced genuine goodness of other human beings. Most of us have had countless experiences of such benevolent intentions of others towards us. This is clearly the case in the play by Raimund. In spite of all these hints of experience to embrace the extremely implausible assumption that the persons who show kindness towards us in the last analysis want us ill, is an insult and an immoral rejection of a sort of fundamental openness and trust with which we ought to turn towards other human beings. In fact, we could say that we have no right to mistrust another human being and to refuse to believe in his good intentions, *as long as he does not provide some positive evidence that we ought to distrust him.* A fundamental esteem *(Achtung)* of other human beings demands that we do not *a priori* distrust them.

Against this background, we can see: The person who refuses *any such fundamental trust towards fellow-human beings and a human person who distrusts completely the author of all being* violates the fundamental trust human beings owe to fellow-humans and above all to God and His providence.

This it is not just a neutral psychological condition, the inability to trust, but the refusal of a morally good trust that will lead to the above mentioned totally neurotic and indeed psychotic condition in which a person is wholly cut off from all human relationships and is tormented by fears, suspicions, and finally will end in an almost total paralyzation of his actions. For the reasons given, to take such an attitude of refusing a kind of natural trust in the goodness of God and in the wise governance of the world is morally wrong and at the same time a source of neurotic or psychotic states. That such a complete refusal of a fundamental trust is objectively morally wrong does not necessarily imply that the person who lives in such a state is acting immorally or is morally evil. For in some persons, especially children who suffered unspeakably, such a distrust in the face of the hellish world in which they lived, may be without guilt of theirs and rather the fruit of the sin of others against them. But in most persons the refusal of this fundamental trust constitutes a despair and hopelessness which is profoundly morally evil. Soren Kierkegaard analyzed this immorality of despair in his book *Sickness unto Death.*

But also a less immoral and less metaphysical and religious level of the refusal of a basic trust, namely, a misanthropic distrust in humanity, is both immoral and mentally sick. Such a radical misanthropist will approach every individual with an unfounded total mistrust and thus both offend his human dignity and end in a mental state worse than that of Ferdinand Raimund's *Menschenfeind.*

At this point it becomes also evident that mental health has certain *metaphysical presuppositions.* For if God were out to destroy us and would not justify our trust, this state of total mental unhealth of complete distrust would be the only one adequate to the world.

Similarly, if all other human beings were as wholly lacking solidarity as the misanthropist thinks, if they were all a hellish folk of liars, deceivers, and murderers, this mental unhealth would be adequate to reality. Then the love which gives a credit to the other person, which contains elements of belief, trust and hope, would be impossible. Without these elements no human love and friendship would be possible. But a person who is incapable of *any love* is also mentally ill. Thus a normal life also has certain social and moral conditions regarding the society in which we live.

Now while the negative moral attitude in this case gives rise necessarily to mental unhealth, the corresponding morally positive trust which is part of mental health can also be substituted by a morally neutral or even by an immoral attitude which still may leave mental health intact. This is the case if one's fundamental trust is given without any rational foundation in the truth or if any other human being, even those who clearly deceive us, is trusted, etc., or if the trust springs from the conceitedness of the subject who trusts, etc. In other words, there are many attitudes which can substitute for the truly morally good trust.

I prescind here from the interesting question as to whether there are many other such attitudes which belong to a human life, for example some form of gratitude, of humility and recognition of our limits, of readiness to forgive offenses, etc. I would think, however, that there is a considerable number of such morally good qualities which are a necessary part of mental health and that there are—even more unambiguously—a great number of related moral evils which constitute immediately a state of mental illness.

I. Combinations of mental illness and moral evil in fetishism and other psychic illnesses

Still another relation between mental disease and moral evil lies in a type of coexistence of both in certain types of living out moral evil by a person afflicted by perverse inclinations which may also be regarded as forms of mental illness. Before we have pointed out the similarity between the moment of irrationality in certain forms of moral evil and the irrationality found in mental abnormalities. Now we consider the very different type of relationship between moral evil and mental illness that consists in the coexistence of both and the close connections and interrelations between them. Take the fetishist man who performs impure acts not with a woman and not even, if he is homosexual, with another man,[41] but with the shoes or blouses of his beloved, let us say, of his neighbor's wife. This is a lesser moral evil than adultery but mentally sick, while adultery as such is not mentally sick. Or take the proud and arrogant commander who, fallen mentally ill, thinks in his schizophrenia that he is Napoleon and shouts abominable orders and lives out his destructive evil arrogance. Here, the immorality of his pride partakes in his madness, which leads to a closely knit but unsightly marriage of both.

IV. Conclusion

To conclude our consideration of the relationships between mental health and morality, we may say with the Socrates of the *Apology* also about mental health that it is not the highest good for man[42] and that "from the virtue of the soul all other goods come." Also the words of Socrates which form the title of a recent paper of Giovanni Reale about Plato's concept of health, entitled "If you want to cure your body, first cure your soul"[43] could be applied and transcribed here: "If you want to cure mental diseases, seek cure and overcome first the moral evil in your soul." In the light of the preceding reflections, and of the whole of Plato's text, this statement must of course not be interpreted in the sense that there is no innocent mental illness caused by brain damage or other factors that are entirely beyond our control, as there are also causes of poverty which do not justify a literal reading of the Socratic word that "wealth comes from virtue." Nonetheless, the Socratic words from the *Apology* retain a deep truth especially in reference to mental health, a truth which I would explain by saying the following: *While a saintly person may be innocently mentally ill, a person not given to the quest for meaning and the good will never be quite healthy, and a demonically evil person is also profoundly sick. Personal health can be defined ultimately only in terms of a full givenness to goods which both transcend the level of health and yet are necessary to realize health: the True, the Beautiful, and the Good in all their forms and especially in their highest forms.*

NOTES

1. In September 1995 the International Academy of Philosophy in the Principality Liechtenstein hosted a conference entitled "Person, Society and Value: Towards a Personalistic Conception of Health." I am indebted to a number of speakers at the conference for enriching my concept of health and mental health. Here I would like to thank in particular Professors Armando Roa, Giovanni Reale, and Manuel Lavados who influenced the development of this paper. These papers will be published in P. Donohue-White, K. Fedoryka, P. Taboada (Ed.), *Towards a Personalistic Conception of Health.* I also wish to acknowledge gratefully many excellent suggestions on this text which I received from the participants in its discussion in Dallas and later from Dr. James DuBois, Mag. K. Fedoryka and Dr. P. Taboada, with whom I could discuss the contents of the paper in a research seminar on the philosophical aspects of health.

2. See Josef Seifert, *Leib und Seele. Ein Beitrag zur philosophischen Anthropologie* (Salzburg: A. Pustet, 1973), "Prolegomena," *What is Life? On the Irreducibility of Life to Chaotic and Non-Chaotic Physical Systems* (Amsterdam: Rodopi, 1993), *Sein und Wesen* (Heidelberg: C. Winter, 1996), ch. 1.

3. In what follows I will sometimes use the technical term 'unhealth' to denote the opposite of health, rather than the more common terms disease or illness. The term 'unhealth' covers all kinds of opposites to health, not only those which are due to illness and disease, but also health-deficiencies of any kind, for example, those which are caused by injury, retardation, deformity, or perverse instincts. Moreover, the term 'unhealth' suggests merely the absence or deficiency of health, whereas the terms 'illness' and 'disease' connotes that which *causes* this absence of health. Such a use of the term of 'unhealth' has been introduced recently as a

technical term into the philosophical discussion of health, while the term 'un-healthy' in ordinary parlance has a very different meaning, referring to food or climatic conditions which threaten health. See, for example, H. Tristram Engelhardt, Jr., "The Concepts of Health and Disease," in: Caplan, A.L., Engelhardt, H.T & Mc Cartney, J.J., *Concepts of Health and Disease. Interdisciplinary Perspectives*, 1981, pp. 31-46.

4. Armando Roa, "The Concept of Mental Health," in: P. Donohue-White, K. Fedoryka, P. Taboada (Ed.).

5. See Roa, *ibid.*

6. Roa refers to R. D. Laing, D. Cooper, and T. Szasz as anti-psychiatrists who deny many forms of mental health or even the very notion of mental health as an invention. See Armando Roa, "The Concept of Mental Health," *op. cit.*

7. See on this Roa, *ibid.*: "all—or almost all—societies distinguished the mentally ill from the delinquent. Both of these disturb the social order, but punishments were established only for the delinquent. This shows that it was not the failure to conform to a social order which constituted the deviation from being healthy."

8. I cannot pursue here a discussion of the exact differences between illness and disease.

9. This is also the view of Armando Roa, who writes: "health is a primary concept, capable of being clarified through comparisons and certain characteristics, but not definable through broader concepts." (*ibid.*)

10. This formulation leaves open the question whether also pure spirits (angels) could be called mentally healthy and ill but restricts the meaning of 'health' to a finite level of personhood, implying that an all-perfect personal life would be beyond the level designated by 'health.' While the supremely living absolute being encompasses the innermost perfection designated by the term 'health,' the full flourishing and actuality of life, and possesses in this sense the archetypical perfection meant by health, the term 'health' designates a form of life which is capable of sickness or illness and a finite form of life which has different levels of perfections (vital values and other higher perfections) which cannot be attributed to divine life.

11. See Marie Jahoda, *Current Concepts of Positive Mental Health* (New York: Basic Books, 1958).

12. On 2 and 3 cf. also Armando Roa, *op. cit.*

13. Roa, referring to Marie Jahoda, characterizes the third and fourth features of 'mental health' in the following way: "consciousness and acceptance of the 'I' and a sense of personal identity." *op. cit.*

14. I refer here to Lavados's paper entitled "Relations between Empirical and Philosophical Aspects of a Definition of Health," to be published in: P. Donohue-White, K. Fedoryka, P. Taboada (Ed.). See the following text : "As illness hurts man in his nature, it hurts him ... doubly. First, by depriving him ... of the exercise of his natural functions...Second, illness imposes a limitation on the free construction of his personal being."

15. "Health is a state of complete physical, mental and social well-being and not merely the absence of disease or infirmity," (from the Preamble of the *Constitution of the World Health Organization*, adopted by the International Health Conference in New York, 1946).

16. See H. Tristram Engelhardt, Jr., "The Concepts of Health and Disease," in: Caplan, A.L., Engelhardt, H.T & Mc Cartney, J.J. ed., pp. 31-46.

17. This is not only true of mental retardation or incapacitation but also of mental illnesses in the narrower sense such as schizophrenia which do have, or can have, purely physiological and other causes that are entirely independent of freedom.

18. Cf. also Armando Roa, *op. cit.*

19. Cf. also Max Scheler's discussion of utilitarianism and an ethics of success (*Erfolgsethik*) in his *Formalism in Ethics and Non-Formal Ethics of Values,* transl. Manfred S. Frings and Roger L. Funk (Evanston: Northwestern University Press, 1973).

20. See Armando Roa, *op. cit.* In his paper, he switches, however, to a position which identifies mental health with many purely moral attitudes and acts, and mental unhealth with certain forms of evil. In what follows, we shall discover a partial justification of this.

21. Possibly the most outstanding investigation into this type of moral value blindness, which is also of deep interest for psychology, is Dietrich von Hildebrand, *Sittlichkeit und ethische Werterkenntnis. Eine Untersuchung über ethische Strukturprobleme,* in: *Jahrbuch für Philosophie und phänomenologische Forschung* (1922), 3rd, revised edition: Vallendar-Schönstatt: Patris Verlag. 1982. (Ed. Dietrich-von-Hildebrand-Gesellschaft).

22. See the moving book on this by one of the survivors and victims of this horror, Wanda Póltawska, *Und ich fürchte meine Träume,* 2. Auflage (Avensberg: Maria aktuell, 1994).

23. This crucial distinction in ethics was first clearly made by Dietrich von Hildebrand. See his *Ethics*, 2nd edition (Chicago: Franciscan Herald Press, 1978); *Moralia.* Nachgelassenes Werk. Gesammelte Werke Band V (Regensburg: Josef Habbel, 1980).

24. See Dietrich von Hildebrand, *Moralia*. Nachgelassenes Werk. Gesammelte Werke Band V. (Regensburg: Josef Habbel, 1980), pp. 445 ff.

25. Max Scheler, *Der Formalismus in der Ethik und die materiale Wertethik*, 5. Aufl. (Bern und München: Francke, 1966): "Wer seinem Nächsten nicht wohltun will— so daß es ihm auf die Realisierung dieses Wohles ankommt—, sondern nur die Gelegenheit ergreift, in diesem Akt selbst "gut zu sein" oder "Gutes" zu tun, der ist nicht oder tut nicht wahrhaft sittlich gut... (der Wert gut) befindet sich gleichsam auf dem Rücken dieses Aktes."

26. Cf. Max Scheler, "Humility," transl. by Barbara Fiand, *Aletheia* 2 (1981), pp. 210-219.

27. Cf. Josef Seifert, "Phänomenologie der Dankbarkeit als Zugang zu einer personalistischen Metaphysik," in: J. Seifert (Ed.), *Danken und Dankbarkeit. Eine universale Dimension des Menschseins* (Heidelberg: Universitätsverlag C. Winter, 1992), pp. 75-95, to be published also in English (Dallas, 1996).

28. One could think here also of the words of the good thief on the Cross which the Catholic Church linked to indulgences: *merito patior* (I suffer deservedly).

29. Paul Vitz, "Hatred and Forgiveness in Psychotherapy," in this volume.

30. See Alfred Adler, *Menschenkenntnis* (Frankfurt a. M., 1966), pp. 189 ff. See also my paper read at the last Conference of the Institute for Personalist Psychology, 1994, Josef Seifert, "Inferiority Complex and Response: Alfred Adler—Discoveries and Errors," in: James M. DuBois, *The Nature and Tasks of a Personalist Psychology* (Lanham/New York/London: University Press of America, 1995), pp. 87-110.

31. Plato, *Gorgias, Phaedo*.

32. "Greek medicine believed that the state of health corresponds to the perfect ordering of the combination and functioning of the four corporal humors. As a consequence of this, health coincided with moral goodness, because being good belongs to health." (Roa, *op. cit.*).

33. See Vitz, *op. cit.*

34. Shakespeare's insights into the origins of the mental breakdown of Lady Macbeth and Dostoevsky's analysis of the roots of severe mental disturbances of several of his characters are splendid examples of this knowledge.

35. See Roa, *ibid.*

36. Soren Kierkegaard, *Die Krankheit zum Tode*, trans. and commented by L. Richter, 2nd ed. (Frankfurt a.M.; Rohwolt, 1986), pp. 18 ff.

37. Frankl's Logotherapy can only be used, I argue, in such cases where either the loss of meaning for nonmoral reasons or free moral attitudes and actions lead to neuroses, psychoses, and other mental illnesses, or where free responses and rational discoveries of meaning can cure them.

38. I must add immediately, however, a point to be explained below, namely that it is possible in these cases to substitute for the genuinely moral virtue which is simultaneously a part of mental health an attitude which also conditions mental health, but which is a pseudo-virtue which has no moral value and possibly even a moral disvalue.

39. "*Excelsior.*—'You will never pray again, never adore again, never again rest in endless trust; you do not permit yourself to stop before any ultimate wisdom, ultimate goodness, ultimate power, while unharnessing your thoughts; you have no perpetual guardian and friend for your seven solitudes; you live without a view of mountains with snow on their peaks and fire in their hearts; there is no avenger for you any more nor any final improver; there is no longer any reason in what happens, no love in what will happen to you; no resting place is open any longer to your heart, where it only needs to find and no longer seek; you resist any ultimate peace; you will the eternal recurrence of war and peace: man of renunciation, all this you wish to renounce? Who will give you the strength for that? *Nobody yet has had this strength!*'" Friedrich Nietzsche, *The Gay Science*, trans. W. Kaufmann, (New York: Random House, 1974), IV, 285. Emphasis added.

40. All classical proofs for the existence of God try to establish this truth with apodictic philosophic certainty. I developed such proofs elsewhere. See Josef Seifert, *Essere e persona. Verso una fondazione fenomenologica di una metafisica classica e personalistica.* (Milano: Vita e Pensiero, 1989); see also my *Gott als Gottesbeweis* (Heidelberg: Universitätsverlag C. Winter, 1996).

41. Also homosexual inclinations have been regarded until recently in most handbooks of psychiatry as a mental disorder but have been eliminated from most lists of mental diseases and anomalies today. See for example the Proceedings of the American Psychiatric Association (1955) and the cited works of R.D. Laing.

42. See the very similar idea expressed by Manuel Lavados, *op. cit*: "In the case of man, ... Health corresponds to the state of perfection of living in man that does not depend on the exercise of his freedom. Health for man is not identical with his total and final good."

43. See Reale, "If you want to cure the body, first cure the soul," in P. Donohue-White, K. Fedoryka, P. Taboada (Ed.), *op. cit.*

II. Dealing With Hatred and Pain

3

Hatred and Forgiveness: Major Moral Dilemmas in Secular Psychotherapy

Paul C. Vitz
Philip Mango

In this paper two major psychological phenomena, hatred and forgiveness, will be discussed and analyzed in the context of psychotherapy. Besides treating their role in the therapeutic process, the paper will also present the argument that important psychological aspects of hatred and forgiveness are intrinsically incapable of resolution by nonreligious means.

The major dilemmas can be briefly described before moving to a more detailed treatment of them. Consider the ubiquitous capacity of human beings to hurt others. Often we even hate those whom we have hurt or harmed. The problem here is that if we are guilty of such actions we will also suffer from genuine guilt as a result. The simple fact is that genuine guilt cannot be removed without our repentance and without God's forgiveness. Certainly the psychotherapist cannot forgive the patient for hurting others, and in the great majority of instances those who have been hurt are unavailable to forgive the patient even if they could be contacted and were willing. Unfortunately, Americans tend to think that guilt is somebody else's problem and not theirs—that is, we are convinced that we are much more sinned against than sinners. Good evidence for this is the widely prevalent narcissism of our self-oriented society, combined with our equally prevalent victim psychology (Sykes, 1992). In short, many Americans see themselves as the victims of other people's abuse. Nevertheless, as Scripture says, and ordinary common sense supports it, "we have all sinned." The problem is that the psychological harm that comes to each person as a result of harming others cannot be removed without forgiveness.

If we set aside the issue of those whom we have hurt and turn to the matter of those who have hurt us, we still face psychological dilemmas. A standard response to those who have hurt us is to hate them. It is argued in Vitz and Mango (1997) that this hatred is itself intrinsically harmful to the person doing the hating, and often to others. (It is claimed by Vitz and Mango that hatred can be considered as a psychological defense mechanism.) In any case, if we wish to get rid of the burden of our victim psychology and our hatred of others, the best known procedure is to forgive the other and to recognize the harm to ourselves and others that our hatred caused. This kind of forgiveness of one's enemies is not necessarily religious, but a religious rationale is often a major support for it. After all, it is very difficult to forgive those we hate. Thus, such forgiveness involves a kind of partial dilemma for secular psychology. No doubt this is why the major approaches to psychotherapy from Sigmund Freud to Carl Rogers have ignored the basic concept of forgiveness. And, of course, repentance and the acceptance of forgiveness from God for the effects of our hatred on others and ourselves are impossible in a secular framework.[1]

A religious perspective on hatred

To begin, we should note some of hatred's basic implications for religious aspects of psychotherapy. Although psychologists often focus on extreme forms of pathology, it is likely that even the most normal of people exhibit hatred close to the pathological when they are under great stress. Most adults at certain times have "demonized"—at least briefly—a particular enemy. In the process we also show "splitting," that is, making someone all bad or all good. (See below.) Furthermore, even when stress is not intense the so-called "normal" hatreds found in the ordinary person's life can be understood as different in degree but not in kind from those found in severe psychopathology.

In addition, the treatment of hatred raises the fundamental issue of sin and its origins. (This is not to imply that psychological theorists think in terms of concepts like "sin.") Certainly, the familiar ease with which human beings develop and then hold on to hatred in response to pain and trauma can be taken as a sign of our fallen nature. A position which is consistent with Melanie Klein's remark that "The repeated attempts that have been made to improve humanity—in particular, to make it more peaceful—have failed, because nobody has understood the full depth and vigour of the instincts of aggression innate in each individual" (quoted by Wolberg, 1988, p. 247).

Psychological origins of hatred

Sigmund Freud proposed that aggression and hatred were intrinsic to human nature and that we were born with a large amount of what he called "thanatos." That is, Freud claimed that the "death instinct" was a basic, innate part of everyone. An important psychoanalyst who developed Freud's view was Melanie Klein (1946, 1957, 1964), who explicitly proposed that "primal rage" and envy were instinctual aspects of human motivation that were clearly present even in the infant. More specifically, she proposed that in the first few months of life the infant was unable to recognize that the good aspects of the mother and the bad aspects of the mother were part of the same person. As a result, the infant constructed a split representation of the mother, namely the "good mother" and the "bad mother." The "bad mother" mobilizes the infant's intrinsic hatred and rage. The good and the bad aspects of the mother are so contradictory that for the infant they can not be combined in the same internal schema. Later, as the cognitive capacities of the child develop, these two contradictory aspects of the mother are combined, and the child no longer shows splitting. This integration occurs both as a result of cognitive maturation and because most mothers are significantly more positive than negative. As a result, for most people, factoring "bad mother" elements into their internal psychological representation is not particularly conflictual. However, if the mother is powerfully negative—and thus bad elements equal or even outnumber good elements—then the conflict is great and it is very hard to resolve the original split. The result is that the child maintains this very fundamental split often into adulthood. This general view of splitting is accepted by almost all psychoanalytically-oriented psychologists although many may reject Klein's emphasis on innate origins.

There is another generally-accepted consequence of splitting—namely projection. Through splitting, the infant maintains the false view that it is not the idealized good mother that frustrates him but some other devalued bad mother. Further, through projection, the infant rids himself of his own aggressive feelings by attributing them to that same bad mother, thus preserving the experience that both self and the primary other are "good."

The major costs of these defenses are that, first, the accurate perception of reality is compromised. Second, the infant has created an external world of persecutory bad objects from whom he fears attack and retaliation, i.e., a paranoid system. Unless the infant progresses beyond this stage, there will be long-term serious difficulties in reality-testing. That is, unless the harmful consequences of splitting are overcome, there will be substantial mental pathology.

People who maintain this split representation of the mother often generalize the same dichotomous thinking to other people, and suffer greatly because of it. The problem is that until we can see important people in our life as a mixture of both good and bad elements we are unable to see people as they really are. It is quite dysfunctional to constantly demonize or idealize others.

Anger and hatred: the difference between them

Anger is a natural reaction to almost any actual or perceived attack, hurt or threat. Anger is both the immediate emotional and behavioral response to such attacks and it is familiar to all. Anger is often normal and appropriate, not psychologically harmful. Hatred, by contrast, is not an immediate reaction, but rather depends upon the cultivation of anger. This cultivation creates supporting cognitive structures, which continue to produce negative affect, causing psychological pathology. It is assumed that hatred sets up splitting much more than does anger. The injunction not to let the sun go down on one's anger is presumably aimed at preventing the development of hatred and the serious problems which go with it.

Hatred as choice

An essential point needs to be made here—a point that is not part of any major secular psychological position—namely that hatred in adults at its core is not affect but volition. Hatred in childhood can exist as an affect, and not as a willed decision, for example as a response to severe abuse. Presumably very little true volition is involved in the experiences that set up fixation and developmental arrest. The point being made, however, is that adults, at some later time, do freely decide either to accept their hatred or to work at rejecting it. Even more important, in psychotherapy itself, the patient is confronted with a choice. Either he or she *decides* to begin or not to begin the process of letting go of hatred and moving toward forgiveness. Hatred, in adults is therefore ultimately a free decision to intend to do evil to others (or to self). It is not intense affect determined by psychological processes such as affective aversion. Indeed, for the adult, much of the affect associated with hatred is not a cause of hatred but a consequence of previously built cognitive structures and of actions of the will. Hatred also involves a decision, a refusal to love and forgive; a refusal to request, accept or give forgiveness. In the willed sense, hatred of others or self is never healthy. It is "natural" in the sense of being common but it never produces psychological health.

Obviously, the patient does not have the freedom to stop hating in the sense of easily or suddenly abandoning pathological structures built up over many years. But, as stated, he or she does have the freedom to *begin* to stop hating. In part, this freedom is demonstrated in the patient's continued participation in therapy. However, at some point, usually after many sessions, the freedom to begin to let go of hate-filled structures arises in more concrete ways.

In psychoanalytic terms, our emphasis on the patient's will can be interpreted as an example of Meissner's (1993) "self as agent." Meissner interprets the self as a super-ordinate structural construct representing the whole person and containing the willing or responsible self as agent, as actor.

The concept of forgiveness

In this paper, the term "forgiveness" refers to a person's conscious decision to give up resentment and hatred and any claims for redress from someone who has hurt him or her. The psychological processes presumed to be involved in the act of forgiveness are a central focus here, since it is clear that the underlying dynamics of a patient can encumber, and may render nearly impossible genuine forgiveness. Certain patients have never or rarely observed, given, or experienced forgiveness. For them, the therapist is often a source of a new understanding. For many, the very fact that the therapist faithfully comes to the sessions constitutes an implicit forgiveness since he or she continues to show support even if the patient is often critical or even hostile.

At times, the therapist may directly forgive a patient for expressing hostility; even more therapeutic may be the occasional times when the therapist may apologize to the patient for the therapist's mistakes or hurtful behavior which were perhaps not intentional, for example, having to be out of town for a particular session. (See Gartner, 1992.) In these instances, the opportunity for forgiveness, even of minor wrongs, is offered to the patient.

In time the patient has examples—implicit and sometimes explicit—of forgiveness, and often the desire now to forgive others. But even here, as the authors have observed, the patient may decide not to forgive, out of fear, pride, selfishness, etc. As Gartner (1992) observed, overcoming splitting can facilitate real forgiveness but, still, the fact that *I can* forgive does not mean that *I will*.

Often in psychotherapy with patients without serious pathologies, there is no hatred projected onto the therapist but rather there is hatred of others such as parents, siblings, peers, co-workers, etc. In this situation, the therapist can use the therapeutic alliance with the patient to facilitate forgiveness by mobilizing the cognitive, affective and volitional ability of the patient. For example, the conscious use of forgiveness exercises has been described as useful. (Fitzgibbons, 1986).

Gartner (1992) proposed that authentic forgiveness is not the replacement of negative affect with positive loving feelings, as is commonly believed. Authentic, mature forgiveness requires, as a precondition, an integrated realistic perception of both the positive and negative aspects of self and others (p. 23). This cognitive dimension of being convinced of our own and of others' dual nature is an essential precondition. That is, splitting must first be overcome, especially with respect to early childhood relationships. But keep in mind that many normal adults under extreme stress or provocation may engage in splitting. One can assume that this mechanism is very common today in (for example) the former Yugoslavia.

Our proposed psychological explanation for why splitting prevents forgiveness goes like this: When the patient is all good and his or her enemy is experienced as all bad, there is a complete *qualitative* distinction between the self and the other. This difference—this conceptual abyss—makes it impossible for the patient to empathize with the other. Only awareness of the other's good qualities and of the self's bad features allows recognition of the other as like the self. Otherwise the other is almost a different species: a demon. And human beings do not forgive demons.

The forgiveness process

Forgiveness is presumed to be the culmination of the stages shown in Table 1. The last stage—stage 5—is rarely examined in detail in psychotherapy. It is the present thesis that pathological early interpersonal relations, trauma-related depression and severe hatred, for example, are never really resolved without two normally religious processes: repentance and forgiveness. Therefore a more thorough clinical understanding of the stages in Table 1—especially the last stage—is needed.

The stages and their sequence shown in Table 1 should be understood as schematic simplifications. In actual psychotherapy, aspects of later stages may occur at the same time as earlier stages. There is often "backing and filling," as well as

Table 1. *Stages in Recovery from Psychological Trauma as Proposed by Different Theorists*

	1.	2.	3.	4.	5.
A. *In Healing a Memory* (Linn & Linn, 1978)	**Denial** I don't admit I was ever hurt (denial, reaction-formation, idealization)	**Anger** I blame others for hurting and trying to destroy me	**Bargaining** I set up conditions to be fulfilled before I'm ready to forgive	**Depression** I blame myself for letting hurt destroy me	**Acceptance** I look forward to *growth* from resolved hurts; I accept self and forgive others; I re-pent for hurting others
B. *In Recovery from Borderline Personality Disorder* (Kernberg, 1992)	**Psychopathic Transference** Deceptive, narcissistic denial of vulnerability and hurt	**Paranoid Transference** Projected anger at therapist for breaking down psychopathic defenses	For Kernberg: No stage; but resistance is recognized	**Depressive Transference** Patient recognizes depth of his hatred, envy. Experiences shame, guilt, depression	**Acceptance** Accept self/others based on empathy with self/others, including negative aspects; positive modifications of super-ego.
C. *In Healing Any Psychological Trauma* (Vitz & Mango, 1998)	**Denial** Same as A or B, depending on depth of pathology	**Anger and Hatred** Same as A or B, depending on depth of pathology	**Resistance** Partial recognition that problem, e.g., hatred, is within self; this creates resistance: narcissistic/anxious avoidance; bargaining is one kind of resistance	**Depression** Similar to A or B, depending on depth of pathology; recognition of self's contribution to hatred. Self blame leads to: (1) guilt/mourning or (2) clinical depression which can block resolution	**Resolution** Accept self/others. repent of hatred and envy that hurt others/self. Accept God's forgiveness of self; forgive others. Qualitative change in super-ego.

complex interaction among stages. But the order shown in Table 1 is generally found to represent the logical therapeutic sequence.

The Linn model

A major contribution to the understanding of the psychology of forgiveness has been made by Dennis and Matthew Linn (1978). (Table 1, top row.) The Linn brothers observed that the five stages of the death and dying process described by Elizabeth Kubler-Ross (1969) can also be applied to understanding forgiveness. According to Bretherton (1992), Kubler-Ross appears to have been influenced by Bowlby's description (Robertson and Bowlby, 1952) of the psychological stages in a child's response to separation from its mother; these were elaborated into four phases of grief by Bowlby and Parkes (1970): (1) numbness, (2) yearning and protest, (3) disorganization and despair, and (4) reorganization.

In working with persons who have experienced psychic injury, the Linns identify, first, the injuries, secondly, the stage of the forgiveness process at which the patient is currently located. They concurrently empathize with patients and help them continue the forgiveness process. We also propose that Otto Kernberg's (1992, ch. 14) model of recovery in borderline patients can be interpreted as another example of the general model shown in Table 1.

Kernberg's Stages 1 and 2 rather nicely parallel those proposed by Linn and Linn (1978). The third stage, called "bargaining" by the Linns, is not explicitly found in Kernberg. However, Kernberg does acknowledge resistance as a kind of intervening clinical situation and therefore we propose that he recognizes something roughly equivalent to this stage. Stage 4, depression, is found in each model in relatively similar form. Stage 5, involving resolution, is similar in all models, but there are important distinctions.

In the model of this process, found in the bottom row (Table 1), we (Vitz and Mango, 1998) accept the first two stages as derived from the earlier theorists. Stage 3 we believe is better described as "resistance," since bargaining is only one form of resistance, and this term is consistent with Kernberg's general understanding of borderline recovery. Resistance is triggered by subjects' growing awareness of their own responsibility for much of their hatred and their sense of the possible emergence of depression in response to understanding how their hatred has hurt themselves and others. There is also an unconscious understanding that they will have to let go of their hatred. The possibility of depression is resisted for obvious reasons, and the many reasons for resisting the letting go of hatred are described in Vitz and Mango (1997).[2]

Resistance can express itself in silence, avoidance of sessions, in arguments with the therapist over the legitimacy of hatred, and in avoidance of further progress toward forgiveness by sidetracking the therapeutic session into irrelevant topics. In short, besides directly resisting and bargaining, it is through various forms of avoidance that this stage is often expressed. Stage 4 is more or less the same in each model, except that we make a distinction between normal grief and mourning and clinical depression.

There are commonly specific signs which accompany each stage. Denial is often accompanied by painkilling, mood-altering activities and addictions such as alcohol, food, drugs, work, or sex. Addictions of all kinds are often attempts to numb the pain at Stage 1. In Stage 2, where anger and rage are expressed, accompanying signs are pervasive self-pity, passivity about other aspects of life, and extreme devaluation of the other and of those similar to the hated person. Defenses such as splitting, fantasy, rationalization, reaction-formation, projection, idealization, devaluation, repression, and obsessive preoccupation with the hated other are also often observable at this stage.

Signs of Stage 3 resistance include: ambivalence toward forgiveness; compulsive returning to expressions of hatred or to the scene of being hurt; resistance to empathy or compassion for the "enemy"; setting of preconditions; a sense of entitlement. Stage 4 signs include deep sadness or tears over harm done to others and self, and depression over lost years and opportunities; expressions of despair.

Crucial issues arise with respect to Stage 5. This stage is not developed in much detail by Kernberg, but one important process in recovery from the depression is acceptance of the self and of others. This acceptance involves the integration of both good and bad aspects of the self, and thus the overcoming of splitting. Certainly to accept oneself and others as flawed human beings is necessary for psychological health because it corresponds to a realistic understanding of people. Along with Gartner and the Linns, we consider this sort of acceptance to be one important component of the final stage, but we propose that another major process is also necessary in Stage 5, namely forgiveness, which involves much more than self-acceptance.

The dilemma of genuine guilt

As mentioned earlier, a major problem arises when the patient must face genuine guilt. When one has, in fact, through one's own behavior, hurt other people and/or hurt oneself in a serious way, self-acceptance is a seriously inadequate response. An initial difficulty, therefore, for a nonreligious psychology is that the patient's self-acceptance is an unsatisfactory response to major harm that he or she has done to others or to the self.

The problem of self-forgiveness

Some psychologists might suggest self-forgiveness. But you cannot forgive yourself for a crime or harm against another: a criminal who forgave himself for his deeds (such as murder, rape or theft) would rightly be seen as self-indulgent, and perhaps even as psychopathic. The problem is a very basic one because we believe that the Judeo-Christian understanding that we have all sinned and that no one is just before God is an empirically accurate description of each person's condition. We all have real guilt—and what are we to do with it? The prominent psychologist O. Hobart Mower (1960) put the problem clearly some years ago:

For several decades, we psychologists looked upon the whole matter of sin and moral accountability as a great incubus and acclaimed our liberation from it as epoch-making. But at length we have discovered that to be "free" in this sense, i.e., to have the excuse of being "sick" rather than sinful, is to court the danger of also becoming lost... Just so long as a person lives under the shadow of real, unacknowledged and unexpiated guilt, he *cannot* (if he has any character at all) "accept himself"; and all *our* efforts to reassure and accept him will avail nothing. He will continue to hate himself and to suffer the inevitable consequences of self-hatred. (pp. 303-4)

The dilemma for a nonreligious psychology is this: if one believes that people cannot forgive themselves, then where are they to find forgiveness? Who can dispense forgiveness? As Freud himself once said: "And now, just suppose I said to a patient: 'I, Professor Sigmund Freud, forgive thee thy sins.' What a fool I should make of myself." (Freud/Pfister, 1963, p. 125).

Even our self-hatred requires forgiveness from God. Patients usually hate themselves because they have failed to meet some self-constructed standard of excellence. I must be rich, married, beautiful, successful, thin, morally perfect... These standards are then used to judge the self harshly when it fails to live up to them. But this is taking over God's role as judge—and it calls for repentance. In its extreme forms, self-hatred leads to the very serious sin of despair, which involves a rejection of God's love and mercy. Another way of defining the problem is to note the traditional definition of sin: it is, first, an offense against God and, second, a sin against our brothers and sisters, and ourselves. From this it follows that self-forgiveness is not really possible.

It is for these reasons that we propose that sorrow or contrition for the harm one has done is not capable of true resolution without forgiveness, and forgiveness of the self requires God's action—or, at the very least, a *belief* in God's action. It is at this crucial point that psychology must defer to religion, since psychology has no effective answer to the problem of genuine guilt or to its correlate, the need for the forgiveness of one's self.

Of course, false or pseudo-guilt—namely, painful "guilt feelings" caused by defective parenting, manipulation by the superego, by environmental forces and faulty cognitive processes—is not healed by forgiveness proper, but by effective psychotherapy, cognitive restructuring, and the acceptance of love from others.

False forgiveness

Forgiveness can, however, be distorted by a patient's conscious or unconscious motives. The result can be a pseudo- or false forgiveness, put in the service of pathology. It is important to describe the more common varieties. Examples of pseudo-forgiveness include the following:

1) *Narcissistic condescension.* For example, "forgiveness" given from an attitude of moral superiority, as when a wife "forgives" her husband because she feels morally superior to him and "forgiveness" is the thing to do. This type of

pseudo-forgiveness is more common in women than in men, on the basis of our experience.

2) *Denial*. For example "forgiveness" given without direct confrontation with one's own hatred of the other. This seems to be more common in male patients, who want to "solve the problem" from a practical viewpoint, but without confronting their own feelings or the relationship in any honest or specific way.

3) *Reaction formation*. This involves giving "forgiveness" along with a forced positive attitude and feeling of affection, etc. However, this covers over a repressed and still strong hatred.

4) *Undoing*. This involves using "forgiveness" as a way to escape guilt based on the following rationale. The person is "forgiven" in order to undo the harm that has been done—to make it magically not have happened. But this is not real forgiveness, not a gift to the other; rather, it is for one's own benefit.

5) *Neurotic dependency*. This is the use of language and behavior of "forgiveness" in order to maintain a pathological dependency on someone, or to maintain a masochistic relation. Such dependency is usually rooted in a painfully negative self-concept.

6) *Symbiosis*. This involves a pseudo-forgiveness in which a person has yet to achieve a secure object constancy. Persons use the language and behavior of forgiveness to ward off deep anxieties about abandonment by the person with whom they are still symbiotically fused. (This is, of course, a serious pathology, found typically in borderline personality disorder).

7) *Manipulative use of power*. For example, this occurs when an appearance of forgiveness is used to put pressure on others, to force them to admit their guilt or wrongdoing, and to escape responsibility for one's own actions (e.g., to hide one's guilt behind the others' forced confession.) One should keep in mind, again, that genuine forgiveness is a free gift without any demand for a return, without any strings attached. Pseudo-forgiveness of others defends against the painful, necessary and healthy process of true forgiveness.

Looking back, we can see that the theoretical psychology of hatred and forgiveness are far from simple and easily understood. The present paper is part of a much larger recent focus on these topics. (See McCullough and Worthington, 1994). Considerably more work needs to be done on methods that facilitate forgiveness. However, there is probably no more central issue for a Christian psychology.

NOTES

1. Yet another serious dilemma arises from the problem of genuine abuse or neglect experienced by a patient, especially when he or she was young. There are of course many children who have been victimized by parents or other adults. The basic problem is that once this information has been correctly identified and discussed, what can psychology do about it? No doubt understanding the past abuse and expressing one's emotions about it can bring some benefit, but the basic problem remains. If you did not get an adequate amount of love and support when you were young, what can a psychologist do about it, many years later? This dilemma is intrinsically unanswerable within a secular psychotherapy. However, from a religious perspective there is a clear answer to the problem: namely, the gain of God's love can make up for the absence of human love in the past; it can heal the wounds caused by a dysfunctional parent or family. Thus, there *is* a spiritual answer to this most fundamental of psychological problems, whereas there does not appear to be a good psychological answer to this problem. This major dilemma is not of concern here, but for a discussion of it, see Vitz, 1990; 1992.

2   For example, hatred makes one feel alive and purposeful; it justifies feelings of moral superiority; it supports the pleasures of revenge; it distracts us from more constructive tasks that carry a risk of failure, etc.

REFERENCES

Bowlby, J. and Parkes, C.M. (1970). Separation and loss within the family. In E.J. Anthony and C. Koupernik (Eds.), *The child in his family: International yearbook of child psychiatry and allied professions*. New York: Wiley, pp. 197-216.

Bretherton, I. (1992). The origins of attachment theory: John Bowlby and Mary Ainsworth. *Developmental Psychology, 28*, 759-775.

Fitzgibbons, R. (1986). The cognitive and emotive uses of forgiveness in the treatment of anger, *Psychotherapy, 23*, 629-633.

Freud, S./ Pfister, O. (1963). *Psychoanalysis and faith: The letters of Sigmund Freud and Oskar Pfister*, E.L. Freud and H. Meng (Eds); E. Mosbacher (Trans.). New York: Basic Books.

Gartner, J. (1992). The capacity to forgive: An object relations perspective. In M. Finn & J. Gartner (Eds.) *Object relations theory and religion*, Westport, CT: Praeger.; pp. 21-33.

Kernberg, O. (1992). *Aggression in personality disorders and perversions*. New Haven, CT: Yale University Press.

Klein, M. (1946). Notes on some schizoid mechanisms. *International Journal of Psychoanalysis, 27*, 99-111.

Klein, M. (1957). *Envy and gratitude*. New York: Basic Books.

Klein, M. (1964). Love, hate and reparation. In M. Klein and J. Riviere, *Love, hate and reparation*. New York: Norton.

Kubler-Ross, E. (1969). *On death and dying*. New York: Macmillan.

Linn, M. and Linn, D. (1978). *Healing life's hurts*. New York: Paulist Press.

McCullough, M. and Worthington, E. (1994). Encouraging clients to forgive people who have hurt them: Review, critique and research prospectus. *Journal of Psychology and Theology, 22*, 30-20.

Meissner, W.W. (1993). Self as agent in psychoanalysis. *Psychoanalysis and Contemporary Thought, 16*, 459-495.

Mower, O.H. (1960). "Sin," the lesser of two evils. *American Psychologist, 15*, 301-304.

Robertson, J. and Bowlby, J. (1952). Responses of young children to separation from their mothers. *Courrier of the International Children's Center, Paris, II*, 131-140.

Sykes, C.J. *A nation of victims*. New York: St. Martin's Press.

Vitz, P.C. (1990). The psychology of atheism and Christian spirituality. *Anthropotes, 6*, 89-106.

Vitz, P.C. (1992). Beyond psychology. In O. Guinness and J. Seel(Eds.) *No God but God*. Chicago: Moody Press, 95-110.

Vitz, P.C. and Mango, P. (1997). Psychodynamic and religious aspects of hatred as a defense mechanism. In press.

Vitz, P.C. and Mango, P. (1998). Psychodynamic and religious aspects of the forgiveness process. In press.

Waldinger, R.S. and Gonderson, J.G. (1987). *Effective psychotherapy with borderline patients*. New York: Macmillan.

Wolberg, L.R. (1988). *The technique of psychotherapy*, 4th ed. Part One. Philadelphia, PA: Grune and Stratton.

4

Becoming Responsible for Pain: Contradictions in Pain Management

Robert Kugelmann[1]

Moral considerations in psychology all too often benignly neglect the fundamental ethical questions, those of psychology itself. Ethics becomes an exercise or a game of self-justification once the scientific and professional status of psychology is taken for granted. Playing this game makes "psychological ethics" an oxymoron. What is needed is an ethical questioning that calls psychology and its received views of human existence into account. For the most part, psychological theories are still deterministic, so that ethical considerations center on how to treat research subjects and clients, but the ethics of determinism lies fallow. Where the view of the human person is more ample, as it tends to be in psychotherapy, the person is defined in terms of freedom and autonomy. Then psychological theory and practice foster emancipation. As David Bakan wrote, "the major function of...psychology should be to make man aware of the forces that operate on him" (1972, p. 13). This view does not deny that freedom is constrained by external forces; psychology liberates the person from these accidents of existence. There is an unreconcilable conflict between freedom and determinism; together they form an antinomy that has had psychology in its grip from its nineteenth-century beginnings.

I will explore this antinomy in psychology through a study of a phenomenon that raises the conflict in an urgent way: the psychological and medical treatment of chronic pain. I will focus on the admonition to people suffering in pain that they become responsible for their pain and its treatment. The theses I will develop are that the modern conception of responsibility is a humble but profound bourgeois virtue; that in its instrumentalization in pain management, responsibility has ceased to be a virtue and become a vice; that to escape the antinomy of determinism and freedom which underlies the call for responsibility, psychology requires a new understanding of existence, one that surpasses the alternatives of freedom and determinism.

I. Pain as a Question to Culture

Chronic pain is an evil. Defined medically as pain "which persists a month beyond the usual course of an acute disease or reasonable time for an injury to heal" (Bonica, 1990, p 180), it "*never* has a biologic function" (Bonica, 1990, p. 181). Bonica, who did much to develop the contemporary understanding of pain and its treatment, calls it "a malefic force" (1990, p. 181). For many sufferers, it is a living hell, inescapable, unexplainable, and perhaps worst of all, invisible. Blotches, growths and running sores have their own horror, but at least they are stigmata of suffering, whereas chronic pain is hidden, not only from the eye, but often from the x-ray and the MRI. Chronic pain has achieved epidemic proportions (Frank, 1993), yet its nature is much debated. However, we must begin with what ought to be most obvious about it: It is an evil. Stories of origin account for the origin of pain in a fall from grace: Adam and Eve's grasping at godhood, Pandora's prideful curiosity. These accounts recollect a time before pain and death, a nostalgia that should not be dismissed as merely infantile. Levinas, who recognizes a truth of this nostalgia, writes that "suffering is a failing of happiness" (1969, p. 115). The story of the Fall and the myths of origin establish that pain enters a world that preceded it.

What we are considering is not first and foremost a personal or subjective problem, but a tenacious *malady* of literally cosmic proportions. Pain is a cultural question, hence an ethical, political, aesthetic, religious, psychological and medical question. Pain is a given in human life, so we ask: How do we suffer pain? How do we respond to the sufferings of others? How do we live in a Fallen World or in the Iron Age? The stories of origins stress that we cannot eliminate these evils; in the Judeo-Christian tradition, their disappearance is tied to messianic hope. Such stories are the basis on which cultures address pain and other evils. Cultures craft arts of suffering these evils, including the means to alleviate them (see Illich, 1976).

Pain begins a discourse of good and evil, although not of black and white. The moment we say categorically that pain is evil, we can also say that pain is good, because without it, we would never be warned of harm, never learn of the world's dangers, of our limits, never find death tolerable, never earn a place at the Wedding Banquet. Of course, in the Garden, those lessons were not necessary— hence the nostalgia. Then again, chronic pain warns of nothing, protects us from no disease, teaches us nothing about the present situation; it is a wraith that refuses to relax its grip.

Reckoning with the evil of pain is the *raison d'être* of pain management. In what follows, I will address the central message of pain management: the call for patients to take responsibility for their pain. After establishing that pain management does preach responsibility, I will examine the concept of responsibility. Finally, I raise some questions about the significance of the imperative to assume personal responsibility for the evil of pain.

II. Responsibility for Pain

Pain management programs treat chronic pain in multi-disciplinary settings, using a biopsychosocial approach to chronic pain. Biomedical management, including surgery, nerve blocks and medication are included, of course, but what makes pain management distinct from earlier types of treatment is the concomitant use of modalities such as group therapy, biofeedback, cognitive-behavioral therapy, physical therapy and occupational therapy. Typically, these programs treat patients when all else has failed.

The Antinomy of Freedom and Determinism in Health Care
One prominent goal of pain management is to enhance the responsibility that patients take for their pain and its treatment. In fact, patient assumption of responsibility is a major goal in all health care today. The call to responsibility for one's own health originated in the holistic health movement of the 1970s. It has entered the mainstream in response to a host of factors, including the chronic nature of many common diseases today, the results of research showing that lifestyle factors play a substantial role in the cause, continuation and the treatment of these diseases, the ever-increasing costs of health care, and the emphasis on patients' rights. Pelletier, prominent in the holistic medicine movement, voiced the new health care ethic: "The patient's responsibility is to become an active participant, exercising his volition in regard to his own health, life style, and further [personal] development" (1977, p. 319). A commonplace today, such a statement was an innovation when written. The prevailing medical model had been the biomedical (Engel, 1977), which viewed the patient as basically passive in the treatment process; the responsibility of a good patient had been primarily to be compliant with treatment (Arney & Bergen, 1984). That position is being superseded by holistic and biopsychosocial models, which insist on the active participation of the patient in the healing process. So what was radical in the 1970s has become an ethical mandate. Thus we read in a text distributed by a Health Maintenance Organization to new members: "Your health is your responsibility; it depends on your decisions. There is no other way... To be healthy, you have to be in charge. Take Care of Yourself" (Vickery & Fries, 1989, p. xix). The result of this mandate is that the object of current medical care is no longer the anatomically defined body, but the patient-as-person, biologically, psychologically, socially, spiritually (Arney & Bergen, 1984; Kugelmann, in press).
The demand for responsibility became urgent in response to what we might call a gospel of irresponsibility that has been spread across the land. You are not responsible for what happens, so this argument goes, because you are a victim (of germs, of the environment, your childhood, your hormones). The passivity of pain, disease and mental anguish lends itself to a deterministic reading. This bias toward determinism has been amplified in recent decades with the assertion of victims' rights. But if victims are not to blame for their plight, then someone or

something else is. This counterpoint to the call for personal responsibility does not escape the terms of the debate: You the victim are not responsible (for your injury, your pain, your disability), someone else is. Abuses of power, unsafe working conditions, faulty design of commodities and the like do exist, and litigation is a nonviolent means of redress. However, the debate over *who* is responsible blinds us to responsibility itself. The experience of chronic pain takes shape in the light of this conflict over the ownership of responsibility.

The question of responsibility is the specific way in which the underlying contradiction between freedom and determinism is played out. Proponents of human agency and free choice subject to moral norms naturally side with the promotion of personal responsibility in health care. Ironically, even those who theoretically maintain a deterministic standpoint argue for the promotion of personal responsibility because it promotes "inner locus of control," which is held to promote health even if it is illusory.

Responsibility for Chronic Pain

Because chronic pain is chronic, because biomedical intervention is often ineffective, what physicians can do for it is limited. This is the context within which pain management "directs the responsibility for the treatment away from the doctor and back to the patient" (Chronic pain, 1980, p. 16). However, the direction of responsibility back to the patient does not inaugurate a delimiting of professional intervention into the patient's life. Quite the contrary, there is greater and more profound intervention. Pain management creates an enlarged treatment field, including an uneasy marriage of psychology and medicine.

So it is no accident that the call for personal responsibility is coeval with the growth of pain management programs since the 1970s. "The goal of intervention [in the treatment of chronic pain] is the patient *per se*, not the pain or the underlying pathology" (Kotarba & Seidel, 1984, p. 1394), meaning that treatment aims to alter the condition by altering the person. In an early rallying cry for pain management, Steven Brena (1978), a physician involved in the pain center movement, described how debilitating the medical and legal responses to pain are, how they trap people needlessly in dependency and convince many that they are disabled. Sparing no one in his critique of how the medical and legal professionals unwittingly promote pain and disability, Brena lamented that: "Our social emphasis is on health, but health is viewed as a gift to be begged for, one involving medical manipulations and drug prescriptions. Instead, health should be a right we earn by our personal commitment to healthy and ethical living" (Brena, 1978, p. 92). By and large, pain clinics foster the attitudes Brena championed. For example, Aronoff and Wagner (1988) summarize the prevailing view in these terms: "Once cure in the passive sense is not seen as a focus of treatment, a patient can be more easily recruited as a 'member' of the treatment team and begin to plan for ways of getting on with life despite pain" (p. 40). This means that much of the work of the pain clinic, in addition to the physical conditioning provided by physical and occupational therapies, is educational: "Processes and strategies by which cognitions and feelings are modified…, monitoring 'automatic' dysfunctional thinking patterns…, and learning and rehearsing new coping strategies" (Aronoff and Wagner, 1988, p. 37). The goal of these programs "is to return responsibility for pain and its management to the patient, who, at this point in the pain career, has placed all responsibility for suffering in the hands of health care workers and workers' compensation officials" (Kotarba, 1981, p. 797). Assumption of responsibility plays a "rehabilitative role" (Aronoff & Wagner, p. 43) in pain management.

Precisely what are patients being asked to be responsible for? Specifically, pain programs stress that "responsibility to keep fit, maintain their individual exercise programme, and remain relaxed…is that of the individual, not of the professionals" (Frank, 1993, p. 906). "Self-managed reduction of drug dependence is a major component" (Gottlieb, Alperson, Schwartz, Beck, & Kee, 1988) of pain programs. Or in general, such programs help "clients to assume responsibility for their own well-being, achieve independence in their lives, and practice healthy coping mechanisms" (Christenson, 1993, p. 13). The appeal of the call for responsibility, its congruence with the American belief in self-reliance, its apparent common sense, seem irresistible.

What is Responsibility?

The concept of responsibility is older than the term. The concept originates with that of the will. The term "will" refers to a person's capabilities to initiate actions from within and to reply to whomever addresses him or her. Three types of responsibility have been distinguished: moral, legal and political (Gablentz, 1968, Vol. 13, p. 496). Moral responsibility is "a correlate of freedom" of the will (Gablentz, 1968, Vol. 13, p. 496), and it refers to "*moral culpability* (blameworthiness) or *moral laudability* (praiseworthiness)" (Shaver, 1975, p. 96). What we do or fail to do without coercion is subject to blame or praise. Legal responsibility concerns liability, and while it overlaps with moral responsibility, it does not coincide with it. Political responsibility "means the right use of power" (Gablentz, 1968, Vol. 13, p. 497). This last type of responsibility can be applied both to ordinary citizen and absolute monarchs. While moral responsibility is the primary emphasis in pain management, the other two meanings shadow it closely.

These three types of responsibility overlap because underlying them is a more general concept, ontological responsibility: "*To exist is to be liable.* Man is, as Heidegger describes it, 'projected into the world' and responsible for his existence. The resultant 'care' which derives from the original fact of his 'being-in-the-world' permeates every aspect of his existence. He is, Heidegger argues, responsible for himself and to himself" (Schrader, 1972, p. 268). This statement emphasizes a factor basic to the concept: Responsibility rests with the self.

The term "responsibility" is of modern origin. It does not occur in English prior to 1787 (Simpson & Weiner, 1989). While it belongs to a family of concepts about comportment that also includes *dharma*, honor, duty and conscience, the type of responsibility that has become important in pain management is a product of the eighteenth and nineteenth centuries and the concept of liberal or autonomous individuality. Mansfield (1994, p. 80) writes that "responsibility" first occurs in *The Federalist*. Responsibility means "taking charge in a situation of risk or drudgery in order to improve it, a situation from which others shrink because they think that inaction is in their interest" (Mansfield, 1994, pp. 84-85). For Mansfield, responsibility arises from the pursuit of self-interest, because a society in which one can pursue one's interests provides the occasion for one to take risks and take charge even though not obligated to do so. For example, if I own my house, I am responsible for its care, and I may also take on responsibilities in my neighborhood and city, these larger responsibilities emerging from my self-interests.

The paradigm of the responsible person, according to Mansfield, is the American president as described in *The Federalist*:

> The American presidency...is concerned with aspects of politics that go beyond the routine and are full of risk; these are long-term enterprises and their opposite, quick strokes in dangerous emergencies. The President's job, if it can be called that, is to do what is no one else's job...The highest responsibility is accepting responsibility for things one has not been responsible for. (Mansfield, 1994, p. 91)

That this office is paradigmatic indicates two characteristics of the modern concept of responsibility: its executive and representative aspects. The responsible person seizes the initiative, even though he may not, strictly speaking, be duty bound to do so. That taking the reins is the executive aspect. And while he must know his limitations, "the responsible person makes himself the representative of nature or God, accepting the situation in which he takes responsibility as his own" (Mansfield, 1994, p. 92). In other words, when I am responsible, I act on behalf of others, even as I act on my own and for myself. The disposition to act in these ways makes of responsibility a "bourgeois virtue" (Mansfield, 1994, p. 79).

Who is Responsible?

Mansfield writes that the notion of the modern individual "has created both the need and the opportunity for responsibility" (1994, p. 93). The very notion of the individual is itself complex, so that it is necessary to specify in what sense the individuality is tied to the concept of responsibility. The "modern self" or autonomous individual is tied to responsibility. The historical origins of the modern self, especially since the seventeenth century, are concurrent with the origins of the notion of responsibility. In Locke's *Essay concerning human understanding*, it was the question of moral and legal responsibility that led him to discuss identity. The modern self is an ideal type defined by highly defined personal boundaries, "radical reflectivity" (Giddens, 1990) or the "prejudice against prejudice itself"

(Gadamer, 1975, p. 240), and an identity that results primarily from personal choices. In addition, the modern self is self-possessive. I own myself, body and mind, and all my abilities. This self-possession is fundamental to modern ethical and legal codes, and it is the basis of modern economic relationships. Because I own myself and my actions, I alone am accountable for them. Neither my family nor my tribe are accountable for my behavior. Being in possession of myself also dictates a type of self-discipline, characterized by Max Weber as "inner-worldly asceticism" (Berger, 1986, p. 107). This discipline inculcates an ability to delay immediate gratification, a desire to be productive economically, and a strong sense of self-reliance.

The same historical matrix that produced the modern self also produced "faith in bureaucratic paternalism" (Illich, 1984, p. 10), in part because of the inevitable failure of some people to be individuals fully (the young, the old, the injured, the demented, the criminal, the poor, etc.). As modern institutions weakened traditional communal forms of caring for the dispossessed, the state and its private equivalents stepped in to provide care for them. The welfare state is the correlative of the autonomous individual.

The vaunted autonomy of modern selfhood is thus shadowed by passivity, an enticement created not only by bureaucratic paternalism, but also by science, technology and modern statecraft. While the sciences promise domination over nature, the power that knowledge gives is accessible only to those in the know; the laity consumes only what the experts deliver. Technology too tempts us to passivity, insofar as machines do what people once did with their own hands and voices. Finally, the modern belief that people are not by nature political animals, that the self has an asocial core, leads to political passivity. This polarization between autonomy and passivity expresses in another way the fundamental antinomy of freedom and determinism that holds us enthralled. So the autonomous individual, source of will and initiative, is tempted to be passive and irresponsible.

The cultivation of responsibility thus accomplishes a virtuous autonomous individuality. Such a person does not heedlessly pursue self-interests in isolation. Responsibility as the primary virtue of this type of individuality serves to relate autonomy to the social situation. Finally, responsibility saves the autonomous individual from the ravages of passivity.

The Notion of Responsibility in Pain Management

What pain management seeks, then, is to strengthen the autonomy of pain patients. One must be either a possessive individual or a ward of the state, and pain management neither escapes this antinomy nor seeks to see past it. Consider again what pain management seeks to accomplish, in light of the above discussion of the modern self:

1) Patients can be responsible only for what they know consciously. The educational emphasis in these programs, which includes biofeedback, stress management, instruction in body mechanics, etc., aims to make the patient more

knowledgeable about the conditions that cause pain. The assumption is that if people know how their behavior causes pain to increase and decrease, they will rationally choose to decrease it.

2) Pain management "subjectifies" pain. Many patients enter a pain management program with the belief that pain is something that doctors can fix with surgery or drugs. What they typically are taught is that their own attitudes, cognitions, feelings and behaviors play a substantive role in creating and alleviating pain. They become responsible for their pain in the strong sense that what they do and fail to do directly affects the level of their pain.

3) The individual alone needs to assume responsibility for his or her well-being. The patient's body belongs to the patient. The body is a possession, to be grasped from an epistemological distance. Patients are taught that medical care has limits, and that it is useless to continue to seek the magic bullet. The time has come to own up to the reality of pain and to own up to the fact that the patient's attitudes and behaviors can make a difference. "Take care of yourself."

4) Pain management seeks to free the individual from the passivity of pain. A patient typically enters the program believing that his initiative cannot make a difference. Pain management operates on the will of the patient, freeing it from the contingencies that control it from without.

5) Pain management affirms the patient's right to treatment for pain, but it stresses the limits of that right. It stresses the self-interest involved in self-management and responsibility.

6) The appeal for the patient to take responsibility either implicitly or explicitly makes reference to the individual as executive and representative: The person must take charge of pain even if the patient did not cause it (the executive aspect), so that the patient, our representative, can resume a "normal" productive life and cease being a social burden (the individual must take up as his self-interest the good of all of us).

III. The Ambiguities of Responsibility

Pain management is essentially a modern moral enterprise. The assumption is that if patients learn to be personally responsible for their pain and its management, they will likely feel less pain, or at least lead productive lives despite ongoing pain. A further assumption is that if patients become autonomous individuals, they will fare better. Therefore, pain management is a moral schooling that teaches a socially sanctioned way of responding to suffering: autonomous individuality. It is also assumed that if patients become autonomous individuals they will be more socially responsible by ceasing to be or not becoming wards of the state. Patients had previously learned a dependent, passive response to pain; they had come to believe that physicians could eliminate their pain with surgery and medication. Pain management must undo that faulty education.

Moral management is an appropriate response to chronic pain because it is an open question "the extent to which chronic pain is or is not strictly a medical phenomenon" (Csordas & Clark, 1992, p. 392). Nachemson (1994, p. S13) cites studies which "have demonstrated quite clearly that work satisfaction played the most important role in the reporting of disabling back pain occurrence in a healthy working population." Disability because of chronic pain fluctuates with economic conditions, is more common among lower socioeconomic groups, among those with little formal education, and among workers with low occupational status (Osterweis, Kleinman, & Mechanic, 1987). Dissatisfaction with work, "the desire to obtain maximum gain" (Chapman & Brena, 1989, p. 1034) from disability assistance, the prodding of attorneys, etc., all contribute to the chronicity of pain. In this light, pain is not something that could be handled "purely" medically. As these statements also imply, the moral management of pain is likewise political.

Pain management, we must conclude, is a political enterprise, a correctional institution designed to instruct deviants from the norms of autonomous individuality. It takes suffering people who can pay for the treatment and seeks to instill in them values and attitudes that promise less pain and greater productivity. To the holders of the purse strings, it promises fewer medical expenses in the future.

The Contradiction of Pain Management

This is not all the story, and thanks to the insights of John McKnight (1995) and others, we can see a contradiction in these programs. The clarion call of personal responsibility has been accompanied by an appeal for a new medical specialty, the pain specialist, and for accelerated growth in the "pain-clinic movement" (Brena, 1978, p. 86-87). Thus, increased personal responsibility for health has led to more, not less, professional involvement in patients' lives. When Brena wrote, the pain management business was still a fledgling enterprise. Since the late 1970s, it has mushroomed (Csordas & Clark, 1992). By all accounts, pain management has been a growth industry, "starting with zero in the 1960s and numbering about 500" (Chronic pain, 1980, p.3) by 1980, and 1500 seven years later (Csordas & Clark, 1992, p. 383). In an article written to acquaint hospital administrators with the benefits of such programs, Souhrada notes that "the demand for pain management is staggering. An estimated 80 million Americans of all ages suffer chronic pain" (1989, p. 52). Moreover, "recently some hospitals have begun to treat the management of pain as a business in itself. And programs that treat both the physical and psychological aspects of pain are bringing in profits and new patients" (Souhrada, 1989). Nor has there been a mass exodus of consumers from the health care system; in fact, as Nachemson (1994) notes in alarm, there have been "drastic increases" in the prevalence of disability from low back pain over the past twenty years, the very years that pain clinics have sprouted worldwide in an effort to reduce disability. There is a strong suggestion here that pain management is, to use the term of Illich (1976), counterproductive. And to use McKnight's term, pain management provides the counterfeit of increased autonomy.

The contradiction in pain management is that pain clinics seek to instill responsibility into people by making them clients of yet another institution. What the clinics really preach and practice is the "therapeutic ideology" (McKnight, 1995, p. 61). Responsibility entails learning how to be a good consumer of professionalized services. Pain clinics have sprouted and spread in the wasteland created by earlier "disabling professions," and have added to personal powerlessness and helplessness. By complaining about the irresponsibility of pain patients, pain professionals forestall the critique that they worsen the enclosure of the commons of compassion.

So pain management inculcates a meaning of pain. Pain, patients are told, is personal. The message is, in effect: "It is your possession, your problem. Once you accept that your pain is yours, it can mean anything else you want it to mean." Prior to this education, patients typically believe that pain is a medical problem, one that can be fixed. Once they accept its new significance, they can, through guided imagery, biofeedback and other treatment modalities, attribute all kinds of personal meanings, construct a private myth or realize that pain is a teacher with harsh messages about the significance or direction of life. Any such meaning, so long as it is compatible with diminished pain behaviors and increased prosocial actions, is acceptable. That pain is personal opens a superhighway for psychology, whose stock-in-trade is the cultivation of elaborate personalized meanings. Cushman (1990) has shown that the idiosyncratic development of the generic personalized meanings of life only deepens the emptiness of the modern self.

A Critique of Responsibility

MacIntyre (1975) argues that virtues can in certain circumstances become vices, and he applied this analysis to medicine, arguing that the combination of changes in the nature of medical practice and the absence of a common moral ground has rendered the physician's situation tragic in the deepest sense. His analysis applies to attempts to inculcate responsibility through psychological techniques. Responsibility as taught in pain management is either a vice or it is a word without meaning.

A virtue becomes a vice when "what was a virtue is transformed into part of a set of technical skills" (MacIntyre, 1975, p. 107). Pain clinics seek to instill responsibility because it may help the person feel less pain, by leading the person to be economically and socially autonomous, and less of a social burden. Responsibility here is already a vice, because it has ceased to be an end, a good, and become a means to augment functional competence. The sought-for goal compounds the viciousness of responsibility, for alleviation of pain and functional autonomy are not two goals, but one: Reduction of pain occurs when one becomes more useful and productive. These techniques for controlling pain are thus inherently economic and political, masked as therapeutic. Especially in cases of pain resulting from work-related and automobile accidents, attempts to teach responsibility means that those who suffer directly the ill-effects of a highly technologized world should bear the brunt of the burden of economic development, because they are our representatives. Responsibility assumed in this situation becomes a vice: Compliance with deception, pride of ownership of what belongs to no individual, exceeding the limits of what one can appropriate by representation. At best, this assumption reflects resignation, an admission that there is nothing else to do. To teach responsibility in this situation is also vicious, because it both scapegoats people in pain and tempts them to self-deification. The pedagogy of responsibility makes of pain the possession or attribute of others, theirs alone, an impediment to their being fully functional members of society. Pain, an evil, a mystery of human life, is transformed into a private affair.

Responsibility has become an empty term because it refers to a disposition that is no longer possible. MacIntyre asserts that "a virtue may become a vice or simply a nonmoral quality by a change in its relationship to a role which it partially defines" (MacIntyre, 1975, p. 107). Responsibility the virtue signified first of all personal accountability in a bourgeois society, and it entailed the taking up of interests in the public trust. That is, responsibility implied a choice. But the person in pain cannot so choose, for pain is a passion, not an action, something undergone or suffered rather than accomplished. Requiring people in pain to take responsibility for their pain and its treatment resembles torture, because of the implicit threat of continued pain if directions are not followed. In this context, being responsible means following orders in the hope of being free of pain and economic dependency. Failure to assume responsibility is tied to liability to punishment. The primal association of pain and punishment, present in the etymology of the word "pain," returns with a vengeance. A sufferer of chronic pain is tempted to experience any increase in pain as a fitting punishment for a lapse in self-management. If patients say that they do assume responsibility under such circumstances, it is as if they lie under duress. Patients "confess" to being responsible, as hostages to crimes that they did not commit. If patients believe that they are responsible, they are tempted to deceive themselves in a setting where the term "responsibility" is doublespeak.

The demand that patients be responsible for chronic pain and its treatment is, therefore, a lure into presumption and deceit, into an anti-language where words no longer mean anything, but where they serve to justify suffering. What makes the situation tragic is that there is no good solution. The pain patient and the therapist can only choose between wrongs: passivity and victimhood on the one hand, and pride on the other. As long as the healing relationship maintains its current structure, so long will responsibility not be a virtue.

I am not the first to call responsibility, and specifically responsibility for health, a vice. Illich (1994) argues that "responsibility" has become an empty term. Responsibility as the personal accountability of an autonomous individual no longer is possible, because the social world that sustained autonomous individuality no longer exists: "In a world which worships an ontology of systems, ethical responsibility is reduced to a legitimating formality" (Illich, 1994, p.9). The call to responsibility is a "legitimizing formality" because in an essential way my actions are no longer mine. Why? Because the conditions for the possibility of responsible action have been undermined by the rise of technological society, according to Illich. Because the consequences of action, despite my best intentions, contribute to the degradation of the social and natural world. Responsibility is illusory because there is no context within which to act responsibly. We live in a time in which responsibility is as foreign as honor, chivalry and the pioneer spirit of self-reliance. We are individually and collectively helpless in the face of a hitherto unimagined evil, a capacity to destroy the natural and cultural world. "Responsibility for pain," then, is meaningless verbiage that numbs the mind to our existential condition.

Like MacIntyre, Illich presents a tragic view of our situation. Responsibility will not do because we cannot effect the change. We are not in charge, and only in the context of reckoning with our helplessness can we begin to envision the world anew. The call for responsibility silences an implicit question about contemporary society, a question that would ask about the epidemic nature of chronic pain. In this regard, pain management is essentially social engineering applied to hellish suffering. Pain management assumes that chronic pain is a side-effect of economic development, a bearable cost. The epidemic nature of pain indicates that progress continues to extract a toll; the preachers of responsibility displace the cost of progress upon its random victims.

IV. The Rehabilitation of Responsibility

Chronic pain is but one price we pay for the continual revolution of modernization. Those in pain feel the cost; the rest of us are more or less numbed by the comforts that development provides. Since the juggernaut of modernity will not stop, we must agree with Illich that we are helpless in the face of chronic pain. It is a great hoax to impose on those who suffer the burden of being responsible for that for which no one can be responsible. Chronic pain arises from an evil, an evil in which we all live.

The requirement that patients be responsible for their pain is a tragic error. But pain management, while it is blind to tragedy, contains an insight: Pain is natural and personal; it is of the nature of the person. The other pole of the antinomy of responsibility also fails to grasp our tragic circumstance. By arguing that others are responsible for pain and its treatment, it indulges the fantasy that a particular agent is in charge when actually no one is. But there is an insight at this pole, too: Pain is social and political. To move past the contradictions in pain management and past the antinomy in which it is embedded, we will have to reconsider these insights in a different context. If anything needs rehabilitation, it is responsibility itself.

I will end with a beginning, which is the only thing possible in tragic situations. For psychology, it will mean abandoning the notion of the autonomous self that underlies the vice of responsibility. It will be necessary to abandon this position without falling back into a position of determinism, which would only keep us within the tragic contradiction. Another conception of self is found in the writings of Emmanuel Levinas. It offers a different beginning for psychology by establishing that the person, prior to being free or determined, is responsible for the other; that I come to be by way of the call of the other which I hear prior to my being free or not free. In these concluding paragraphs I will sketch this notion of the self, a notion born of our tragic time and in response to the horrors of the twentieth century. With this renewed notion of the person comes a renewed sense of responsibility.

The freedom of the self, its autonomy, and its subjection to external causal factors, giving most of our living the quality of situated freedom, are true, but according to Levinas, the self originates in responsibility. What "originates" the person is a yearning, a risk taking, a vulnerability, exposure to the other, and a response to a call before I am. As Strasser (1968) expresses it, the You is older than the I, and calls me into being. I am Thou before I am I (Rosenstock-Huessy, 1970). "It is in this non-objectifiable response-ability prior to being that the com-ing-to-be of the subject occurs" (Walsh, 1989, p. 271). The implication of Levinas's analysis of existence is that the most primary orientation of the person is not free-dom, as maintained by both the philosophies of freedom and of determinism. At the core of the person is obligation to the other, who "invests" the freedom of the person (Levinas, 1969, p. 84).

This call to respond to the other defines human existence: "I am I in the sole measure that I am responsible, a non-interchangeable I. I can substitute myself for everyone, but no one can substitute himself for me. Such is my inalienable iden-tity of subject" (Levinas, 1981, p. 101). The other, the other's pain and suffering, summon me to be, to be for him, and I am to the extent I am for him. For Levinas, "No one may remain in one's self: man's humanity, subjectivity, is a responsibility for the other, an extreme vulnerability" (1972, quoted in Chalier, 1993, p. 68). The other's pain infects me, obsesses me, before I decide if I will act on it, ignore it, or seek to kill the other who touches me. This response-ability concerns how *I* reply to the suffering of others.

In light of this conception of the person, responsibility means my answer to the appeal of an other who faces me (Levinas, 1969). There is a responsibility beyond the vice of responsibility. This deeper responsibility is not a virtue, i.e., a power or disposition at my command. It is a responsibility other than one depen-dent upon the freedom of the individual from efficient causes of behavior. This responsibility surpasses the antinomy described above by avoiding its terms: *your* responsibility for *your* pain (the pain management position; the self as free and autonomous); *their* responsibility for it (the biomedical position; the self as deter-mined). We begin again by examining *my* responsibility *to you.* "Here I am" are the first words of responsibility. The indigence, neediness and superiority of the other commands me. Levinas insists on the asymmetry of this responsibility (i.e., mine and not yours) in order to avoid an all-too-easy leap outside the actual face-to-face encounter with an other.

Because it concerns my and not your or his responsibility, it cannot be imposed or prescribed. There is no programmatic implication in this assertion of a responsibility beyond responsibility. It is a realization that even in tragedy, something remains. Pain is an evil, a mystery of disorder, failure, abandonment, privation, unhealable wounds. Pain manifests the evil of the world, of all our works. Another in pain calls out to us, and helpless, we answer. Because we are human selves, we are in this way condemned, before being free, to be responsible for others.

Therefore, reckoning with the tragedy in which we participate, reckoning with the viciousness of demanding that others be responsible for their suffering, the viciousness of demanding that they suffer the meaning of being responsible in addition to their other burdens, this reckoning of suffering endlessly from pain requires of me "pity, compassion...and proximity" (Levinas, 1981, p. 117). It requires, moreover, continual questioning and questing in the face of an evil that challenges the basis of culture.

NOTES

    1.   I thank my colleague, Lance Simmons, at the University of Dallas, for his helpful comments and criticisms of this paper.

REFERENCES

Arney, W., & Bergen, B. (1984). *Medicine and the management of living: Taming the last great beast.* Chicago: University of Chicago Press.

Aronoff, G. M., & Wagner, J. M. (1988). The pain center: Development, structure, and dynamics. In G. M. Aronoff (Ed.), *Pain centers: A revolution in health care* (pp. 33-54). New York: Raven Press.

Bakan, D. (1972, March). Psychology can now kick the science habit. *Psychology Today,* 10-13.

Berger, P. (1986). *The capitalist revolution.* New York: Basic Books.

Bonica, J. J. (1990). *The management of pain,* Vol 1 (2nd ed.). Philadelphia: Lea & Febiger.

Brena, S. F. (1978). *Chronic pain: America's hidden epidemic.* New York: Atheneum/SMI.

Chalier, C. (1993). Emmanuel Levinas: Responsibility and election. In A. P. Griffiths (Ed.), *Ethics* (pp. 63-76). Cambridge: Cambridge University Press.

Chapman, S. L., & Brena, S. F. (1989). Pain and litigation. In P. Wall & R. Melzack (Eds.), *Textbook of Pain* (2nd ed., pp. 1032-1041). Edinburgh: Churchill Livingstone.

Christenson, J. L. (1993). Chronic pain: Dynamics and treatment strategies. *Perspectives in Psychiatric Care 29,* 13-17.

Chronic pain: The endemic disease of an industrial society. (1980). Washington, DC: U.S. Government Printing Office.

Csordas, T. J., & Clark, J. A. (1992). Ends of the line: Diversity among chronic pain centers. *Social Science and Medicine 34,* 383-393.

Cushman, P. (1990). Why the self is empty. *American Psychologist 45,* 599-610.

Engel, G. (1977). The need for a new medical model: A challenge for biomedicine. *Science 196,* 129-136.

Frank, A. (1993). Low back pain. *BMJ 306,* 901-909.

Gablentz, O. H. v. d. (1968). Responsibility. In Sills, D. L. (Eds.), *International Encyclopedia of the Social Sciences.* (Vol 13, pp. 496-500). New York: The Macmillan Co. & The Free Press.

Gadamer, H.-G. (1975). *Truth and method.* New York: Seabury Press.

Giddens, A. (1990). *The consequences of modernity.* Stanford: Stanford University Press.

Gottlieb, H., Alperson, B. L., Schwartz, A. H., Beck, C., & Kee, S. (1988). Self-management for medication reduction in chronic low back pain. *Archives of Physical Medicine and Rehabilitation 69,* 442-448.

Illich, I. (1976). *Medical nemesis: The expropriation of health.* New York: Vintage Books.

Illich, I. (1984). *Gender.* New York: Pantheon.

Illich, I. (1994). Brave new biocracy: Health care from womb to tomb. *New Perspectives Quarterly 11,* 4-12.

Kotarba, J. (1981). Chronic pain center: A study of voluntary client compliance and entrepreneurship. *American Behavioral Scientist 24* (6), 786-800.

Kotarba, J., & Seidel, J V. (1984). Managing the problem pain patient: Compliance or social control? *Social Science and Medicine 19,* 1393-1400.

Kugelmann, R. (in press). The psychology and management of pain: Gate control as theory and symbol. *Theory & Psychology.*

Levinas, E. (1969). *Totality and infinity: An essay in exteriority* (A. Lingis, Trans.). Pittsburgh: Duquesne University Press. (Original work published 1961)

Levinas, E. (1972). *Humanisme de l'autre homme.* Montpellier: Fata Morgana.

Levinas, E. (1981). *Otherwise than being or beyond essence* (A. Lingis, Trans.). Dordrecht: Kluwer Academic.

MacIntyre, A. (1975). How virtues become vices: Values, medicine and social context. In H. T. Engelhardt & S. F. Spicker (Eds.), *Evaluation and explanation in the biomedical sciences* (pp. 97-111). Dordrecht: D. Reidel Publishing Co.

Mansfield, H. C. (1994). Responsibility and its perversions. In W. L. Taitte (Ed.), *Individualism and social responsibility* (pp. 79-99). Dallas: University of Texas at Dallas Press.

McKnight, J. (1995). *The careless society: Community and its counterfeits.* New York: Basic Books.

Nachemson, A. (1994). Chronic pain—the end of the welfare state? *Quality of Life Research 3* (1), S11-S17.

Osterweis, M., Kleinman, A., & Mechanic, D. (1987). *Pain and disability.* Washington, DC: National Academy Press.

Pelletier, K. (1977). *Mind as healer, mind as slayer: A holistic approach to preventing stress disorders.* New York: Delta Books.

Rosenstock-Huessy, E. (1970). *I am an impure thinker.* Norwich, VT: Argo Books.

Schrader, G. A. (1972). Responsibility and existence. In Jung, H. Y. (Ed.), *Existential phenomenology and political theory: A reader.* (pp. 265-293). Chicago: Henry Regnery.

Shaver, K. G (1975). *An introduction to attribution processes.* Cambridge, MA: Winthrop Publishers.

Simpson, J. A., & Weiner, E. S. C. (1989). *Oxford English Dictionary* (2nd ed.). Oxford: Clarendon Press.

Strasser, S. (1968). *Toward a dialogal phenomenology.* Pittsburgh: Duquesne University Press.

Souhrada, L. (1989). Pain programs offer opportunities for hospitals. *Hospitals 63,* 52.

Vickery, D. M., & Fries, J. F. (1989). *Take care of yourself: Your personal guide to self-care and preventing illness.* (4th ed.). Reading, MA: Addison-Wesley Publishing Co.

Walsh, R. D. (1989). *The priority of responsibility in the ethical philosophy of Emmanuel Levinas.* Unpublished doctoral dissertation, Marquette University.

III. Morality and the Challenge of Naturalism

5

Can Psychology Discover Moral Norms?

A. Psychology, Ethics and the Naturalistic Fallacy

Howard H. Kendler

When I last attended a conference on morality[1] I had the good fortune to be enlightened about the nature of science by a postmodern anthropologist . He had objected to my conception of natural science methodology as an exquisite interaction between rationalism and empiricism in a search for "scientific truth." He forcefully stated that the scientific method is equivalent to the procedure used to identify witches in 1692 in Salem, Massachusetts. Realizing that our discordant preconceptions would prevent a constructive exchange I diplomatically suggested that I was tired and needed to retire.

My refusal to continue the conversation with my postmodern colleague is not offered as a not-so-subtle hint that I desire only to engage in discussions about morality with those who share my view of science. Nor did I wish to suggest that an analysis of ethics must be intertwined with science. The anecdote represents a first, hesitant step in acquainting the members of this conference with the various segments of my belief system relevant to ethics. The intellectual core of this system stems from my being a psychologist. But that does not say much because psychologists can have a variety of epistemological commitments, some of which inevitably conflict with those of other psychologists. Thus I am forced to describe the kind of psychologist I am and the epistemological context within which I operate.

My undergraduate education in psychology was combined with an active interest in the philosophy of science especially with issues that were relevant to the task of the psychologist as an empiricist and theorist. As my psychology education progressed it became obvious that psychology was not a unified discipline in which all members of the profession were operating within a common methodological orientation. Such a conclusion appeared beyond dispute for a student who took courses from animal psychologists, biopsychologists, gestalt psychologists, psychoanalysts, humanistic psychologists, and those "literary psychologists" whose primary psychological assumptions were expressed in quotations from great, and not-so-great, works of literature. In addition I discovered that some of my professors' psychological beliefs reflected political agendas while others were completely apolitical. Although this cacophony of views was disconcerting, the essence of psychology nevertheless became clear for me. I had the opportunity in an undergraduate experimental psychology course to plan and execute a study that was designed to evaluate my hypothesis about how the passage of time would influence a set way, an *Einstellung,* of solving a series of similar mathematical problems. My hypothesis was proved wrong but instead of disappointment, elation ensued. I could formulate a psychological theory and design an experiment to test it and discover whether my hypothesis was confirmed or disconfirmed. The entire project proved sufficiently fascinating to convince me that I had discovered my life's work!

With greater sophistication I gradually became aware that I had stumbled on the kind of psychologist I wanted to be, *a natural-science psychologist.* One of the basic methodological controversies that has occupied center stage in the history of psychology is the meaning of the term *science.*[2] Most people think of *science* as a general method to discover truth but are unclear about the method itself. A question about which psychologists disagree is whether the *scientific method* consists of a single basic method or a collection of different methods, each specifically designed to reveal valid knowledge in different disciplines. The first 50 years of American psychology was dominated by the single-science view that assumes the methods that have been used in physics, chemistry, and biology can be successfully employed in psychology. The single-science view has been rejected by so-called human scientists because they insist that the method to investigate physical events from the outside is inappropriate for understanding humans beings. Humans must be understood from the inside, from the perspective of conscious experience. Instead of trying to emulate the natural sciences, the argument goes, psychologists should face up to their task of understanding the essence of humanity which is embedded in human consciousness. Kierkegaard expressed this attitude when he proclaimed that natural science methodology can deal with stars, animals, and plants, "but to handle the spirit of man in such a fashion is blasphemy" (p. 182).[3]

Frankly the argument between a natural science psychology and a human science psychology is not worth pursuing any longer. It cannot be resolved because the opposing viewpoints fail to share a common standard against which to evaluate the methodological differences. Like my discussion with the postmodern anthropologist the argument is tiring and I wish to retire from it. I can only suggest that those who are undecided about the relative merits of each orientation can evaluate them by their accomplishments. To abandon the argument does not excuse me from facing up to the complex and much debatable issue of what is *natural science methodology.*

If a single word were needed to distinguish natural science methodology from other methods of interpreting the world (e.g., religious, intuitive, rational, literary) that word would be *empirical.* Observable phenomena are both an essential component in scientific discourse and the final authority in science. *Natural science methodology* in contrast to other interpretive orientations, demands factually-based explanations.

Natural science methodology is a product of an ongoing process that will never end. It represents a historical accumulation of ideas and strategies that generations of problem solvers employed in their efforts to reveal and understand the world in which they lived. The scientific approach has its roots in a naturalistic view of the world; the assumption that the cause of all phenomena reside in the material world itself. In an effort to understand scientific methodology by rational means, philosophers of science have sought to abstract from an epistemological analysis of scientific knowledge and the history of science those techniques and procedures that natural scientists used. Not surprisingly, this rational analysis did not produce general agreement about the essential nature of science, nor will it ever.

Science is not a product of a book of fixed rules but instead is a set of historical conclusions tainted by ambiguity and vagueness. Nevertheless natural science methodology is discriminably different from other forms of psychological inquiry. I would suggest that even though I am unable to offer a precise delineation of scientific psychology from nonscientific psychology the two are mutually exclusive in a functional sense. An elaborate context of factors is necessary to make the distinction but for our needs only one factor will be mentioned. Popper's concept of falsifiability is a useful criterion to separate natural science psychology from other forms if one appreciates that a time perspective is required to apply this litmus test.

I. Behaviorism and Natural Science Psychology

My natural science approach to psychology can simply be described as being *behavioristic* but doing so creates a risk of generating confusion. No concept in psychology is more misunderstood. Behaviorism's critics have been more interested in attacking the concept than understanding it, while leading behaviorists have been more concerned with imprinting their own personal stamp on behaviorism than clarifying its basic structure. To make matters worse the idea, emanating from sloppy scholarship, is that behaviorism is equivalent to Skinnerian psychology. This is rapidly becoming the dominant view of behaviorism.

Behaviorism is fundamentally a methodological orientation that prescribes an *objective (intersubjective)* observational base for psychology. It rejects the notion that a natural science psychology can be intrinsically phenomenological in the sense of being based on the observations of one's own consciousness. The suggestion that behaviorism extirpates the mind from psychology, however, is contradicted by the creative efforts of one of the most sophisticated behaviorists, E. C.

Tolman (1886-1959). Tolman formulated a cognitive theory of learning in which the "mind" was an inferred theoretical concept, not a directly examined entity. Thus the problem Tolman raised for theoretical psychology was whether a model of the mind was a necessary ingredient for a satisfactory theory of psychology, a question that still has not been answered. Another misunderstanding of behaviorism is that it assumes that behavior can be shaped into any form by the control of environmental influences. Genetic influences are plainly acknowledged by the cognitive behaviorism of Tolman and the neobehavioristic conception of Hull, Spence, and Neal Miller[4]

II. Forms of Understanding

My emphasis on natural science methodology as a distinct orientation in psychology can easily be misinterpreted to imply that psychological truth, or any other kind of truth, must emerge from scientific analysis. Such a conclusion is contradicted by the apparent ease with which humans are able to convince themselves, and others, about a variety of truths that do not meet the demands of science. Religious truths vary from one religion to another and are denied by non-believers as well as members of different religions. Similarly the conceptions of *human nature* and *common sense* are not dictated by some innate human capacity but instead by belief systems that are strongly influenced by family, culture, and personal experiences. The point is that one can *understand* without any assistance from natural science methodology. The thesis being advanced is that *understanding* is a psychological process that refers to the manner in which life's events are comprehended. *A sense of understanding can be achieved in a variety of ways.* In my methodological analysis of psychology[5] I described four kinds of understanding that are relevant to our analysis of morality:

Deductive explanation—understanding an event by deducing it from one or more general propositions—is the form of comprehension commonly associated with natural science methodology. The dramatic story of the discovery of the planet Neptune in 1843 illustrates this kind of explanation. The planet Uranus had been noted to follow a peculiar and variable path around the sun. Astronomers deduced from the theory of gravitation that some unknown celestial body of a given size must be exerting gravitational pull on Uranus. As a result, the location of a heretofore unknown planetary body, later to be named Neptune, was predicted, and subsequently discovered. The hypothesis was judged true because its empirical implication was confirmed.

Interpretive consistency is a form of understanding that results from explicating natural phenomena within a coherent and meaningful conception. It is different from *deductive explanation* because it is incapable of being falsified by objective evidence. Nevertheless a compelling sense of understanding is provided. Religious systems fall into this category of understanding. Psychoanalytic systems, proposed by Freud and others, also offer for some an integrated and compelling interpretation of human nature in spite of their inability to meet the natural-science criterion of falsifiability.

Intuitive knowing is a subjective conviction of understanding that is independent of any rational justification. It has been described as "a spontaneous process of integration."[6] *Humans are basically good* is a compelling intuitive truth for many philosophers and psychologists. Their subjective reality indicates the validity of the belief and no need arises to demonstrate its empirical truth value.

Phenomenal control represents a form of understanding that is equated with the ability to control a phenomenon. This kind of understanding represents an important tradition in the philosophy of science. Ernst Mach (1838-1916) was a distinguished physicist who became interested in the philosophical underpinnings of science. Mach's aim was to rid science of metaphysical notions that were, for him, any event or concept that could not be *directly observed* by the senses. For Mach, the demonstration of functional relationships among directly observed variables represent the ultimate form of scientific explanation. In psychology, B. F. Skinner (1904-1990) adopted the Machian view and rejected the notion that theories are necessary. For him, only facts are important. Thus if one can eliminate the fear of high places among acrophobics by appropriate conditioning procedures then one understands the positive effects of the therapy by knowing its procedures.

In concluding my treatment of the concept of *understanding* it becomes necessary to emphasize that my aim was only to describe different methods of comprehending life's events. No effort was made to place a value on each or to rank them. If however, one operates within a specific epistemological framework, such as natural science methodology, then one would value more those forms of understanding that are consistent with one's preference. Thus the *understanding* resulting from *deductive explanation* and *phenomenal control* are scientifically more valuable than hypotheses based on *interpretive consistency* or *intuitive knowing*.

III. The Naturalistic Fallacy

My decision to operate as a natural science psychologists has implications for my analysis of ethics. Again this statement requires qualification because I do not want to imply that natural science psychology demands a specific conception of morality or an acceptance or rejection of religion. A natural scientist can discard his empirical orientation and assume a different perspective for coping with problems of morality. In my case, however, for numerous personal reasons, I feel it is necessary to analyze morality, a psychological phenomenon, within the epistemological stance of natural science methodology.

Once morality is analyzed within this framework, moralists are confronted with a most perplexing and disturbing problem: *the naturalistic fallacy*. The *naturalistic fallacy*, more clearly described as the *fact/value dichotomy*, states simply that facts do not logically lead to values. The *naturalistic fallacy* represents a confusion of the propositions that assert something *is* with the prescription that it *ought* to be. Because there is no logical connection between the natural *is* and the moral *ought*, between *facts* and *values,* the idea that moral conclusions can be drawn from empirical evidence is erroneous. For example, if a study revealed that bilingual education for Hispanic children showed stronger ethnic identification but inferior academic performance, such findings from an ethical point do not justify either bilingual or monolingual English education. Facts do not logically generate values. Psychology is incapable of judging the relative moral value of enhancing ethnic identification or improving academic performance. Psychology can, however, provide reliable information so that social policy can be determined in light of available evidence. But it must be clearly understood that social policy cannot be logically dictated by empirical facts.

I have indulged in an exercise in critical ethics, the analysis of the nature of moral arguments. The conclusions drawn are intellectually appealing but morally frustrating. The critical approach has led to the conclusion that science in general, and psychology in particular, can offer no unqualified authority upon which to base an ethical system. If this critical conclusion is combined with the acknowledgment that ethical commitments profoundly influence individual behavior and the functioning of an entire society, then psychologists, like myself, are caught on the horns of a disturbing dilemma; ethical commitments are psychologically important, but moral truth is alien to the science of psychology.

What can scientific psychologists, like myself, do in face of such a dilemma? One obvious choice is to seek ethical guidance from sources outside of scientific psychology. Such a choice would be consistent with but *not demanded* by my critical analysis of ethics. Because psychology cannot offer valid ethical imperatives when some are needed, it does not logically follow that psychologists should encourage people to seek values through religious faith or political fervor. A pragmatic alternative is to renounce the critical conclusion that psychology cannot offer ethical imperatives that humanity needs. Any critical conclusion, no matter how impeccable the logic may be, that counters the fundamental needs of humanity, the argument goes, must be rejected. An additional alternative is to finesse the disturbing dilemma by failing to recognize it. By uncritically insisting that psychology offers special insights into moral truth, psychologists can delude themselves into believing that they are serving the public interest while simultaneously enhancing their own sense of social responsibility and self righteousness. This ploy, used too often, has damaged psychology by undermining society's confidence in it.[7]

Those psychologists who demand intellectual rigor need not abandon the study of ethics to those who do not, but they do have to contemplate the distressing thought that their epistemological stance creates a moral vacuum that can be employed to justify anything and everything as history so painfully reminds us. By accepting the verdict that science cannot meet our demands for the ultimate values of life, the door is opened to the opportunity for humankind to shape its own moral destiny. Of course some would argue that this condition prevailed at the birth of humankind and all moral systems are human creations. But let us avoid becoming entangled in this metaphysical issue and focus only on the problem of a humanly designed moral code.

Any particular ethical system that has been readily accepted by some is guaranteed to offend others. Perhaps humankind's moral needs cannot be satisfied by a single ethical system. Instead of engaging in a fruitless search to find one, perhaps our energies should be directed at creating the option of a diversity of ethical systems so that people, in principle, can pick and choose. That would require a sensitively designed system that minimizes the negative effects of the inevitable ethical conflicts that would arise. The justification for such a goal is not to achieve an ethically ideal society but only a morally effective one. For the time being a *morally effective society* will be defined as one in which a variety of moral codes operate with a minimal amount of conflict among them. In other words I am endorsing a moral pluralism which, within a pragmatic frame of reference, dovetails with a democratic ethic.

IV. Psychology and Ethics

My conception of a morally effective society stems from my effort to analyze the intersection of science, psychology, and ethics. I have concluded that natural science methodology is a distinctive form of inquiry that evaluates its interpretive conclusions on the basis of its match with empirical evidence. I have also assumed that natural science methodology can be productively applied to the study of behavior. Finally I am convinced the fact/value dichotomy cannot be breached; facts cannot *logically* generate values. If psychological facts cannot lead *directly* to the design of a morally effective society then an indirect approach is necessary. Psychological knowledge cannot dictate ethical values but it can assist in their formulation.

In this effort to blend psychology with ethics certain philosophical orientations offer useful psychological implications: *traditional morality, consequentialism, egoism, utilitarianism,* and *instrumentalism. Traditional morality* expounds the view that behavior is moral when it is consistent with the ethical traditions of a society. Tradition seems a weak standard to justify a moral code especially if one considers the ethical foundation of repressive authoritarian regimes. But the positive aspects of traditional morality come to the fore when one considers the virtues of tradition in a democratic society that provides opportunities to choose among competing social policies. Unless that choice is available, partisan views can breed social conflicts and chaos, as the recent history in eastern Europe testifies. Traditional morality within the context of a democracy can be perceived as a productive starting point for the effective airing of moral conflicts and their resolution. *Consequentialism* reorients ethics by shifting the focus of attention from moral principles to their consequences. In this manner ambiguous metaphysical concepts such as *goodness* can be transformed into observable empirical ones, thus allowing for the objective evaluation of competing moral policies. *Egoism* and *utilitarianism* are ethical systems that direct attention to significant psychological processes that operate in social behavior: self interest and communal demands. These ethical systems suggest that morality should serve the needs of individuals and the whole community. *Instrumentalism*, an offshoot of *pragmatism*, is the ethical system that has most to offer in the integration of morality with science and psychology. The reasons are threefold. First, *instrumentalism* is concerned not with ivory tower metaphysical issues but with practical solutions to life's problems. Second, it views morality not as a set of absolute principles but instead as a group of ideas that has functional value. Third, *instrumentalism* emphasizes the scientific approach to the solution of social problems. John Dewey who proposed *instrumentalism* favored the term *experimentalism* because he viewed attempts by individuals and society to cope with problems as experiments the outcomes of which could provide reliable information for the design of a better society.

The intersection between morality and psychology raises the issue as to whether humanity is preprogrammed to operate within a universal set of ethical imperatives. From a scientific point of view such a question must be answered in the negative. But that does not mean that humans do not have some fairly strong behavioral predispositions that can be described as moral. The family is the context where many of these predispositions are expressed. The amazingly strong bond between parents and their children is a good example of the kind of moral predisposition to which I refer. The love and responsibility that parents exhibit toward an offspring is amazing, even more so when the offspring is a stinker! But no matter how powerful this morally right and good behavior is exhibited by most humans, it falls far short of being universal. Two compelling reasons can be offered to deny its omnipresence: Environmental inputs and individual differences. The murder of offspring occurs throughout the world for a variety of reasons: gender bias, economic deprivation, certain religious laws, parental gain, etc. To diagnose such behavior as abnormal misses the scientific point that environmental and genetic factors can influence parental behavior. A naive environmentalism prevails among many moralists, encouraging the belief that with proper teaching and upbringing, everybody can be trained to be moral.

The phenomenon of homosexuality should destroy the optimistic hope of those who believe that everybody can be trained to meet the standards of a conventional sexual moral code. The evidence now, which is consistent with my experience as a clinical psychologist during World War II, is that homosexuality is not a matter of choice anymore than is heterosexuality. Homosexuals have the same sexual appetites as do heterosexuals but their drives demand different instrumental acts to achieve satisfaction. A reasonable summary of the evidence is that certain innate predispositions, combined with some environmental inputs, make people homosexual or heterosexual or bisexual. Don't misinterpret my point! I am not preaching a tolerant sexual morality because a scientific psychologist, *as a psychologist,* should not preach morality. I can only suggest that when society deals with sexual morality, benefits could accrue from considering the psychological consequences of the social policy. Not that the consequences can justify moral principles but they can estimate their psychological effectiveness.

By now it should be clear what the role of scientific psychology can be in shaping morality. It can provide information about the consequences of competing moral principles. When such information becomes available, a moral criterion is needed to choose among the competing social policies. One such standard that can serve as a *litmus test* is the democratic ethic of *majority rules*. Thus the scientist can provide information that will enable a democratic society to select one social policy among several in the light of their consequences.

The psychologist who operate within the strictures of science has certain responsibilities in estimating the social consequences of different policies. These obligations are no different from those operating in the laboratory; design and execute research in a fair and objective manner. This is not to say that the problems of evaluation research—measuring the consequences of different social policies—is not more complicated than doing laboratory research. But the point being made is that the same critical intelligence and scientific integrity that operates in ivory-tower laboratory studies can also operate in evaluation research. To meet this goal demands that the research psychologist be motivated to reveal the truth, not to obtain results consistent with a particular political agenda.

The distinction between value-free and politically-biased research is not accepted by all psychologists. Postmodern psychologists would deny the existence of any psychological truth. Some humanistic and social psychologists would insist that their profession entitles them to judge the moral rightness of social policies. For example the American Psychological Association, with a membership of over 60,000, dedicated to the promotion of *human welfare* passed a resolution in favor of *abortion rights*. Equating *human welfare* with *abortion rights* is a moral judgment that cannot be validated by facts or logic. But arguments can be proposed in a democracy favoring a pro-abortion or anti-abortion legislation based on their consequences. Let us analyze how this can be done.

All researchers have value systems that extend beyond the confines of their scientific life. Few, if any, are neutral about the morality of abortion. In my own case, I fall in the ambivalence camp. The wide use of abortion, I suspect, coarsens a society. At the same time I can think of no greater personal tragedy than a rape victim, especially one who is knowledgeable about genetics, who is forced to bear the offspring of her torturer. I should also confess to a view of democracy, as previously indicated, that is consistent with the empirical denial of a single ethical system that is appropriate for all humankind. If no such universal code exists then a democracy, for pragmatic reasons, should provide the widest latitude of moral behavior that allow people to practice their own morality without impinging on the morality of others. A difficult goal but nevertheless one that can be fashioned by democratic processes.

Now let us return to the problem of determining the psychological consequences of abortions. Can a psychologist with a moral view about abortion conduct value-free research about its consequences? Yes, if the researcher is committed to the ethics of science. Science and society, in a common cause, can develop research procedures that will minimize the influence of bias. Can such evaluation research offer a complete description of the consequences of a pro- or anti-abortion policies? Absolutely not! The number of outcome variables that could be measured are infinite therefore forcing society to select those that are the most important. Several years ago an administration that opposed abortions leaked the results of a study that reported that women who underwent abortion had a higher rate of depression than those who did not. The aim of the study was reasonable but not the manner in which it was carried out. It was inadequately designed and executed in order to promote political goals, not psychological consequences. In principle, it would be possible to measure the relationship between abortion and depression but only with rigorous natural-science techniques. And the information from a research program designed to reveal the consequences of abortion and *not having an abortion*, would provide those pragmatic members of society an opportunity to base their policy preferences on facts, not fiction.

The potential contributions of a scientifically-oriented evaluation research program can extend far beyond the confines of the abortion debate that rages in our country. *Affirmative action, welfare, gender conflicts*, and many other policy clashes, emerging from fundamental ethical conflicts, can be subjected to an empirical analysis that will reveal their potential consequences. The knowledge gained will always be incomplete, and somewhat distorted by sampling and measurement problems, but at the same time one must recognize that such information is far superior to complete ignorance or politically biased preconceptions.

Now that I have endorsed the application of psychology to the resolution of ethical and policy disputes, allow me to confess some unease. If there is a weak link in my analysis, it belongs to psychologists, not psychology. The conviction among many psychologists that ethical principles permeate their entire discipline and research should be the servant of political goals has robbed psychology of its scientific reputation. Only if society can distinguish between the findings of natural science psychology and forms that do not seek to meet these standards, can society reap the benefits of psychological data that estimate the consequences of competing moral and policy conflicts. And in that effort it is important to recognize that scientific psychology can help, but cannot dictate.

NOTES

1. Kurtines, W. M., Azmitia, M. & Gewirtz, J. L. (Eds.) *The role of values in psychology and human development.* New York: John Wiley & Sons, 1992.

2. Kendler, H. H., *Historical foundations of modern psychology,* Pacific Grove, CA: Brooks/ Cole, 1987.

3. Kierkegaard, S. In A. Dru (Ed. & Trans.), *Journals.* London: Oxford University Press, 1948, p.182.

4. The meaning of behaviorism and its numerous theoretical forms is described in my book *Historical foundations of modern psychology,* Pacific Grove, CA: Brooks/ Cole. 1987. A more condensed analysis is contained in my article "Behaviorism and psychology: An uneasy alliance" which appeared in S. Koch & D. Leary (Eds.) *A century of psychology as science.* New York: McGraw Hill,1985.

5. Kendler, H. H. *Psychology: A science in conflict,* New York: Oxford University Press, 1981.

6. Polyani, M. Logic and psychology. *American Psychologist, 1968, 23,* 27-43.

7. A brief statement of this kind of moral chutzpah is expressed in a comment (Prilleltensky, I. Psychology and social ethics. *American Psychologist ,* 1994, *49,* 966-967) to an article of mine (Kendler, H. H. Psychology and the Ethics of Social Policy. *American Psychologist,* 1993, *48,* 1046-1043). My response to Prilleltensky is carried in a general rejoinder to four comments (Kendler, H. H. Can psychology reveal the ultimate values of humankind? *American Psychologist,* 1994, *49,* 970-971). I'm amazed and repelled by those psychologists who modestly accept their qualifications to identify moral imperatives for all humankind. They do not imply that they are God, only that they are qualified to play the role.

B. Response to Kendler's
"Psychology, Ethics and the Naturalistic Fallacy"

John F. Crosby

I thank Howard Kendler for joining us for this conference on moral issues in psychology. His presentation is well suited to opening what I expect will be a fruitful discussion. I must admit that I was made a little nervous by what Kendler told about the last time he was involved in a conference on psychology and morality; you will recall that, as he said, he suddenly withdrew from the discussion, thinking that he and his discussion partners were too far apart to continue talking. This makes me think that I should begin with surveying our common ground, and should put my critical questions to our colleague only after assuring him that we—he and I and most of those in attendance here—are indeed in a philosophical position to have a real discussion together.

And so I begin by saying that I quite agree that there is such a thing as the "naturalistic fallacy," just as G.E. Moore taught, and that, as a real fallacy, it is to be avoided. The idea of the fallacy is this: you never lend valid support to an ethical position by any empirical observation that you make about human behavior. Take the ethical teaching about the wrongness of suicide. If you were to try to support this teaching by appealing to the strong instinct of self-preservation in every human being, you would commit the naturalistic fallacy. From the fact that we have a strong instinct to preserve ourselves in being, it in no way follows that we morally ought to preserve ourselves and that we act immorally in directly taking our lives.

C.S. Lewis explains the naturalistic fallacy when, in *The Abolition of Man*, he considers the theory that certain basic human instincts like this one of self-preservation can provide *moral* direction for us. Lewis asks:

> But why ought we to obey instinct? Is there another instinct of a higher order directing us to do so, and a third of a still higher order directing us to obey *it*?—an infinite regress of instincts? This is presumably impossible, but nothing else will serve. From the statement about psychological fact 'I have an impulse to do so and so' we cannot by any ingenuity derive the practical principle 'I ought to obey this impulse.' Even if it were true that men had a spontaneous unreflective impulse to sacrifice their own lives for the preservation of their fellows, it remains a quite separate question whether this is an impulse they should control or one they should indulge.[1]

As Lewis explains elsewhere in this splendid little study, only if we factor in the *value* of our fellow human beings, and the *value* of our acting on their behalf, can we make sense of the moral imperative to help them. Here is the main source of the moral ought—it lies not in empirical facts about human behavior, but in the good and bad of human acting.

From my agreement with Kendler about the naturalistic fallacy follows my agreement with him about the limits of the behaviorist psychology to which he is committed. He is right that such psychology, working only with the methods of natural science, can have nothing to say about good and bad, and so also can have nothing to say directly for or against any ethical proposition. If, with its characteristic methods, behaviorist psychology should attempt to derive any ethical conclusion, it would commit the naturalistic fallacy. By the way, in a recent article, "Psychology and the Ethics of Social Policy," which in many ways underlies the briefer presentation that we have just heard,[2] Kendler convincingly shows that psychologists such as Wundt and Maslow have committed the naturalistic fallacy in some of their central psychological teachings. Even if they did not limit psychology as strictly as Kendler does to the empirical study of human behavior, they nevertheless tried to derive "good" and "ought" from materials that can never imply anything properly ethical.

And I must say that there is something admirable in the intellectual self-restraint that Kendler practices on the basis of his respect for the naturalistic fallacy. He would undoubtedly like to be able to appeal to his professional knowledge as psychologist in advocating ethical and political positions which are dear to him. It is not easy to acknowledge one's limits to the point of saying: as a psychologist working only with the methods of natural science, I have nothing to say about the great questions of good and evil, of right and wrong. Kendler seems personally to support, with fairly minor reservations, the present legalization of abortion in the U.S., and yet he has said to his colleagues in the American Psychological Association: you have taken an official stance in behalf of abortion rights, but as psychologists we are not entitled to any such stance; none of our empirical results will ever establish the right or the wrong of abortion. Let us not discredit our profession by posing as moral teachers when in fact we as psychologists have no ethical wisdom to teach. As I say, I can only admire this intellectual abstinence of Kendler, this conscious acquiescence in the fundamental limitations of what he knows as psychologist. You will remember how Socrates complained that the shoemaker, for example, simply because he knows something about shoes, usually thinks he is thereby wise about all kinds of ultimate matters. Well, Kendler is not like this; he practices the Socratic ignorance of knowing what he does not know, and what lies beyond the reach of his science.

If now I proceed to raise some critical questions to Kendler, it is clear that I do so on the basis of having some considerable common ground with him.

I.

First I ask whether Kendler himself always succeeds in avoiding the naturalistic fallacy.

Whether there is one moral order of the world, the same for all human beings, is one of those properly ethical questions that empirical science can never answer. When C.S. Lewis, in the same book in which he takes such care to avoid the naturalistic fallacy, argues that there is indeed one moral order, binding universally on all human beings, he is clearly conscious of basing himself on specifically moral experience and not on the empirical experience of natural science.

Now Kendler seems to deny that there is one moral order within which we all live; he speaks of multiple moral systems devised by human beings, and says that the conflicts arising among them are to be dealt with, not by appeal to any higher, all-encompassing moral system, but by adjustments hammered out through democratic processes. My difficulty with his position is this: his denial of one universal moral order of the world seems to rest far more than it should on certain empirical observations which he makes. It is after all only an empirical observation when he says that parents, though they usually provide for their offspring, do not always do so, and it is only an empirical observation when he says that men and women do not always come out with heterosexual inclinations. And yet Kendler seems to find in these empirical facts confirmation for his denial of a universal moral order of the world. On his own principles he should recognize that even given these facts it may still be the case that all human parents without exception are morally bound to provide for their children, and that all men and women without exception are bound to limit the sexual intimacy they practice to heterosexual relations. A moral norm is not called into question when people fail to live in accordance with it, any more than the laws of logic are called into question when people reason illogically.

To conclude: would not Kendler be more faithful to his own commitment to avoiding the naturalistic fallacy if he would frankly say: for all I know as a psychologist, all those moral teachers from Cicero to C.S. Lewis who have affirmed one universal moral law may well be right? Should he not be saying something like this: my psychological findings about homosexual tendencies, or about parents destroying their children, in no way call into question such a moral vision?

II.

The next critical question which I put to Kendler concerns the extent to which his empirical research in psychology can in fact remain value-free. While I grant that such research cannot *establish* values and moral norms, I would think that it *presupposes* values and moral norms and in fact cannot be carried on apart from them. But I must make my meaning perfectly clear to him, for I can see from his article how he is liable to misunderstand me. I do not mean that psychologists inevitably wear ideological blinders which prevent them from being objective in their research. I do not mean that psychologists cannot help manipulating their research so as to advance some political agenda that they bring into their research. I rather mean something like this. Kendler must recognize some value in being objective in research, some value in getting at the real facts, some value in the intellectual integrity of communicating them truthfully. No one can miss the moral pathos of this sentence of his: "To meet this goal [of objective empirical research] demands that the research psychologist be motivated to reveal the truth, not to obtain results consistent with a particular political agenda." Of course, this moral imperative cannot be derived from psychological research as Kendler practices it: but the research cannot be carried out without the imperative. And this is not just a moral consideration like the one whereby a person is led to choose psychology as the area of his professional work; it is a moral consideration inherent in the activity of conducting psychological research—in a sense it controls this activity from beginning to end.

And there are other values and moral norms that are almost as intimately inherent in such research. Let us think of the moral norm never to use persons as mere instruments; this norm right away imposes moral limits on the kind of research that can be undertaken by the psychological researcher. Participants in an experiment, for example, may not be given potentially harmful experimental drugs without their knowledge and consent; nor may they be coerced or intimidated into participating. Even if the researchers must forego the most useful information which they might have gathered by applying some coercion, there is morally nothing to be done. They are entitled to gather their information only on certain moral conditions. Again we find that moral considerations in no way deriving from psychological research, nevertheless control the way in which it is rightly carried out. My question to Kendler is whether he is prepared to admit this presence of values within the kind of research that he is committed to. He certainly cannot allege that this presence of values commits the naturalistic fallacy. But it goes far beyond the only relation of research to value that he seems to consider, namely the relation whereby such research can help us think through the consequences of some proposal involving value, as illustrated in his example of research into bilingual education.

III.

Let us look beyond the behaviorist psychology of Kendler. If we think, for example, of Viktor Frankl's logotherapy, then we find all kinds of values entering into the work of the psychologist. If we think of *the will to meaning* in terms of which Frankl understands the human person, and of the frustration of this will in which he sees the source of many neuroses, then we see how psychology can involve itself in a rich world of value, for much of what Frankl means by meaning is nothing other than value. In this realm of psychology we see psychologists helping patients re-establish contact with value, or establish it for the first time. It is still true even here that the values to which the patients are directed are not themselves established by logotherapy; it is philosophy that establishes them, and logotherapy can only presuppose them. But logotherapy presupposes all kinds of them, and does so in such a way that no one can suspect it of the naturalistic fallacy; it is value-laden without trying to derive values illegitimately from facts.

Now the question to Kendler is why we should not recognize the likes of logotherapy as psychology no less than we recognize the behavioral research and behavioral modification to which he has dedicated his life. Why should psychology not be as concerned with the way in which people understand themselves as it is with their publically measurable behavior? Why should it not be as concerned with the subjectivity of human beings as with the objectivity of their behavior? If there are such things as conscious self-understanding and the will to meaning, how can it be right to ignore them in favor of an exclusively behavior-centered psychology?

I think I know his answer, though I find it not so much in his presentation as in that article of his underlying much of his presentation. He will say that a psychology that deals with consciousness and self-experience deals with that which only one person has direct access to, namely the person having the self-experience. Behavior, by contrast, is open to public inspection; it can be directly observed by as many people as care to turn their attention to it. As a result, behavioral research can establish a level of intersubjective agreement that seems impossible for a psychology which looks to the inner self-experience of persons and relies on reports based on introspection. Let me explain why I cannot accept Kendler's reason for preferring behavioral psychology to all the other forms that psychology can take.

a) First of all, when he thinks of the study of conscious experiencing, he thinks too exclusively in terms of people reporting what they find in introspection. But a reliance on such reports is by no means the only way for psychology to study conscious experiencing. For example, through the bodily expression of the inner life of persons we can directly experience something of their inner lives. Or through the various forms of sympathy and empathy, which Max Scheler has analyzed with such subtlety, we can enter into their inner lives. Again: through our common human nature we can almost experience others in ourselves, as has been said; we can experience that in ourselves which is not limited to ourselves. Furthermore, through our understanding of the essence of personal acts, we can come to understand what is not only true for ourselves but for every possible person. But let us make this point more concretely: however you explain it, Paul Vitz in his lecture at this conference said many things about hatred and forgiveness that we can all verify in ourselves. Though hatred, with its strong volitional character, exists in the first place not in our behavior but in our innermost subjectivity, he has not merely given us the results of his own introspection or of that of his patients, but has succeeded in speaking as if he were speaking first of all of ourselves and not of himself. Our reading of psychological authors like Vitz shows that broad intersubjective agreement can be reached in the psychological study of conscious experiencing. This means that even if we share Kendler's high esteem for intersubjective agreement, we still have no good reason for letting authentic psychology consist only or even primarily in behaviorist psychology.

b) And then I might point out that Kendler himself has the greatest difficulties in establishing intersubjective agreement about points that are all-important to him. For recall that he not only does empirical research, but has a theory about the value-neutrality of such research, and this theory is for its part not based on empirical research. Now many of his colleagues do not accept this theory, they do not accept the naturalistic fallacy and the consequences which he draws from it. Just look at that article of his that I have already mentioned several times. In the next issue of the *American Psychologist*, where his article appeared, six of his colleagues responded expressing various critical stances towards his argument,[3] and only two of these six agreed with him about the naturalistic fallacy. Some of them said that of course you can draw ethical conclusions from empirical facts. Kendler is far from intersubjective agreement with his colleagues on the theoretical axis around which his entire understanding of psychology and ethics turns. The cornerstone of his psychology does not enjoy anything like the agreement which can be achieved in any empirical investigation of behavior. But he does not withdraw from the discussion saying that, in the absence of such agreement, there is probably little scientific value in his understanding of the relation between ethics and psychology. What then can Kendler object to those psychologists who propose to deal with more than behavior? Will he object that, dealing with data of consciousness, they deal with that which cannot be publically inspected in the same way in which behavior can be publically inspected? Kendler himself works with first principles which suffer from exactly the same epistemological disadvantage. Should he not admit that their work, as far as its intersubjective verifiability goes, can have as much scientific integrity as his has, and that theirs can have as much right to count as psychology as his does?

Let me return to my point of departure in this third and final part of my comments: if there is no compelling reason to exclude non-behavioral, experience-oriented forms of psychology, we will find, as we take account of these, that the value-laden character of psychology immeasurably increases. But at no point does this increase of value involve the naturalistic fallacy, for it is always a question of presupposing values and norms, and not of deriving them.

IV.

One last question for Kendler: these values and norms must have some foundation, even if psychology does not provide it. If they have no foundation, if values are all ultimately subjective or relative, then psychology, to the extent that it presupposes them, is itself corrupted with subjectivism and relativism. It certainly would not exceed the scope of our conference if in the discussion which now follows, we also entered into the philosophical question of the grounding of objective and universally valid values and norms.

Kendler is ready with an objection to any attempt to ground objective values; it is just like his objection to forms of psychology other than behaviorism. He will say that each person has his or her own intuition of good and bad, and that, though you don't commit the naturalistic fallacy in having your own sense of good and bad, you fail to have anything like universally valid knowledge. For when somebody disagrees with your value intuitions, the two of you cannot iron out your disagreement by appealing to some objective fact like human behavior. You may think you have grasped some objective reality, but there seems to be no means of intersubjective verification through which you could settle value disputes. Thus you should realize that your values are not objective, are not universally valid, and certainly cannot provide society with an ultimate standard by which it could order the common life of its members.

To which I reply just as I did above. Kendler is the last person to be arguing like this; he has no means of settling his disputes with his colleagues over the naturalistic fallacy. But he does not think that the truth that he immediately grasps is relative or subjective, or sub-scientific. He is sure that, if only his colleagues will look at the matter with an open mind, they will agree with him; in the meantime, he stands by his insights, being more interested in truth than in consensus. But this is just the position of those who argue for objective value; there is nothing in their stance which should disturb the scientific conscience of Kendler.

To make the same argument in a slightly different way: Kendler affirms the value of truth, and the moral obligation to respect it and to transmit it faithfully, as we saw. But as he probably knows, Nietzsche does not agree with him. Nietzsche called into question as nobody ever had before the value of truth. Many of you know the famous passages in which he asks why we should not prefer error to truth. After all, he said, error will often be far more *lebensfoerdernd* than truth, that is, it will often do more to promote an abundance of vital life in us, which is for Nietzsche the supreme good. Kendler and Nietzsche, if they were to argue about this value, would not be able to settle their dispute like two laboratory scientists disputing over the weight of some chemical substance. And yet I daresay that Kendler would persist in his certainty of the objective validity of this value, persist in thinking that Nietzsche could recognize it, and should recognize it. Why then could he not show the same persistence in dealing with other values? In the above-mentioned article, "Psychology and the Ethics of Social Policy," Kendler mentions his revulsion at the idea of "mass rapes, gassing political opponents and shooting innocent bystanders."[4] What should hinder him from recognizing objective moral evil in these things? What should hinder him from recognizing that the wrong of these things, whether it is *in fact universally accepted*, is in any case *worthy of universal acceptance*? Why should he not recognize that the process of coming to agree about what is really there in the moral world, is only *different* from the same process in natural science, but that it can occur in its own way with values no less than with facts?

NOTES

1 C.S. Lewis, *The Abolition of Man* (New York: The Macmillan Co., 1968), 47-8.

2 Kendler, "Psychology and the Ethics of Social Policy," *American Psychologist* (October, 1993), vol. 48, no. 10, 1046-1053.

3 *American Psychologist* (November, 1994), 966-971.

4 Kendler, *op. cit.*, 1047-48.

C. Religion and Science

Howard H. Kendler

My response to Crosby's evaluation of my paper will initially take the form of a sermon. The text comes from a 1981 pronouncement of the National Academy of Science:

> Religion and science are separate and mutually exclusive realms of human thought whose presentation in the same context leads to a misunderstanding of scientific theory and religious belief.

I carefully walked on eggshells to abide by this stated principle not only to maintain the important distinction between contrasting ways of *understanding* but also to exhibit a tolerance which is too often missing among some scientists who feel no hesitations in offering answers about anything and everything. In contrast Crosby feels no such inhibition and enters the fray with a heavy-footed demolition of the epistemological wall that separates religion and science.

I.

The problem is that Crosby cannot escape from his role as a religious philosopher which encourages him to answer scientific questions in a theological mode. This leads to a conflation of issues in his treatment of the *naturalistic fallacy* . Our mutual adoption of this principle allows him to gloss over our fundamentally different views of the *fact/value dichotomy*. Within the context of natural science methodology, the *naturalistic fallacy* prohibits the logical deduction of values— what is good and bad and right and wrong—from facts. Crosby's commitment to the naturalistic fallacy does not stem from a desire to eliminate the confusion of facts with values in scientific discourse but instead to emphasize the theological principle that facts cannot contaminate a universally valid moral code which he, and those who share his views, are privy to. He mistakenly presumes that the naturalistic fallacy is committed when the hypothesis of a single valid morality for all humankind is challenged by the counterfactual evidence of a variety of moral codes throughout the world. Crosby misunderstands the naturalistic fallacy if he believes that it excludes studying moral development. Seeking how moral principles develop is not equivalent to validating them. One should realize that denying the empirical existence of a universal moral system is not equivalent to ethically condemning such a code.

Crosby is disingenuous when he urges me to acknowledge the possibility of one universal moral law. Such a hypothesis, within the realm of empiricism, assumes an innate morality with other factors operating to prevent its universal acceptance. To make such a theory meaningful requires the identification of these other factors and their *modus operandi*. Otherwise the innate theory is unfalsifiable and like many other theological assumptions, scientifically meaningless. Crosby appears to be more interested in scoring a debating point than in pursuing the empirical validity of an innate human moral sense.

II.

The fact that the scientific enterprise is guided by important values does not mean that one cannot do value-free research. Basic values required by the scientific method have pragmatic roots. The scientific method is an elaborate problem-solving technique devised to understand the world and in order for science to be effective, scientists must adhere to these pragmatically-created values. As one example is the value of *honesty* which is not simply the best policy, but the only policy for science to achieve its goal of empirical truth. Added to the values that are intrinsic to the functioning of science, such as honesty, are extrinsic values that are imposed by various segments of society. Some of these are justified, others are well-intentioned, while still others can be destructive to science such as the excesses of the so-called *animal rights* movement. One should maintain a sharp distinction between intrinsic and extrinsic scientific values in order separate pragmatically imposed values from metaphysical norms that play no role in uncovering empirical truth. Crosby's conflation of the two could be seen as an attempt to infiltrate the scientific method with his own metaphysical biases such as the ambiguous moral norm of never using persons as mere instruments. By so doing he clouds the difference between science and religion allowing him to reach conclusions that serve his theological agenda. The important point to recognize is that one does not have to moralize to empirically investigate morality.

III.

Crosby repeatedly notes that values operate in science and psychology, a point with which I do not disagree. My point is that scientists and psychologists can operate in a value-free environment by carefully distinguishing between empirical events and value judgments. Crosby objects to such a detached view for psychotherapy because people need the right values to live by. I do not disagree that moral commitments are important for individuals and society but the overwhelming problems that are associated with defining what is right are ignored by Crosby who knows what is right for himself and everybody else as well. Some experiences as a military clinical psychologist during World War II highlight this problem. Soldiers with strong fundamentalistic religious convictions often experienced difficulties in adjusting to the free-wheeling uninhibited Army environment. They were sometimes treated by therapists who tried to help them by reducing the pressures from their strict religious upbringing. This sometimes backfired producing disabling panic attacks. I made a practice of avoiding dealing directly with obvious religious conflicts by seeking assistance from a chaplain of my patient's faith. But such gambits had risks. I requested the assistance of a Catholic chaplain to talk to a patient who felt that "excessive masturbation" doomed him to eternal damnation. Unfortunately the Catholic Chaplain confirmed my patient's hypothesis who promptly succumbed to a psychotic episode that required closed-ward treatment. I became sophisticated about choosing chaplains and after rejecting one Catholic chaplain who was too psychoanalytically oriented, I discovered another one who was sensitive, reasonable, compassionate, and cooperative. In retrospect I wonder what would have happened if I did not abstain from giving advice to my guilt-ridden patient. Would Woody Allen's moral judgment have been psychologically helpful or harmful: "What is wrong with masturbation? At least you are having sex with someone you love!" In sum, Crosby's endorsement of a value-laden therapy reflects not simply a prescription for value intervention, but for ones that meets his standards of validity.

I have had my full say about the role of consciousness in a natural science psychology.[1] My analysis aimed to distinguish between a psychology based on natural science methodology and forms of psychology designed to be consistent with a particular set of religious, metaphysical, or political belief systems. My basic thesis is that "there are no interacting minds"[2] thus preventing the accumulation of reliable knowledge from the *direct examination* of consciousness either in a naive fashion or by trained introspection. This methodological point does not exclude consciousness and mental processes from a behavioristic psychology. The direct examination of one's own consciousness can be viewed as a form of behavior instead of a veridical reflection of consciousness. The mind can be interpreted as a theoretical model, the truth of which can be appraised by the match between its empirical implications and observable behavior. Finally, conscious experience can be correlated with neurophysiological processes to evaluate the relationship between the two. In any case Crosby's complaint that I failed to achieve intersubjective agreement among psychologists is misdirected because he conflates empirical evidence which requires intersubjective agreement with theoretical truth that consistently generates some disagreement.

IV.

I tried to suggest that my epistemological playground—natural science psychology—was different than Crosby's playground—moral philosophy and theology. Our respective playgrounds required different rules of conduct to achieve the kinds of truth we sought; empirical truth in my case and moral and theological truth in his. I was willing to let him alone in his playground because I can understand people pursuing his goals even though I cannot accept their conclusions. He however persisted in invading my territory and confusing and distorting the natural science game I was playing. I can even be tolerant about that, realizing that his absolutist orientation makes it difficult to deal with ideas that do not fit within his philosophical commitments. And I have also found that philosophers who never engaged in empirical research and theory construction experience difficulty in understanding the meaning of science.

Now I must drop my detached attitude toward Crosby's critique of my natural science analysis of morality because his comments extend beyond the bounds of science into the realm of a political democracy, an area in which we are both active players, and in this case, opponents. And I should note that my opposition does not stem solely from my commitment to natural science methodology because I cannot live by science alone. To live a full life requires for me inputs from such philosophical orientations as humanism, existentialism, and on occasions, sheer hedonism. But I must emphasize that my critical view of his moral philosophy stems from my scientific orientation.

Although Crosby has every right to be guided by his theological beliefs, I have every right, and obligation, to resist the imposition of his absolutist moral beliefs that I believe can threaten a political democracy. I can understand where his absolutist beliefs come from but their consequences endanger a society that can function more effectively with a moral pluralism that is in tune with the full range of human variability and potential. The full impact of his views began to frighten me when on page 116 he makes an apparently innocuous remark about an "authentic psychology." The word *authentic* operates as a red flag because it reminds me of the Marxist use of the concept *authentic consciousness* which suggests that a real human consciousness exists from which absolute moral principles can be derived. In contrast, I distinguish among different psychologies in terms of their methodological orientations coupled with a strong preference for a natural science psychology not because of its "authenticity" but instead because its empirical superiority has many uses. Just imagine what would have occurred to science if Aristotle's emphasis on *final cause* was judged to be an "authentic" component of scientific explanation. The knowledge claims of those who make judgments about *authenticity* in regards to psychology or morality, should be examined with great suspicion.

My fears of absolutism, within psychology and society, are furthered by Crosby's two final points, one to be answered concretely and the other abstractly. He urges me to recognize objective moral evil as a natural consequence of my revulsion to "mass rapes, gassing political opponents and shooting innocent bystanders." Let me add an equally repugnant moral outrage: denying a victim of rape the opportunity to have an abortion. Will Crosby continue to ask "What should hinder him [Kendler] from recognizing objective moral evil in these things?" Who resolves disagreements about "what is really there in the moral world"? I cannot do so because within the framework of natural science epistemology a world of value cannot be found that is comparable to the natural world of facts.

Why has not the human world embraced a universal morality? My psychological guess is that an ethical code, mediated by a legal system, has functional value and if ethical principles create intolerable difficulties their moral "validity" will be challenged. Witness the turmoil in the Catholic Church about birth control! A universal morality with strong, restrictive demands can not serve all societies regardless of their cultural background and social and physical environments. Even in the same society, such as the United States, genetic predispositions plus a broad range of philosophical and religious commitments will create resistance to any ethical system that demands complete acceptance by all. Only a moral pluralism can meet the demands of a democracy. But how a satisfactory and effective moral pluralism can be created is an overwhelmingly complex task, far more difficult than formulating a universal ethical code. Moral pluralism does not contain intrinsic moral limits that are needed to prevent chaos and nihilism and the resulting destruction of the functional value of moral pluralism. Moral boundaries are demanded in an ethically pluralistic society but they cannot be set in stone. They require constant evaluation to determine their consequences so that the functional value of moral pluralism can be retained. One must fully recognize that the delineation of moral boundaries in a pluralistic democratic society can only be approached, but never finalized. But however great the difficulties moral pluralism creates it has the redeeming virtue of resisting a moral absolutism that can lead to a Torquemada, Lenin, or Hitler.

NOTES

1. Kendler, H. H., *Psychology: A science in conflict.* New York: Oxford University Press, 1981; Kendler, H. H., *Historical foundations of modern psychology.* Pacific Grove, CA: Brooks/Cole, 1987.

2. Bergmann, G. (1956). The contributions of John B. Watson. *Psychological Review, 63,* 265-276. p.266.

D. Response to Kendler's Response

John F. Crosby

I.

The first misunderstanding I find in Kendler's response concerns the naturalistic fallacy. Kendler does not know how to recognize it as well as I thought he did, and in fact he sometimes commits it. He commits it when he refers to the "variety of moral codes throughout the world"and says that this fact does indeed "challenge" the claim that there is "a single valid morality for all humankind." If Kendler had not said, "a single valid morality,"but rather "a single system of human mores,"he would have spoken about an empirically verifiable quantity and would have avoided the naturalistic fallacy. But he made bold to say "validity,"which is not an empirically verifiable quantity. We can certainly infer no objection to the validity of some moral norm from the fact that many people deny the norm. What people think about moral validity is a matter of moral psychology; as an empirical psychological fact, it implies nothing about validity itself. Or if with Kendler you think it does, then with him you commit the naturalistic fallacy.

II.

I fear that Kendler still does not understand rightly my claim that there is no such thing as a *purely* empirical psychology. He thinks that with this claim I am letting theology intrude into empirical psychology. In fact I am making an entirely secular claim that has nothing to do with theology and everything to do with scientific integrity. Perhaps I can make myself better understood by restating my idea as follows.

In order to carry out an empirical study, the scientist has to presuppose all kinds of truths that for their part are not empirically verifiable. For example, they have to presuppose that one must never commit the naturalistic fallacy, and no one can empirically show that the inference from is to ought is a fallacy (because no one can deal empirically with an ought). Indeed, no one can empirically justify any of the laws of logic (such as the principle of contradiction and the principle of excluded middle) that are constantly presupposed in any empirical study. And yet they must be justified, for they impart to any empirical research, not indeed its content but its rational form. If they are just arbitrarily postulated, if they could be replaced by different equally arbitrary postulates, then the empirical research that is informed by them is all infected with this arbitrariness. Thus the scientific integrity of Kendler's research rests in part on the justification that only philosophy can provide for those formal principles of rationality that he presupposes. If he thinks he can play his "natural science game"without any debt to philosophy, then I say that he remains ignorant of his own presuppositions. If he confuses this debt to philosophy with a debt to theology, then it is he and not I who is conflating faith with secular matters.

III.

I also doubt that Kendler understands rightly what I wanted to say to him about the presence in his research of certain values, such as the value of truth, which is altogether intrinsic to any empirical research project. Suppose we called into question whether it is really better in research to find out what is the case than to ignore what is the case and to postulate only what we human beings want to be the case. Then we would have to call into question all the painstaking efforts of the empirical researcher to achieve objectivity; we would have to wonder whether his ideal of objectivity is a superstition that impedes him from doing some different thing that he really ought to be doing.

He tells me in his response that such values as are immanent in empirical research "have pragmatic roots"and are "pragmatically imposed." We get a sense of what he must mean when he mentions the value of honesty and the necessity of practicing honesty for the sake of getting objective empirical results. But this will not do. When any of us, Kendler included, are indignant at a colleague for deliberately falsifying his or her research, we are not in the first place indignant at the technical fact that an ineffectual means has been chosen by the colleague for getting results. Indignation would not even be an appropriate response to a mismatch between means and desired end. We are rather indignant at the very fact of the dishonesty. It is a thoroughly non-pragmatic indignation; we would still be indignant if the falsified results turned out to be true and to have a salutary influence on other researchers.

Furthermore, the value of honesty rests on the more basic value of objectivity in research. But what could it mean to say that *the value of objectivity itself* "has pragmatic roots"? If pragmatic here means empirical, then Kendler had better beware of committing the naturalistic fallacy again. Or does Kendler mean that we cannot survive without aiming at objectivity? Nietzsche thinks that we can survive far better by forgetting about objectivity and by "spinning out ideas as the spider spins its web,"as he says. But perhaps Kendler disagrees with Nietzsche and esteems scientific objectivity for the sake of survival, which then becomes for him as researcher the foundational value. But what does it mean to call this value "pragmatic"? Think of the objections to the value of survival raised from the point of view of philosophical pessimism; the objection that there really is no point in prolonging the existence of the human race is not a pragmatic objection, nor is there any pragmatic way of dealing with it. Thus Kendler has to recognize sooner or later some self-evident value without which he could not do his research-aimed-at-objective-results. He will not be able empirically to verify this value, nor will he be able to present it as more or less "pragmatic"than any other objective value.

I find it hard, then, to understand why Kendler has such difficulty agreeing that there is no such thing as purely, exclusively empirical research; that such research is embedded in different kinds of non-empirical intuition and understanding; and that if these for their parts cannot be rationally (and non-empirically) justified, then the rational pretensions of empirical research collapse. By registering such agreement he would not undermine anything dear to him as empirical researcher, nor would he be making any theological commitments: he would simply be signing on to that which alone founds and grounds his research.

IV.

Kendler shudders at my "absolutism"and, in a highly imaginative and original move, invokes Torquemada and Hitler so as to put me in the company in which he thinks I belong. Here, too, I think that he does not understand my position, or even the consequences of his own position. I would ask him to consider these well-known words of Mussolini, who, I submit, draws out quite correctly the consequences of Kendler's "anti-absolutism":

> If relativism signifies contempt for fixed categories and men who claim to be the bearers of an objective and absolute truth...then there is nothing more relativistic than Fascist attitudes and activity... From the fact that all ideologies are of equal value, that all ideologies are mere fictions, the modern relativist infers that everybody has the right to create for himself his own ideology and to attempt to enforce it with all the energy of which he is capable.[1]

From the rejection of moral absolutes Mussolini concludes to none of the nice liberal-democratic positions of Kendler; he concludes instead to a license for violence. Mussolini thinks here more clearly than Kendler. How does Kendler propose to take a moral stand against some future fascist grabbing for power if Kendler has sworn off all absolutes? On what will Kendler base his protest if he recognizes no absolutely inviolable rights, no absolute imperative to practice tolerance? People who rail at moral absolutes only help to create the moral vacuum into which thugs like Mussolini can enter unopposed.

V.

Kendler asks, "Who resolves disagreements about 'what is really there in the moral world'?" He answers by saying that a natural science epistemology cannot help to settle moral disagreements. Of course it cannot; empirical methods cannot settle non-empirical questions. But certain non-empirical methods, methods well adapted to the moral world, *can sometimes lead to far more intersubjective agreement than can be reached in empirical research*. Almost everyone will agree, for example, that promises ought to be kept and that benefactors ought to be thanked and that persons ought never be owned as slaves. We can get a broader agreement among human beings about these moral principles than we can get among empirical psychologists about the causes of certain neuroses, or about the factors that give rise to the superego. Thus moral absolutes need not always be as divisive as Kendler fears when they come up in public discussion; it is still possible for a broad moral consensus to form around many of them, even though such consensus does not constitute their validity.

NOTES

1.   Mussolini, *Diuturna*, 374-77. Quoted from Hellmut Kuhn, *Freedom Forgotten and Remembered* (Chapel Hill, N.C.: University of North Carolina Press, 1943), 17-18.

6

Psychology and Philosophy: Points of Contact and Divergence

A. Is Psychology a Part of Philosophy?
The Problem of Induction in Empirical Research

Richard W. Cross

I. The Problem

I believe we can shed considerable light on the relationship between the sciences and personalist psychology if we are prepared to admit that there are two kinds of psychology. One psychology is scientific and is as such part of the empirical tradition initiated by Newton and brought into psychology by Fechner and Helmholtz. The other psychology is a part of philosophy of which Plato seems to be the primogenitor. The support for the distinction between the two psychologies resides in both the respective subject matters and methods. It is toward the method of each that I will devote my attention, and specifically that part of method known as induction. As a basic activity of the mind from which generalities proceed by a consideration of specific instances, induction can give rise to the first principles and other premises of psychology. A sketch on the nature of induction, with particular attention paid to its two different modes, relates to the development of questions within personalist psychology, no less on questions of morality. Is it not the quest of much of contemporary humanistic psychology to uncover, to redefine, or to highlight that which is the nature of man? And does not our understanding of the morality of the human person flow from our understanding of the nature of man? It is in these considerations that pertain to matters of definition, which are after all the starting points of psychology, that the problem of induction is most keenly felt.

Psychology is characterized today by many of its expositors as a science because it proceeds by way of principles and methods adopted from the physical sciences. As a basic component of method, science must devote itself to the study of things as they are subject to public scrutiny, in as much as the public knowledge is empirical. From this public knowledge the starting points emerge from which generalizations follow. These starting points are proffered in contradistinction with those of philosophy which are not from the start available to empirical observation as defined by the sciences. Philosophy has its own methods of discovery and explanation which vary from those of the physical sciences. In light of the fact that psychology has until this century been conceived as a part of philosophy, such a preliminary disposition by the empirical psychologist of today would place into doubt the classical relationship between psychology and philosophy; that is, that it is a part of philosophy.

This point is briefly addressed by DuBois (1995), in his paper delivered at last year's Institute for Personalist Psychology conference, on whether the human person is innately defective. In the midst of his paper, DuBois seeks to justify his method of argument in comparison to those of the sciences. He enunciates four marks of scientific knowledge, and illustrates correctly, I think, how the philosophic mode of explication is similar in several respects to the scientific. Allow me to summarize briefly these four marks of science. (1) Science seeks to generate laws. (2) It aims at a coherent body of knowledge. (3) It draws from public evidence. (4) It is empirical. DuBois wishes to qualify this fourth criteria asserting that not all valid scientific knowledge derives directly from the 'empirical' in the sense used by the physical sciences.

This qualification touches upon the first of the ten principles of the Intitute for Personalist Psychology. In light of the fact that much of what passes for psychology today issues forth from empirico-scientific research, DuBois'(1995) qualification gives rise to the question, is psychology a part of philosophy.

The first principle, entitled the nature of evidence, asserts the following:

> Because human beings are complex beings, and because each scientific procedure has its limitations, we encourage the use of a wide variety of methods of studying the person. This requires the psychologist to espouse a broad notion of evidence, to view evidence as any way in which a truth reveals itself. Such a notion of evidence will serve to justify supplementing the traditional empirical methods of psychology with the use of philosophical methods of research in psychology, particularly as one approaches peculiarly personal phenomena such as love, freedom, ethical action, and religious practice. (p. 185)

It is significant that this statement of principle leaves open the question of the exact relation of philosophy and psychology, except to suggest that no science is entirely adequate to grasp the central characteristics of the human person. I wish to contend here, that the physical sciences as valid forms of truth, cannot adequately grasp the human person because of the mode of induction that science demands as the indispensable starting point precludes from the complete grasp of the nature of the human person.

II. Method & Induction

The provisional character of induction, also called the inductive inference, has been a matter of considerable debate among philosophers of science (Salmon, 1971.) My use of the term here is in the classical sense where the mind moves from particular instances to generalities. Some suggest that this is done in two ways. To paraphrase DeKoninck (1957), one kind of induction, the *natural* or *ordinary* induction, is as natural as breathing. Think of those basic and universal truths which influence so much of our thinking, without reflecting them. When did we first come to understand that 'the whole is greater than its part,' or that 'it is impossible to be and not be at the same time and in the same respect?' This is the kind of induction that goes virtually unnoticed but which everyone does. It seems at the base of our common experience of things, and brings with it a high degree of certainty.[1] The other kind of induction can be more deliberate and considers the specific instances of a general rule. In this kind of induction "The rules serve as principles, but they are not the reason for the regularities which they enounce." (DeKoninck, 1957, p. 139) The first kind of induction is at the basis of philosophic psychology, particularly as it relies upon our capacity to reflect upon ourselves, that activity which is so critical to establishing the validity of the psychological proposition. The other induction, sometimes called *inductive enumeration*, seems to be at the base of all scientific inquiry. Ordinary or philosophical induction may not be always easy, as in the case of intuiting the evident prescriptions of the moral law; so I don't wish to suggest here that all ordinary induction is arrived at without some effort or without some experience. But it should be emphasized that the basic propositions that could arise from ordinary induction are certain propositions that are in no way preceded by any form of complex reasoning.[2]

Let's look at a few illustrations of the different kinds of induction. We may recall our high school geometry days where the geometric proof proceeds from principles, such as the parallel postulate, to the conclusion about the properties of mathematical figures. For example, in Euclid's deductive proof on the sum of the interior angles of a triangle, we observe a demonstration from the parallel postulate that the interior angles of a triangle are equal in sum to 180 degrees (or in Euclid's parlance, 'two right angles'.) The parallel postulate states that if a straight line falling on two straight lines make the interior angles on the same side less than two right angles, the two straight lines will meet at some point. This postulate seems to be self-evident. Once we correctly apprehend the meaning of the terms, we understand its validity. We grasp its truth by way of what DeKoninck calls ordinary or natural induction.

But suppose we would proceed by way of inductive enumeration. We would find ourselves making numerous measurements of the interior angles of the lines that intersect to discover that these angles never sum to a value equal to or greater than 180 degrees. Which is to say—if the protractor is accurate—that the average value of all measured angles will be less than 180 degrees. This result is the same result we acquired through simple apprehension. But note the difference between these approaches. In the measurement example, we simply determine by way of an operational definition whether 'two lines meet' and measure with a protractor the interior angles of the transversal. We repeat this operation on numerous different examples.

These are two very different ways of approaching the same truth. One is by way of an inductive enumeration, the other is by way of ordinary induction. The ordinary induction is not provisional, it is certain to the extent that one apprehends the nature of matter under consideration.[3] The protractor measurement yields an inherently provisional type of knowledge, since, the understanding of the 'parallel' is only known through the measurement of its angles, or rather, through the measurement instrument, the protractor.

From psychology we can derive another example that should further help illustrate the distinction between the two types of induction. Suppose we wish to ascertain the validity of the following proposition 'Man is risible.' As an empirical approach, we would have to generate an operational definition of risibility. Then we would have to proceed to evaluate the presence or absence of this attribute in a sample of people. We would undoubtedly find statistically significant results; i.e., for example, of the 1000 persons evaluated, all demonstrated laughter, or reported having laughed in the last four weeks.

By way of ordinary or natural induction, we simply reflect on the evident fact that we are all at least potentially able to enjoy the incongruous. Which leads to 'Man is risible.' Each mode of induction yields the same result materially, but the approaches are different. The certainty accorded by the ordinary induction is much greater than that of the inductive enumeration.

Of the examples so far, some of us may think that a principal characteristic, if not a defining characteristic of ordinary induction is that it is always more certain than inductive enumeration. This may not be so. The next example, a little more mundane perhaps, illustrates how ordinary induction, will yield somewhat less certain, but still knowable/reasonable propositions, and in a manner that is qualitatively different than inductive enumeration. It is apt that this example stems from the areas of ethics or political philosophy but clearly also relates to social psychology. Suppose one wishes to assess whether or not the major political players in world politics are part of a global conspiracy. One way to evaluate this claim would be to assess major bureaucratic organizations to see how well they run, to note that as organizations become larger, the more difficult they are to control. Now this type of argument is a demonstration by way of an inductive enumeration. It requires one to have some considerable experience with bureaucracies, particularly large ones, to conclude, by way of enumeration, that it is unlikely that a small syndicate of individuals could exert such significant influence over such unmanageable organizations. The conclusion on the unmanageable quality of bureaucracies issues directly from the enumeration. Now let's take an entirely different approach that involves philosophic induction, perhaps from ethics or political philosophy. By definition we know that a conspiracy must involve more than one person, perhaps, two or more. We reflect that by the very nature of a conspiracy these two or three people must agree between themselves on all the essentials, in order to conform to the definition of conspiracy. Now from the mere experience of life, we understand that people, particularly those in positions of influence, are much inclined to dominate others for their own benefit, without much regard for the others. We also know that the more powerful we become, the less likely we will be to succumb to the desires of another, and in fact, the more inclined we will be to relish a contest with our competitor. This competitive urge is a universal impulse of humanity. From playgrounds to corporate boardrooms, any person who reflects upon their common experience sees the desire for power as embedded in the human person. We can see that a conspiracy requires an enormous amount of cooperation, where power sharing seems to presuppose competition. The joint occurrence of both would seem, not impossible or logically incoherent, but clearly an utterly unlikely state of affairs. So we can see scientifically and philosophically that a conspiracy of a few elite power-brokers is an unlikely event. Again, both the empirical and the philosophic approaches yield the same conclusion, but the modes of demonstration are quite different.

If ordinary induction yields knowledge with greater certainty, why would we content ourselves to use inductive enumeration? Because ordinary induction cannot validate some propositions. These types of propositions do not lend themselves either to ordinary induction or to demonstration by way of deduction.[4]

Examples of such findings, though probably true via inductive enumeration, but still open to revision would be propositions like:

All crows are black.

The ratio of the moon's axial rotation to its orbit about the earth is 1-to-1.

The capacity to grasp the distinction between right and wrong emerges at the age of seven.

Men are more prone to depression in mid-life than women.

A behavior that is punished at one point in time is less likely to appear at some future point in time.

These propositions are clearly reasonable, but far from certain. They are by nature tentative. The reason for their tentative nature lies in the inability to understand what it is about the nature of the thing that requires that it have a certain attribute. We don't know what it is about 'crowness' that requires that we predicate 'black.' We can only conclude that our findings of crows' blackness is true, but tentative. Similarly, although we may grasp the nature of man, we don't thereby know that depression is a consequence, let alone depression in males during mid-life. We have to admit the possibility of being in error because we lack a certain understanding of the nature of depression. Similarly, it is evident by way of ordinary induction that man is a moral animal, but it is not evident that from the nature of the child that the attribute of moral awareness arises by a child's seventh year—this is gathered from considerable experience of knowing children.

Virtually all scientific knowledge, and certainly knowledge gleaned from most of scientific psychology is of this tentative form. This is the major limitation of scientific induction. The principle of falsification forwarded by Karl Popper is a formal development of the nature of inductive enumeration. Scientific propositions must be framed in a manner that they are testable or falsifiable. The test arises by looking at illustrations of the proposition in question.

III. Experience and Science

One of the distinct marks of scientific experience which sets it apart from the experience of the layman is that it requires a kind of systematic observation. The information upon which science bases its claims is of a special sort. Either by way of using special instruments, or some other method, which yields information that is by its very character unavailable to the layman who lacks access to the scientist's specific tools and observations. For the psychologist, these special tools consist of systematic observation, clinical experience, or psychological tests. The data that science derives from such observations have a special quality that places them outside the reach of ordinary experience. The method of acquisition itself creates the data and thereby produces the experience.

Simply carefully observing or measuring research subjects is not enough if science is interested in making generalizations—which it almost always is. To achieve generality science usually has to go to great lengths to get a good sample of subjects. This is so the results can be reasonably generalized to some group or population of interest. Here, the ability to generalize the findings from specific findings of say specific persons who were examined, to all persons with similar characteristics, is referred to as statistical induction. This is a rather special kind of knowledge that is based upon enumeration, much the way one would come to conclude, say, that all crows are black, but in a controlled fashion. Virtually all political polling uses a refined version of this kind of induction, as do the better conceived sociological and psychological researches. They can be quite accurate if the conditions of measurement are right. Even so, this kind of knowledge always yields propositions that are inherently tentative.

The specialized experience of science differs in kind from what philosophy calls common experience. Common experience is something accessible to anyone without recourse to some special instruments of science and it is the basis of our ordinary induction. Of course, the experiences of any two people are hardly the same, but to the extent that we all live in the same world of objects, and apprehend these objects with the same senses and an intellect, and are capable of reflecting on our relation to these objects, then our experience is a shared or common experience.

> The distinction between common and special experience is thus seen to be a distinction between natural and artificial experience. Scientific method, from its best

experimental to its crudest empirical forms, is the art of creating experiences which men do not naturally have. The value of experience, whether common or special, whether natural or artificial, is the same: it is the immediate source of inductions, of generalized knowledge of the world of experienceable objects... The maxims of common sense, the axioms or principles of philosophy, the general facts and laws of science, all arise from experience, but not the same kind of experience, because the method of ordinary and philosophical knowing is thoroughly natural, whereas the method of scientific knowing involves operations of art in the production of special experiences. (Adler, 1937, p. 131.)

Both the principles of philosophy and the findings of science arise from fundamentally different kinds of human experience. The scientific experience is the result of a specialized manner of observing small facets of nature, whereas the experience of the philosopher stems from the experience of living that is common to all. Scientific experience entails recourse to special experience, which in its own turn utilizes inductive enumeration. Statistical estimation is the mathematically rigorous expression of inductive enumeration, and thus we see its use throughout the sciences, but not at all in philosophy. Perhaps some facets of common experience arise from inductive enumeration, but of itself, this would not yield the special experience that science requires. Further, not all facets of common experience are utilized by philosophy. Philosophy seems to have a special interest in those experiences that stem from ordinary inductions which give rise to the apprehension of the intelligible nature of the thing under consideration.

If we are to understand that the point of departure for the science of psychology is fundamentally different than philosophic psychology, and if we are further to understand that the kinds of conclusions that one may deduce depend upon these inductive starting points, then we can see why it is that psychology is really of two different sorts. Philosophic psychology is part of philosophy in that its methods conform to those of philosophy with the starting point being ordinary or philosophic induction. Scientific psychology relies upon the kind of provisional inductions consisting of special experience. The advantage of the former, philosophic psychology, is its reliance upon the ordinary induction which yields general but certain propositions. Its disadvantage, as philosophic, resides in its inability to specify in detail some implications of its propositions. The advantage of scientific induction, (inductive enumeration) is the capacity to descend into specific details, and to test those facets of common sense that arise from sources other than ordinary induction. Of course, this carries with it the disadvantage of a corresponding reduction in the certainty of the more general proposition. For example, we may grasp by way of philosophic induction the general proposition that the capacity to distinguish between right and wrong belongs to children—that they have a conscience. We may also understand philosophically that the conscience arises from the person's capacity to grasp or to comprehend prescriptive truth with the desire to do good for its own sake. We may also understand that the capacity to exercise the conscience depends upon the capacity to reason, and this in turn depends in some way on the material principles which contribute to the conscious state. So we know that conscience is not used at those times when we are asleep, or comatose, or drugged, or otherwise impeded due to some state of matter. But these essential insights, important as they are, reveal none of the specifics under which the attribute of conscience comes into being, the material conditions of its exercise, nor the time-line of development which is an important educational concern with children. And it is precisely these limitations that can be addressed both by the experience of living and also by scientific induction, since each of these sources of experience reveal those factors not otherwise known except through an immersion into the particulars. However, the inductive enumeration sheds no further light on the *nature* of conscience, as such, but it certainly clarifies or illustrates some of its properties.

IV. Some Examples

At this point, allow me to give some examples of where the distinction between philosophic and scientific psychology pertains. As we listen to the brief development of each example, we should ask ourselves two questions: First, on what kind of experience are the claims based? Second, what seems to be the character of the general statements? The first two examples arise from very different branches of psychology, one from cognitive neuroscience, the other from humanist existential theory. Despite the very different subject matters and perspectives, the inductive errors are remarkably similar—each entails the use of scientific experience to yield conclusions which appear to be inherently philosophical.

In our first example, we turn our attention to the recent work in cognitive neuroscience. One of the preeminent thinkers of this program is Roger W. Sperry, a once committed positivist (his own description), who is attempting to redefine the role of science in the realm of ethics and religion, or perhaps another and more apt way to put it would be to say that he is attempting to redefine religion in the realm of science.

This is a significant departure from the tradition of experimental psychology through the behavioral reign, where psychology is clearly not a part of philosophy or religion. Historically, the experimentalist conceived of philosophy—particularly philosophy in its analytic garb of the twentieth century—as subsumed under psychology as science. In this respect, philosophy simply provides the canons of reasoning and testability. Experimentalists have until recently cast philosophy as the positivist, where philosophy has no truth value, apart from its relationship to the empirical and mathematical sciences.

The paradigm shift leading to cognitive neuroscience, has created a reappraisal of the traditional materialist assumptions so dominant in experimental psychology, and suggests some fundamental realignment between philosophy and science (Baars, 1986.) Roger W. Sperry's work on the mind-body problem is illustrative in this regard with what he calls the "interactionist" view of causal determinism.

According to Sperry, research in cognitive science cannot be made reasonably coherent without assuming that meta-material properties are significant factors in cognitive functioning.[5] These meta-material properties appear to arise out of the brain processes themselves, and in turn affect the brain processes. In other words, when the physical brain functions, it creates these meta-material processes which in their own turn affect brain processes. Sperry further contends that consciousness emerges out of this interactive mixture of mind and brain. But he also sees emerging out of the two-way street of brain and cognitive process reflections of a larger order of the universe, where:

> ...it is not possible to physically separate the forces of creation from creation itself; the two become inextricably interfused. A Spinoza-Einstein-like concept of the cosmos is supported in which ultimate respect naturally centers, as in most religions, in the forces that made and control the universe, *but these forces are conceived scientifically in emergent macrodeterminist terms.* (Sperry, 1988, p. 611. Emphasis added.)

It is not clear here how to evaluate Sperry's reassessment of the relationship between science and religion. His casting religion in the realm of philosophy, personal belief, and morality, can be seen in perhaps one of two different ways. It can be a more measured or nuanced type of materialism, where belief is simply a manifestation or emergence of material forces. Or it can signify the reemergence of a kind of Cartesian dualism that rejects simple materialism by conceding the existence of some other dimension of reality. But what does seem clear is that Sperry fails to address the distinction in method between the disciplines.[6] He gives weight to scientific conclusions drawn from empirical investigation on an inherently philosophical subject. Sperry's chief inductive error is that he takes the special experience of science as primary and subverts the common experience of philosophy. It is the same kind of mistake that is so common among the materialists of recent vintage

Our second example comes from the humanist psychologist, Carl Rogers, who certainly ranks as one of the most influential of the humanists both by way of the development of his therapy but also by way of his theory. The substance of his views have been critiqued by members of the Institute, and so I will not add to them here.[7] But by way of his method of discovery, I think that he errs in a manner similar to Sperry, even though his subject matter is quite different.

Rogers' main genius was his ability to tap into a simmering sentiment in clinical psychology against the philosophical excesses of the behaviorists and the psychoanalysts, who ruled the theoretical roost from the 1930s to the 1950s. Rogers had a deep suspicion of thinkers like Skinner, who was a philosophical materialist. Even though he was unable to sustain a critique of Skinner, he was extremely successful at magnifying the suspicions against him that were harbored by many psychologists. In large measure he succeeded in creating a school of thought that supplanted the determinism of the behaviorist with his doctrines of personal freedom and autonomy. In so doing, however, Rogers appeals to a series of philosophic impressions that he contends were generated by his clinical experience.

Rogers' philosophic views were, for example, that if one's personality is allowed to develop with only support and encouragement from the family and society, adjustment and happiness would inevitably result. People become conflicted, unhappy, or destructive only because each person's innate capacities are not allowed to come to their natural fruition. People are good so long as they're not forced to do things that they do not want to do; that is, as long as their autonomy is not encroached. Any external influence to the good is purely accidental to the good which arises from within. Nature is such that we are each born with these inner potencies to autonomous fulfillment (or what fellow humanist A. Maslow called self-actualization.) Each of us strives toward autonomy in our own peculiar way, but never in conflict with others who are themselves seeking autonomy. Conflict-free activity is possible since its origins are from nature as an evolved adaptive tendency within the human species. The autonomous person cannot help but contribute to the benefit of man. This inner impulse to autonomy is like an inner calling, a psychological vocation, or a moral instinct, as it were. Each of these views has the strong ring of ordinary induction. It is rather natural if not easy to see how each of these statements could arise in some fashion, out of ordinary experience.

But Rogers contends that he came to his views, especially those on guilt and autonomy, by way of his therapeutic experience. He contends that it is in virtue of that special and unique experience of the non-directive therapeutic relationship that the view of human nature arises, as a philosophic awareness. In other words, special experience (science) produces philosophy.

> The essence of some of the deepest parts of therapy seems to be a unity of experiencing. The client is freely able to experience his feeling in its complete intensity, as a "pure culture," without intellectual inhibitions or caution, without having it bounded by knowledge of contradictory feelings; and I am able with equal freedom to experience my understanding of this feeling, without any conscious thought about it,...When there is this complete unity, singleness, fullness of experiencing in the relationship, then it acquires the "out-of-this-world" quality which many therapists have remarked upon... I am often aware of the fact that I do not know, cognitively, where this immediate relationship is leading, (but) its rewarding character lies with the process itself, and that its major reward is that it enable both the client and me, later, independently, to let ourselves go in the process of becoming. (Rogers, 1961, p.202-203.)

It is, of course, this process of becoming as he calls it that serves as the philosophical grid-work upon which his system of human nature is constructed. So from the idiosyncratic clinical experience seems to arise a view of the human person with broad philosophical implications. The great appeal of Rogers was in part due to his grasp of the inadequacy of the positive science to grasp the human person. But his thinking is confused. He recognizes the distinction between the science of psychology and philosophical psychology, and the inadequacy of science as it is conceived by Skinner. But in other places he muses that the science of psychology uncovers by way of a pragmatic realism the source of human happiness scientifically formulated in a manner appropriate to Dewey or Comte. (Rogers, 1961, p. 399) His confusion arises from the failure to distinguish between common experience and special experience.

Rogers' psychology is both philosophy and empirical science, but, it would seem that neither is well-conceived. His views of the human person are clearly philosophical in character, but their discovery is explained in a way that would suggest a kind of special induction appropriate to the clinician. This poses a problem when seeking to cast his thinking as philosophical, since its method of discovery/induction is not authentic as a philosophic induction. If this be the case, then in the pursuit of a philosophic psychology, one would be most mistaken, on the basis of methodology alone, to rely upon Rogers' basic views as a point of departure in the philosophical pursuit.

Our next example is drawn directly from Professor Crosby's paper on conscience and the superego, delivered at last year's conference. (Crosby, 1995) The main point of his paper was to draw a clear distinction between the two while refuting the Freudian notion of conscience being reducible to superego. But he also illustrates the distinctive character of philosophic psychology, as a discipline that addresses those characteristics of the human person that are accessible directly only through a considered reflection and philosophic/ordinary induction.

> It is widely thought by psychologists and philosophers that conscience is nothing more than what Sigmund Freud called the superego. Indeed, Freud himself thought this, or more exactly he thought that conscience is one of several functions of the superego. I want to argue that one can never hope to understand the deep personalist meaning of conscience if one reduces it to the superego, and that a truly personalist philosophy as well as a personalist psychology have to distinguish between superego and conscience as fundamentally different things. {and later}..
> *we are capable of understanding moral imperatives, of understanding where they come from and why they can bind us; we are capable of approving them with our own insight. This means that in obeying them we need not be yielding to the pressure of another person, whether of another outside of us or of another introjected person speaking in our own mind, or rather speaking in place of our own mind; we are quite capable of obeying in such a way as to think with our own mind and act in our own name.* (p.48, 54)

Crosby distinguishes between the conscience and the superego in a manner that escaped Freud and his disciples. It didn't escape Freud in the sense that he could not understand the proposition. Rather, Freud chose to impose his restricted sense of human motive—the motive of fear of loss of physical comfort or safety—

as the defining characteristic of human conscience.

Unless we are prepared to believe that Freud had no understanding of the deeper meaning of human love, of loving something for its own sake, it would appear that Freud left his common experience at the door of the clinic. One may insist on the scientific point that the superego remains a significant component in the behavior of the human person—no doubt the preeminent motive for the neurotic, or for the person who is completely captivated by what philosophers have called servile fear.[8] But such a point that places the superego as the main mechanism of motive is gleaned principally from inductions arising out of the idiosyncratic settings of psychoanalysis. Most certainly, such an assertion is incomplete as it applies to man's nature, and fails to account for that inner awareness of conscience so aptly described by Crosby. The Freudian mistake would reside in our willingness to ignore or deny the ever-present elements of ordinary induction as they pertain to matters of right and wrong. Here again, the philosopher (or theologian) should refrain from depending upon Freud's view of the superego as a basic component in any philosophical argument. Of course, Freud's clinical descriptions of the superego could be used as illustrative, rather than demonstrative of some philosophical point. For example, in ethics the philosopher might make recourse to the psychoanalyst to provide illustrations of disturbed behavior.[9]

Finally, consider for a moment how utterly different Freud's view of the person is from Rogers'. If we assume that these are both gathered from their respective clinical experiences, we need not doubt the validity of either set of experiences, seeming as they do to be contradictory. Since it is in the nature of the scientific experience in its preliminary stages, and in the nature of enumeration, to yield divergent results depending upon the type of sampling that is utilized. Surely, as a foundation for understanding the human person, the very uniqueness of the clinical experience of a particular therapeutic modality disqualifies that experience as philosophically fundamental.

The last example consists of two parts, each of which I think underscores the significant benefits attached to the proper understanding of the relationship between philosophic and scientific psychology. In the first part we see the works of Anna Terruwe.[10] Her clinical researches on the neurotic patient were greatly illumined by her understanding of some important philosophical distinctions on the nature and the division of the appetites in man. These basic divisions, perhaps first suggested by Aristotle but further developed by way of philosophic induction in St. Thomas' *Treatise on Man*, specify the desires, or appetites of man into the rational, the concupiscible, and the irascible. Many animals possess both the concupiscible and the irascible appetites. It is only man who possesses the rational appetite (the will). At the risk of over-simplifying the description of these appetites and the subtlety with which they are understood by Terruwe and Aquinas, a simple example in the small child may suffice to illustrate my point. A child engages in the act of eating based upon its concupiscible appetite, which inclines or drives it to respond to the need for food. The irascible appetite is linked to the execution of behaviors that allow the child to acquire the food not yet within its reach, or to overcome obstacles that prevent its acquisition. In some cases, this appetite spurs the child to try methods of opening up cabinets, or to climb onto counter tops, or other such behaviors which provide access to the cookie jar. At other times, the irrascible appetite could involve the expression of anger or aggression, especially if the food, once obtained is now taken away. Terruwe articulated a theory of neurosis based upon the breakdown of the normal relationships that pertain between the irascible and concupiscible appetites, thereby providing a more coherent account of the clinical phenomenon of repression first observed by Freud. It remains to be seen whether the precise illustration of these insights will prove fruitful specifically in regards to repression itself. What is significant, is that Terruwe does not set out to prove the basic division of the appetites, nor does she attempt to derive a view of human nature from her clinical experiences. Rather, she begins with this division of the appetites as an assumption which is given by philosophical induction, and then proceeds on this assumption to provide a reasonable account of clinical phenomena. She accounts for the clinical phenomena by using scientific induction. Terruwe's development of neurosis is based upon the clinical experience which she interprets within the context of philosophical starting points.

In our second example of this ancient philosophic division of the appetites, we find, I believe, some stunning illustrations forthcoming from the behavioral school. It is well known that classical behaviorism and its variations in psychologists like B. F. Skinner had a major influence over experimental psychology for several decades. These scientists, much like their counterpart Freud, held to the position that the functions of man are all reducible in essence to the operations of the animal. In the more zealous proponents, such as Guthrie, all behaviors, from thinking, to feeling, to reflexive responses were reducible to their material constituents. There were some who resisted this reduction of man to animal, and animal to inanimate matter, but there was a decisive philosophical influence in behavioral psychology, a metaphysics of materialism, that straight-jacketed the manner in which they posed their empirical queries, and thereby greatly limiting the scope of their empirical findings. The materialistic metaphysics of the behavioral school blinded them to a consideration of empirical phenomena that would illustrate the relationship between the various powers of the soul, such as cognition, emotions, and desires.

A group of learning theorists are acquiring a growing body of evidence that punctuates the intimate relationship between an animal's drives—to fulfill its physical needs such as food gathering—with its cognitive capacities of estimation and memory on how to go about such activities. The study of drives and reflexes, or their operational counterpart in the terminology of behavior modification and classical conditioning, has long been the focus of learning theory. The traditional views assumed that the animal was essentially a passive machine-like object, stimulus in—response out. Significantly learning theory now recognizes that its own empirical evidence could not be reasonably accounted for unless it included the notion of cognitive estimation that resides in the animal's memory and imagination, as an active process within animals. (Schwartz, 1989) Ancient views of the irascible and concupiscible appetites, receive elegant illustration in contemporary researches in learning theory. The clinical significance of the relationship between the appetites and the power of estimation or prediction, has been long suspected, at least since Seligman's classic discoveries of learned helplessness in clinical depression. However, the theoretical rationale has now tilted to include the essential activity of estimation.

V. Closing Remarks

I must emphasize here that a proximate or direct consideration of matters proper to the person and to the soul do not belong in the empirical sciences, such as experimental psychology. Also, the philosopher should not be called upon to study matters open to empirico-scientific investigation. Perhaps a different way of saying this would be to insist that it is not up to the philosopher to frame questions that the empiricist sets about to answer, any more than it is up to the empirical psychologist to pose empirical questions for the philosopher, except those that would pertain to matters of the empiricist's first principles. However, science's awareness of the philosophical truth encourages it not to foreclose on the investigation of certain phenomena that are readily within its investigative grasp. I believe that a particularly impressive example of this can be seen in the evolution of learning theory to its current state. It did not draw upon philosophically derived assumptions in any direct way, but it has proposed some findings that are certainly consistent with an ancient philosophical division.

To conclude, we may benefit in the clarity of our thinking if we keep before us the distinction between the two branches of psychology, which here we differentiated by way of method. The principles, data, or conclusions from each branch are not simply interchangeable. One type of data does not simply flow into the other type, since their inductive sources are different in kind. Philosophic psychology, as a part of philosophy, utilizes the ordinary induction we find in philosophy. This is the kind of induction that is the basis of common experience. Scientific psychology, not being a part of philosophy, utilizes a special experience that produces a different kind of induction, from which only provisional conclusions can follow.

Each discipline can draw from the other if the proper qualifications are attached. The philosophical psychologist can avail himself of scientific finds as a way of illustrating some philosophical point. The scientific psychologist can avail himself of the philosopher's truth as a way to frame empirical inquiry—as in the manner of Terruwe. In this regard, both philosophic and scientific psychology provide a context for each other not to direct the researches of the other discipline but rather more to inspire and to illustrate.

NOTES

1. See especially p.138-144.

2. I am indebted to Dr. John Crosby for commenting on an early draft of this paper in this regard.

3. Arguably, depending on the subject of induction varying amounts of experience may be required to arrive at the induced proposition. The degree of certitude might also vary.

4. This would not preclude the usual way of forming the proposition in a *modus tollens*. See P. Meehl (1991) p.272-283.

5. There is some hint here of the classical notion of formal cause, where the action of the agent manifest the formal characteristics of the matter.

6. This presumption of scientific superiority is particularly striking since the quote above was excerpted from a talk to Roman Catholic bishops in the mid-1980s. Of course, that a group of prominent clergy would seek some fundamental insight from an empirical researcher on such spiritual matters would hint at the depth of the problem on how the divisions and methods of the sciences are understood. Sperry comes from the tradition clearly marked by scientists such as B. F. Skinner in his popularized literature (such as *About Behaviorism*, and *Walden Two*) where he devoted considerable attention to reducing the moral dimensions of behavior to its functional principles. Auguste Comte is certainly at the forefront of the idea that science defines moral value by defining that which is useful.

7. I allude to several Christian critiques of Carl Rogers' views, and address some epistemological difficulties in his work. See my paper "Can Catholics Counsel? The loss of Prudence of Modern Humanist Psychology." *Faith & Reason*, 20, No.1, p. 87-111.

8. For example, see St. Thomas Aquinas, *Summa Theologica* II-II Q19, Art.2. Aquinas asks "Whether fear is fittingly divided into Filial, Initial, Servile and Worldly Fear?" Here is an example where he provides a concise description on the types of fears as a philosopher would distinguish them.

9. An example of this can be seen In his *Ethics* Bk 7 ch 5., where Aristotle comments: "Of natural pleasures, some are delightful to every taste, others to different classes of men and animals of the pleasures that are not natural, some become delightful because of sickness or privations, others because of customs or vicious natures. And to each of these pleasures there will be a corresponding habit."

10. Here I will refer only to her early work since it is with this that I am most familiar. See her *The Neurosis in the Light of Rational Psychology*.

REFERENCES

Adler, M. J. (1937). *What Man Has Made of Man : A Study of the Consequences of Platonism and Positivism in Psychology* . Boston: Longmans, Green & Co.

Aquinas, T. (1981) *Summa Theologica*. Westminster, MY: Christian Classics.

Baars, R. J. (1986). *The Cognitive Revolution in Psychology*. New York: Guilford.

Crosby, J. (1995). Conscience and Superego : A Phenomenological Analysis of Their Difference and Relation. In J.M. DuBois (Ed) *The Nature and Tasks of a Personalist Psychology*. Lanham:University Press of America, pp.47-58.

Cross, R.W. (1994) "Can Catholics Counsel? The loss of Prudence in Modern Humanist Psychology." *Faith & Reason*, 20, No.1, p. 87-111.

DeKoninck, C. (1957). Abstraction from Matter. *Laval théologique et philosophique*, 13(2), 133-196.

DuBois, J. M. (1995). Are Human Beings Innately Defective? In J.M.DuBois (Ed.), *The Nature and Tasks of a Personalist Psychology*. Lanham:University Press of America, pp.3-22.

Meehl, P. E. (1978). Theoretical risks and tabular asterisks: Sir Karl, Sir Ronald, and the slow progress of soft psychology. *Journal of Consulting and Clinical Psychology*, 46, 806-834.

Meehl, P. E. (1966 & 1991) Some methodological reflections on psychoanalytic research. In C.A. Anderson & K. Gunderson (Eds.), *Paul E. Meehl: Selected Philosophical and Methodological Papers*. Minneapolis: University of Minnesota.

Rogers, C. R. (1961). *On Becoming a Person*. Boston: Houghton Mifflin Co.

Salmon, W. C. (1971). *Statistical Explanation and Statistical Relevance*. Pittsburgh: University of Pittsburgh Press.

Schwartz, B (1989). *Psychology of Learning and Behavior.* New York :W.W. Norton.

Sperry, R. W. (1988). Psychology's Mentalist Paradigm and the Religion/Science Tension. *American Psychologist,* 43(8), 607-613.

Terruwe, A. (1960). *The Neurosis in the Light of Rational Psychology* (C. Baars, Trans.). New York: P.J. Kennedy & Sons.

B. ON INDUCTION: RESPONSE TO CROSS

John R. White

I. Introduction

Professor Cross raises many excellent points for discussion, many of which are worthy of mention. However, because of time constraints, I shall discuss only the main point of Cross's paper, namely, the notions of induction proper to philosophical and scientific psychology. In its main outlines, I find myself mostly in agreement with Cross. My comments here shall concern a clarification of the nature and lines of demarcation with respect to these two forms of 'induction.' I shall then introduce some comments concerning the interaction between scientific and philosophical psychology.

II. Cross's Conception of Induction

A. Let me begin by qualifying the subject matter of our discussion. Cross characterizes induction as a mental process, a process through which the mind rises from particulars to general, scientifically justified propositions. This process is one well known to empirical investigators and perhaps does not need much elucidation. I would note, however, that our discussion concerns one very particular sense of 'induction,' which is by no means the only sense of it: we speak here of induction as a *scientific method.* Thus we are not speaking, for example, of what has been called since the time of Mill, *inductive inference*, i.e., a deduction from examples to generalities.[1] Rather, we are concerned with induction as a method of scientific justification, a method through which we gain rational grounds for holding some general proposition to be true.

We need also note that we speak of this method in its simplest form, taking as examples cases such as establishing propositions such as 'all crows are black.' In order to focus our discussion only on the inductive method in its general outlines, it is important to use such simple cases and not render our discussions more prolix than necessary by taking more difficult cases. However, one should not assume that the case of induction we speak of can be applied without further qualification to the subject matter in question.[2]

Finally, it needs to be pointed out that simple cases of induction in which justification for a proposition arises *exclusively* through the induction are not often met with in science. Most inductively justified propositions are not isolated cases of truth-claims but exist as part of a larger web of theoretical and empirical propositions which themselves either justify or disconfirm, directly or indirectly, totally or partially, the proposition in question. Thus we rarely treat of propositions according to this simple case, although it may well be necessary to consider induction from this point of view for clarity's sake.[3]

B. What qualifies a method as inductive? As I understand Cross, the most characteristic feature of induction is that "the mind moves from particular instances to generalities"(p 131). This seems the only feature essential to all forms of induction, and is thus applicable to both forms which Cross develops and, I take it, would apply to any other form of induction, were there any other form. The precise nature of this motion from particulars to generalities Cross does not illuminate. But I suppose we could characterize Cross's position generally by saying that induction consists in the process whereby the knowledge we attain of some set of particulars gives us grounds for holding some general proposition, law or rule concerning those particulars as true.

After offering his brief characterization of induction, Cross turns immediately to a distinction between two different types of induction, according to which he later distinguishes philosophical from scientific approaches to psychological questions. These are termed, on the one hand, "natural or ordinary induction"—which he later refers to also as "intuitive induction"—and "deliberate or enumerative induction." The two approaches or methods seems to be distinguishable in the following ways:

First, natural or ordinary induction seems characteristic of our natural approach to the world. Referring to DeKoninck approvingly (p 131), Cross proffers propositions such as 'the whole is greater than the part' and a version of the principle of contradiction as examples of propositions derived from this sort of induction. This form of induction—as I understand Cross—is constitutive of our basic or everyday experience of the world: it yields what we might be inclined to call *prima facie* truths, truths which are evident, even self-evident or *per se nota*, as I take it Cross means by pointing to Euclid's postulate. Also, this mode of approach affords a high degree of certainty, according to Cross. Thus intuitive or natural induction, could be characterized as a simple approach to basic truths constitutive of our experience, and which affords a high degree of certainty.

This is in contradistinction to enumerative induction. The latter is "deliberate," by which I understand Cross to mean 'systematic' in the manner of science, as opposed to a non-systematic approach to the propositions in question. Later on, Cross mentions that this approach does not yield certainty: rather we are, necessarily, tentative with regard to inductive propositions of this sort, because "we lack a certain understanding of" the nature of the object, as the example of 'all crows are black' shows (p 133). Hence, I take it, the truths which this enumerative induction is supposed to yield do not have the character of evident propositions, but their evidence is supposed to arise from the induction.

C. I wonder, however, if we do not need to be more precise in characterizing induction: the formulation of a "movement of the mind from particulars to generalities," while in some sense a real feature of both forms of induction, seems to conceal very different relations obtaining between particulars and the generalities they are said to generate in these two cases of induction; this difference is so great that one might be inclined not to call them both by the same name. This becomes clear, I think, when we see the following points:

1. In the case of enumerative induction, at least when we speak of a simple case, such as 'all crows are black,' the question is not simply of a *motion* of the mind, but of a particular type of motion which is grounded in an objective, epistemic relation obtaining between the examples enumerated and the general proposition in question. The epistemic relevance of the particulars consists in the fact that the knowledge of these particulars and, more precisely, of the general, relatively stable structure which these particulars display, gives a sufficient *justification* for a *broader, general truth-claim.* To keep with Cross's example, the truth claim in question could be 'all crows are black.' If this latter is a true, inductively justified proposition, this justification is based on the knowledge of an objective epistemic relation which obtains between the relatively stable, structural moment of crows—that they are black—and the truth-claim of the proposition that 'all crows are black.'

Now this epistemic relation is not so easy to characterize. In order to characterize it, we must first understand the nature of the inductively justified proposition. If we take the proposition 'all crows are black' as an example, the induction is *not* aimed at the quantifier, '*all,*' though at first glance it might seem that way. Were that really the point of the induction, we would, first, necessarily have to discover whether each and every crow is in fact black in order to establish it. And, surprisingly enough, were we to do so, we would not be performing an induction, strictly so called. Rather we would be giving a strict, deductive inference, based on the principle that if each case of x has property y, then all x's are y. This is a strict deduction, based on an empirical premise, to be sure, but nevertheless a strict and valid deduction and not an inductive justification at all. Furthermore, were this proposition established, we still would not know if it tells us anything about the crow. After all, any number of purely factual propositions could be established about the crow in general ("All crows are such that they cannot easily wear wire-rimmed glasses"), but it is neither the fact that these could be quantitatively justified nor even the fact that they are true, which renders them of scientific interest or such that they are the object of induction.

Induction, strictly so called, is not aimed at *quantity:* taking a poll is not an induction. This is the case because induction does not aim simply at stating a fact, such as that, '*as a matter of fact,* all crows are black.' If the predication of 'black' to the crow has any scientific interest at all, it is not because it *happens to be the case* that crows are black, but because one assumes that their all being black *says something about what the crow is.* In short, the inductively justified predicate must show that there is some *intelligible* connection between the predicate (black) and the subject (crows), a connection concerning some feature *genuinely determinative* of the subject, not merely some *factual* connection. Induction aims, then, not at just any, factual proposition about some being, but at a proposition of *principle,* i.e., a proposition which either elucidates a feature proper to the object of investigation or one explanatory of some feature. This cannot be done by mere

enumeration. At rock bottom, therefore, though induction uses quantitative enumeration, it is not for the purposes of establishing quantity.

What then does the enumeration achieve? The quantitative enumeration aims
at giving sufficient grounds for judging that the predicate in question really is a
natural feature of the subject. In other words, the enumeration is not to establish
the quantity in the proposition 'all crows are black' but to give sufficient grounds
for thinking there is a *principle* underpinning the quantity, e.g., it would aim to
show that it is normal for the crow that it be black and, thus, its being black is
either a natural feature of the crow or proper to it under certain conditions. Underlying this conception of induction is the assumption that nature is uniform,[4] that if
there is a constant repetition of some state of affairs in nature, there must be some
stable principle underlying that fact. Thus the investigator in the case of our proposition must assume that, if crows are in all cases black, it must somehow be bound
up with the nature of the crow such that it is black or with some causal principles
essentially connected to the crow (e.g., environmental principles): the uniformity
in question does not admit that something arbitrary has occurred here.

Thus the epistemic relation which seems to obtain in this case can be formulated in this way: if there is a constancy in nature, there must be some intelligible
explanation for it, grounded in the nature of the thing or in causes connected to that
nature. The enumeration, then, attempts to show *that there is* such a uniformity
which can in turn ground the judgment that the predicate in question is somehow
bound up, according to principle, with the subject of the judgment.[5]

The inductive procedure by no means *consists in* the enumeration; the enumeration plays only a part, albeit a significant one, in the process as a whole. It is
this enumeration which justifies the general proposition, at least in the link between the feature and the subject of that feature, a justification which presumably
the proposition cannot otherwise have. But the process as a whole includes more
than just the enumeration. Indeed, induction as a general process of scientific justification seems to presuppose a broad complex of elements, including the cognition of an objective, logical connection between the enumerative examples and the
general proposition, as well as several other non-inductive cognitions—cognitions
whose immediacy inclines me call them forms of *insight*—such that the knower
can actually *see* or *be given* the insight that this enumeration, derived from this
particular stock of examples, specified by such and such conditions, actually *can*
justify the general proposition, as well as the further insight that, *in fact, in this
case*, these examples *do* justify the proposition in question.

But the important point for our purposes is that the enumeration of particulars
does play an essential, justifying role in the induction, so much so that one cannot
claim to have scientific knowledge, i.e., *justified* knowledge of general facts, without the enumeration.

But it seems to me that no such justifying relation obtains in the case of
general propositions such as 'Every whole is greater than its part' or 'No feature
can be affirmed and denied of the same thing at the same time and in the same

respect' etc., even when they are derived from what Cross has termed 'intuitive induction.' We have here, I believe, cases of propositions which are 'a priori' propositions, in a non-tautological sense. In these cases, the so-called induction is not a case of actual examples in any sense *justifying* a general truth-claim: the actual experiencing of some whole being greater than a part, for example, does not and indeed can in no way justify the general proposition that 'the whole is greater than the part,' if this latter is an a priori proposition. This central insight has colored elements of the epistemology of Duns Scotus and many philosophers since, not least Kant, Scheler, and Hildebrand. For such authors, 'a priori' knowledge is not necessarily a knowledge *genetically* independent of all possible experience; indeed a priori knowledge is normally *genetically* dependent on some sort of experience, in the sense that the experience acts as a means for achieving a priori knowledge.[6] But it is knowledge whose *cognitive value* is independent of experience, because experience has no role in justifying (or unjustifying) such knowledge.[7]

Thus whatever role the experienced particulars play in intuitive induction, it is not one of justification: such propositions are neither justified or unjustified by the knowledge of particulars, even if the experience of particulars is our first access to them. The nature of these two forms of induction and the kind of movement from particular to universal are very different—so different that one might be inclined not to use the same term for both activities. Indeed, other than having reference to scientific cognition, these two types of induction seem to bear very little similarity; and, in any case, the inductive moment they share seems to be only some connection to experience, though very different connections. Experience seems by no means a defining element in the intuitive induction of those facts referred to by a priori propositions, whereas it is defining for propositions justified by enumerative induction.

2. A further difference between these two types of induction, if we wish still to call them both that, rests on the kind of *adequacy* of cognition which is proper to each. An enumerative, inductive approach cannot yield a knowledge which is fully adequate to the object in question, whereas, in a sense, philosophical cognition can. This 'full adequacy' in the case of philosophy is obviously not to be understood as a godlike comprehensive adequacy—no finite knowledge can attain to that—but rather an adequacy where the object is sufficiently intelligible that there isn't a *gap* between the immanent truth-claim of the proposition and the givenness of the object in question.[8] Thus, if I claim that 'every whole is greater than its part' or that 'being and non-being exclude each other,' to the extent that these are philosophical propositions of the sort I have termed 'a priori,' to that extent are these propositions possessed of what Husserl called an 'inner evidence' or Kant an 'inner truth': they are self-justifying, because the states of affairs referred to by them are given with this inner evidence correlating exactly to the truth-claim of the proposition. They are *per se nota*, as the Scholastics put it. Much of the most fundamental philosophical knowledge—including in philosophical psychology— aims at this kind of ideal, philosophical adequation, however close in fact the

philosopher comes to this ideal.

Enumerative or scientific induction, on the other hand, implies a certain gap between the generality of the proposition to be justified and the experiences and objects through which his truth claim can be justified. The proposition 'all crows are black,' when understood as what I have called a proposition of principle, cannot be fully and adequately justified through induction, even were all possible crows tested. Precisely the point of the induction is to give *sufficient* grounds for holding to the general proposition, because the state of affairs cannot be given with inner evidence, but must be justified by means of the indirect cognition which cannot *establish*, in the strict sense of the term, the proposition in question.

D. This leads to another point of possible disagreement between myself and Cross. Cross seems to say that the reason we need an inductive approach to scientific objects is that we "lack a certain understanding" of the connection between the induced feature and the nature in question (see p 133): that is, "in the inability to understand what it is about the nature of the thing that requires that it have a certain attribute." I read this as saying that there is always some kind of *requirement*, some kind of *necessity*, between the feature in question and the attribute. But we do not always know what this necessity consists in and when we don't, we need to have induction.

I wonder if that point is true and if induction only arises as an indispensable method because we do not *understand* the kind of necessity in the state of affairs we seek to know and justify. It seems to me that it need not be the case that there *is* an actual necessity in question, or at least not a pure necessity, but there can be a kind of intelligible, but non-necessary connection. This latter non-necessary kind of connection even seems to me to be the main object of scientific investigation. It is not an accident, I suppose, that crows are black. But one need not infer from the non-accidental character that it is therefore "required by the nature" that it be black, at least if by 'requirement' we refer to necessity: couldn't it be that, so to speak, God simply made it that way, but could also have made it another way? This, I think, would not imply no intelligible connection, as if it would be a case of a purely accidental connection between the nature and the attribute, but would simply deny that this connection is a necessary one. It seems to me that it is chiefly states of affairs of the latter sort which science and psychology investigates and it is more properly because of this essential structure that one approaches the objects through induction, not because we do not see some actual necessity. Moreover, were it a case of necessity, it seems that we would approach these facts rather by means of 'intuitive induction' or a priori cognition. Perhaps the very reason we need an inductive approach is that there is no necessity involved and thus the connection is not open to a priori cognition.

E. As a final point with regard to Cross's conception of induction, I wish to point out and indeed to applaud the idea that the kind of experience which is proper to the philosopher is different from that of the scientific, empirical investigator and, further, I want to insist with Cross that philosophy begins with immediate experience, such as that he speaks of with regard to intuitive induction.

At the same time, I think one needs to differentiate this notion of an immediate—let us say a *prima facie* experience—of the sort Cross describes as 'intuitive induction' from that of a philosophical experience, strictly so called. The latter is, in most cases, rooted in the former, but it is not therefore reducible thereto. Here I would introduce the distinction of Scheler between the philosophical and the natural attitude.[9] The natural attitude refers to our everyday, scientifically and philosophically naïve experience of the world. This is to be distinguished from the approach of the philosopher, who aims at the experience of general facts, though those facts are often rooted in natural, everyday experience. A specific form of experience—what Scheler referred to as 'experience of genuine essences'—occurs, when this originally naïve experience is approached with the philosophical attitude. While the experience, in the sense of the objects which are the sources of knowledge in the natural and philosophical approaches may be the same, the philosophical attitude admits of a variation on this natural experience, rendering it a source for evident, philosophical knowledge.

I would therefore be inclined to distinguish not only between immediate, 'intuitive induction,' as Cross refers to it, and scientific induction, but would distinguish at least two different sorts of knowledge which seem to be covered by this notion of intuitive induction: the realm of the natural approach and attitude to the world of everyday experience and that which arises through the philosophical attitude, which focuses on gaining a critical and systematic knowledge of its objects.

III. Closing Remarks

Cross has mentioned important ways in which a philosophical and a scientific approach to the data of the mind are different. This important task, in my opinion, needs to be augmented with raising the question of how these two disciplines complement and, to some extent, interpenetrate each other. This is all the more pressing a task for this Institute, since the achievement of its aims obviously presupposes an interdisciplinary approach to psychology and thus assumes that philosophy and scientific psychology are not simply two adjunct disciplines but can, in some way, mutually fructify each other.

I can begin by agreeing with Cross about the distinctness of subject and method by which we can contrast philosophical and scientific psychology. But it is important to see the *way* in which these two disciplines are distinct. The Scholastic distinction between formal and material objects of a discipline is perhaps apposite here. The material object of psychology in both cases is, or at least a large portion of it is, the same in both scientific psychology and philosophical psychology. This is clearly the case at least to the extent that they both deal with personal acts, the construction of the ego, the nature of good and bad motivations, the ideal and the defective cases of acts and so forth. Still there are formal differences not only in the manner of treating these acts but also, to some extent, in the way in which *elements* of these acts are treated.

First, philosophy deals with intelligible natures, which are accessible through pure philosophical insight. Of course, psychology too needs forms of insight, as I pointed out with regard to the nature of the induction which a scientific approach assumes, which includes insight with regard to the connection between enumerated examples and the general thesis in question, the actual connection, and, I would say, also with respect to the specifications according to which the psychologist would produce his or her research group and chosen examples. Thus insight is not a method used only by philosophy but must be used also in psychology. And indeed, there is some overlap, in my opinion, in these two disciplines. For example, while the philosopher can delineate what a proper act of cognition, willing, affective response or reaction, and other acts might be, he or she can also philosophize about spheres of personal activities which are not essentially necessary. In a certain sense, the great Medieval treatises on logical fallacies were examples of this, when they approached deviations in logical reasoning based not on purely logical problems but also on epistemic problems, based in defective acts of the mind, such as errors. But more relevant to our purposes are cases such as Scheler's *Ressentiment* or Hildebrand's *Graven Images*, both of which deal with actual types of distortion which are typical to us fallen moral agents. Indeed, many treatises on vice are of a similar character. Here we must be careful not to draw the distinction between sciences of the real and sciences of essence too sharply. In *Ressentiment* and in *Graven Images*, Scheler and Hildebrand typify real, contingent types of psychological distortions, types which would be wholly without interest if they were not real.[10] On the other hand, the psychologist must use philosophical concepts, even if they need not be fully clarified in a philosophical manner, in order to undertake his or her discipline at all. Thus notions such as 'mind,' 'act,' 'motivation' (as well as methodological concepts such as 'induction,' 'evidence,' 'justification' and the like) are philosophical in nature, yet necessary both for the content and the method of psychology. In fact, in many cases, it seems that the scientific and philosophical psychologist are thematizing different aspects of the same thing, focusing on different elements given by their own proper methods.

Because of this partial overlap in object, it seems to me, scientific and philosophical psychology can have a relation of mutually purifying each other's concepts. This task supposes the important distinction between the object of study in a discipline and the analytic language through which the object is theoretically articulated. The analytic language of any science can always be more or less adequate to the data analyzed; the chiefly inductive approach of scientific psychology and strongly a priori approach of philosophy with respect to the same objects allows each to help purify and test the other's analytic language.

Finally, and this is perhaps the most important point, though we cannot enter into it here: philosophy and psychology must work together to analyze the connections of the person to value. Philosophy, according to its own methods, can delineate the nature of activities, motivations, value and the ideals immanent to these natures, as well as highly intelligible deviations from it. But the 'search for meaning' which is implicit in a truly personalistic psychology assumes not only essential laws but a personalistic reading of those laws, i.e., a doctrine of the actual state of the person, of how these essential laws ought to apply to him or her, and how the deviations from these ideals can be corrected, and the like. Here we must have a discipline which both acknowledges absolute necessities—especially of the 'ought' variety—and which characterizes and analyzes the actual cases of distortion and healing which are possible.

In conclusion, then, I would say to Cross that I also do not think that scientific psychology is a part of philosophy; I also think that the formal objects and the methods differ, in general. But I do think that there is overlap, similarity, and important cooperation necessary in full-fledged personalistic psychological research.

NOTES

1. There are of course many senses in which 'induction' has been used in the tradition, including inductive cognition, inductive syllogisms, and inductive scientific methods. To my knowledge, the best development of the nature and kinds of induction, as well as analysis of what must underlie induction, is found in Coffey *The Science of Logic* (New York: Peter Smith, 1938), a reprint of the original text (London: Longmans, Green & Co., 1912), volume 2, pp. 1-119. This is a veritable masterwork of neo-Scholastic logic.

2. Thus many qualifications must be added before one can apply this method to human sciences like psychology. This shall become clear below, when I develop the point that in induction the knowledge of particulars and the kind of knowledge possible of them plays a constitutive role in the justification of general propositions. Thus it makes quite a difference if the particulars in question are accessible through simple perceptions, such as cognizing that crows are black, wherein prejudices or other obstacles to knowledge do not easily creep in or if, on the contrary, the particular in question is something accessible only through more complex, difficult and often less certain means, such as cognitions of someone's inner life mediated through their own testimony, as is sometimes the case in psychology. The fact that the object of investigation is not only not immediately and perceptually present to the scientist, but may be mediated through the judgments, e.g., of untrained subjects being investigated, or subjects whose judgment cannot necessarily be trusted, or whose value cognition is limited, requires that much more rigorous conditions be fulfilled before one can claim that one has an inductively justified conclusion.

3. Cohen and Nagel stress the importance of this point for the development of science: the more a proposition to be inductively established can be connected with the web of previously established propositions, the greater the justification possible. See Cohen and Nagel *An Introduction to Logic and Scientific Method* (New York: Harcourt, Brace and Company, 1934).

4. See Coffey chapter 4 and Cohen and Nagel, pp. 279-285, for their — very different — developments of this assumption.

5. Compare Coffey, pp. 27-32.

6. See especially Hildebrand *What is Philosophy?* (London and New York: Routledge, 1991), chapter IV and Seifert *Back to Things in Themselves* (London and New York: Routledge & Kegan Paul, 1987), chapter V for recent expositions of a priori knowledge. See also my "Kant and von Hildebrand on the Synthetic A Priori: A Contrast," *Aletheia. An International Yearbook of Philosophy*, vol V, pp 290-320.

7. Indeed, even the sources of this sort of knowledge may be mistaken. I may, for example, discover after I have understood that every whole is greater than its part based on some experience that what I took to be a whole and what a part of that

whole was mistaken; but the knowledge of the general thesis is neither more nor less justified by virtue of this fact: actual, concrete experiences can neither confirm nor disconfirm such propositions, if they are truly a priori.

8. See Scheler "The Theory of the Three Facts," in Scheler, *Selected Philosophical Essays*, trans. by David R. Lachterman (Evanston: Northwestern University Press, 1973), pp 202-287. Relevant points for this discussion are found throughout the article.

9. Scheler "The Theory of the Three Facts," pp. 222-252.

10. Max Scheler *Ressentiment* trans. Lewis A. Moser (New York: Schocken Books, 1961); Dietrich von Hildebrand *Graven Images: Substitutes for True Morality* (Chicago: Franciscan Herald Press, 1957)

7

The Gnostic Core of Jungian Psychology: Radiating Effects on the Moral Order

Jeffrey Satinover

I. Jungian Psychology as a Substitute Religion

The distinctive danger of psychology is that it tends to establish itself not merely as a narrow discipline with access to but a part of the truth concerning man's nature, but as a total *Weltanschauung*, or worldview. A psychological worldview is necessarily one that depends upon radical subjectivity, precluding the possibility (inter alia) of a morality determined by something outside of man's own psyche. One mode in which this totalizing worldview has become widely established is via materialism, that is, via psychologies that ultimately reduce man to the mere deterministic interaction of lower level mechanisms (e.g., instinctive drives; biomolecules). The other mode—the one advanced by C. G. Jung and his increasingly large number of followers—is via Gnosticism, the ever-recurrent counter-spirituality with which Jung explicitly identified himself. In this latter mode, the instincts and drives of human nature are experienced and related to as gods, and in effect, worshipped. In brilliant fashion, this latter mode shines what appears to be a light of spirit into the long darkness of pure materialism from which so many people nowadays are understandably seeking relief.

At least up to the time of the Cartesian revolution, Christianity provided the almost unchallenged worldview common to Europe and the New World. Its foundational principle was of an absolute, divinely-ordained moral law that constrained and modified what man invariably became when left solely to his own devices. This conception persisted as the dominant worldview well into the twentieth century, but coexisting uneasily with a rapidly-rising materialistic worldview framed, and seemingly confirmed, by pre-twentieth century physics.

Reflecting this tension, and claiming somehow to have resolved it, the depth psychology of C. G. Jung claims at times to be faithful to Christianity—yet views Christianity as fatally naive and flawed from the start, and views both Jesus and his followers as hopelessly neurotic; and then again, it claims not to be a religion at all, but a modern "science of the soul" rooted in empiricism—even though not one of its major tenets has ever been subjected to experimental scrutiny, nor could it be.

Nonetheless, because it promises so much, and because we are so parched, innumerable well-intentioned, spiritually-thirsty Christians (predominantly but not exclusively Roman and Anglican) have fallen unwitting prey to Jung's hugely successful version of "spirituality." It's expressed goal is to become the world's final, unitary religion (though, like Marx, Jung expressed this not as a personal goal of his, but as an historical inevitability which he had merely stumbled upon and now proclaims).

It is the rare seminary, especially in the Anglican world, that does not reserve for Jung and his methods a place of high honor in the pastoral curriculum; there are many whose spirituality consists exclusively of unadulterated Jungianism with a patina of Christianity. Not a few (the more intellectually consistent ones) have scratched off the patina entirely. Innumerable Episcopal Priests in the United States have formally trained as Jungian analysts; many are the cream of the leadership stratum; many Catholic "spirituality" programs have long been dominated by Jungian practices.

Is Jungian psychology in fact an improved version of Christianity, as he claimed? In fact, from his student days until the end of his life, Jung's consistent and unabashed goal has been to present *Gnosticism* as an improved version of Christianity, and his own psychological method as the modernized heir to Gnosticism (both by his own acknowledgment). What follows will show, on the one hand, that Jungian psychology is indeed, as he claims, heir to Gnosticism; but that neither are, nor improve upon, Christianity.

But that so many sincere, searching Christians confuse Jungian "Christianity" with the genuine article should be unsurprising; the confusion is ancient and ever-recurring. The words of Iraneus are as fitting today with regard to Jung and Jungianism they were with regard to Simon Magus and Gnosticism 1,800 years ago: "[A] clever imitation of glass [that] casts contempt as it were on that precious jewel, the emerald, unless it comes under the eye of one able to test and expose the counterfeit."[1]

The widespread loss in the twentieth century of a clear understanding of the genuine Christian (originally Jewish) supernatural has laid us open to this imitation; it is no less seductive—and destructive—now than it was at its origin. In the words of Sir Thomas Browne: "Heresies perish not with their authors, but like the river Arethusa, though they lose their currents in one place, they rise up again in another. (*Religio Medici*)."

With Browne's epigram in mind, the baleful strength of Jung's present influence is readily explained by Pope Pius X's concise skewering of *modernism* : "the synthesis of all heresies."

Jung's particular modernist synthesis is the blending of psychological reductionism with Gnostic spirituality. The result is a modern variant of mystical, pagan polytheism in which the multiple "images of the instincts" (Jung's most concise definition of "archetype") are worshipped as "gods."

Jung equated the "Self" (capital "S") with "the God-image" in man. The "Self" is Jung's term for a hypothetical union of all the various instincts into a single whole. Philosophically this quasi-mystical idea reproduces on a psychological plane the essential construct of antique Hermetic philosophy which likewise considered "the One" as the unity of "the Many." But this "One"—and the idea that the one "God" is but the synthesis of the many "gods"—has in fact no relationship to the God of Judeo-Christian monotheism. On the other hand, the intense subjective experience of this "whole," as Noll documents, is identical to the "Aryan" mystery initiations of the Mediterranean basin and India; an experience in which by "synthesizing the opposites," the initiate above all else transcends good and evil.

Jung specifically identifies his "Self" with "Christ" as well, thereby seeming to place his ideas within the framework of Christianity. In this he is following in the footsteps of a long line of so-called "esoteric" Christians for whom "Christ" is but a variant of "cosmic consciousness" rather than a genuinely suffering and atoning Messiah and Son of the Holy One of Israel. One reason that the atonement has thus been abandoned these days (as it was by many in the days of John) is of course the great difficulty people have in believing in the reality of such a Messiah; another is that as a school of psychotherapy Jungianism has had and continues to have about as much actual—often impressive—therapeutic success as most other schools of therapy, all of which therefore tend naturally to convince their followers that their entire scheme is wholly correct even when the truth they have is but partial.

The important fact for Christians is that whatever secular therapeutic benefits Jungian psychotherapy can indeed afford, Jung's Christ is *not* the Christ of Christianity. It is that of the Gnostics. Like theirs, the presumed superiority of Jung's "Christ" consists in his *not* being one "in whom there is no darkness at all," but on the contrary, he who incorporates both light and dark, a god both benign and malignant. Neither does Jung mince words on this score: "...the Christ-symbol lacks wholeness in the modern psychological sense, since it does not include the dark side of things but specifically excludes it in the form of a *Luciferian* opponent."[2]

For one initiated into this "Christ-consciousness," "the original state of oneness with the God-image is restored," in Jung's words, and brings about: "...an integration, a bridging of the split in the personality caused by the instincts striving apart in mutually contradictory directions."[3]

Thus although itself intensely "spiritual," (indeed stripped of any meaningful physical reality) this Gnostic Christ plays no role in mediating a genuinely non-instinctive dimension to human life, hence its utter disregard of a morality that need often take a stand opposed to the instincts. The "integration" fostered by this "Christ" is simply the more efficient orchestration of instinctive gratification (consistent with purely secular psychoanalytic goals, as also with "Luciferian" ones). But its description in the language of the mystery religions lends it an aura of "spirituality" that effectively obscures its fundamental tendency toward hedonism and amorality.

The practical consequences of this species of spirituality is well-illustrated by one of Jung's prominent followers, Jungian analyst Ginette Paris, in her fittingly-titled book, *The Sacrament of Abortion*:

> It is time to call back the image of Artemis, the wild one, who...chooses to belong only to herself...[t]he Artemis myth manifests itself in our lives...by a...movement away from...fusion with others, the most extreme example of fusion being the connection between a mother and her young children. Artemis...invites us to re-treat from others, to become autonomous.

> Our culture needs new rituals as well as laws to restore to abortion its sacred dimension...I've heard women address their fetus directly...and explain why it is necessary to separate now. Others write a letter of farewell and read it to a friend, a spouse, or indeed to their whole family. Still others invent their own farewell ritual, inspired perhaps by rituals from other cultures, like offering a little doll to a divinity as a symbol of the aborted fetus...the pro-lifers see the spiritual dimen-sion but keep it imprisoned within official orthodoxies, as if no other form of spirituality existed. What if my religious beliefs are pagan?[4]

Morton Kelsey is the Episcopal churchman most responsible for bringing Jungianism into the church. The title of Kelsey's latest book, like Paris' above, says it all: *The Sacrament of Sexuality*. Not, you notice, *marriage*, but *sexuality*. This trendy sacralization of everything natural is, of course, the end result of Jungianism. Between the covers of Kelsey's book one finds stamped as "Chris-tian" the entire, predictable, left-wing "revolution" of statist politics and sexual polymorphism. Is such an approach "spiritual?" Indeed it is. Is it Christian? Only if, following Jung, you consider Lucifer to be what Christ lacks in "wholeness."

II. The Occult Roots of Jungian Doctrine

As psychologist and historian of science Richard Noll recently demonstrated, Jung's intellectual roots are not in Christianity at all, but rather in pseudo-Chris-tianized variants of occult doctrine.[5] These doctrines found fullest expression in Jung's explicitly-stated belief that he and his work had inherited the ancient Gnos-tic and alchemical traditions. There is little difference, Noll illustrates, between a Jungian "Christ," with its romance of instinct and incorporation of Lucifer into a supposedly superior whole, and the "Aryan Christ" of the pre-Hitler Wagnerians and Nietzscheans. There has been a strange blindness to the true nature of Jung's worldview, and to the moral problems that follow, in spite of the obviousness of Jung's entanglement with the occult. Even a cursory examination from a critical perspective, and with an eye fixed on Orthodoxy by contrast, can be jolting. What follows is a mere sampling of what is available to the careful reader.

Jung's fascination with the occult, and the extent to which it integrated him, rather than he it, can be seen in descriptions by Jung's admirers and disciples, few of whom seem fully to understand the darkness of the forces they, following the master, seek to "integrate" into a "higher unity." Thus, Miguel Serrano, Chilean diplomat and biographer of Hermann Hesse, visited C. G. Jung on May 5, 1959, two years before Jung's death. During their conversation about dream interpretation, Jung began to muse out loud. (The following citations and commentary by Serrano, incidentally, were cited approvingly in a biography of Jung by his closest and most prominent disciple, Marie-Louise von Franz—lest readers consider it aberrant). He says to Serrano: "Still, nothing is possible without love, not even the processes of alchemy, for love puts one in a mood to risk everything and not to withhold elements."

Alchemy, of course, was the particular variant of occult doctrine which Jung, having explored them all, settled on as the one closest in spirit to his own school of depth psychology. In isolation, this passage is benign enough. But consider the details. Jung arose to show Serrano some paintings from a case study of one of his "patients" from the 1930's.[6] Serrano reports their conversation as follows (I have added the names of the discussants for ease of reading):

[JUNG:] "These were made," he said, "by a woman with whom we planned a process of individuation for almost ten years..." In the centre ... were drawn a king and queen who were taking part in a mystic wedding, holding fire in their hands. "The...mystic wedding..." Jung explained, "...is...like the Opus Alquimia. For this union is in reality a process of mutual individuation which occurs...in both the doctor and the patient."

[SERRANO:] As he spoke of this magic love and alchemic wedding, I thought of Solomon and the Queen of Sheba, Christ and his Church, and of Siva and Parvati on the summit of Mount Kailas—all symbols of man and his soul and of the creation of the Androgynous. Jung went on as though he were talking to himself:

[JUNG:] "Somewhere there was once a Flower, a Stone, a Crystal, a Queen, a King, a Palace, a Lover and his Beloved, and this was long ago, on an Island somewhere in the ocean five thousand years ago. Such is Love, the Mystic Flower of the Soul. This is the Centre, the Self."

[SERRANO:] Jung spoke as though he were in a trance.

[JUNG:] "Nobody understands what I mean; only a poet could begin to understand."

In the Jungian secondary literature is there is no more concise an explanation of what lies at the semi-secret core of Jung's creation of "analytical psychology" than Serrano's following commentary on these remarks. They must be read carefully, however, to register. I have broken up some of the long paragraphs to make it easier to read. I have also made comments, set in separate, regular text, paragraphs, to draw the reader's attention to certain critical points easy to miss in the strange and sentimental language. Serrano continues:

> [SERRANO:] As one who revitalized the work of the Gnostics and the alchemists, [Jung] himself had to take part in their mysteries, even though he may originally have intended to remain outside of them.

Serrano is alluding to and addressing the common, but mistaken, belief that Jung's use of alchemical and "hermetic" language was exclusively metaphoric. Though it was that, it was not only that. He put certain of the metaphors into actual practice. Which ones, Serrano will make clear below.

> [SERRANO:] For neither the Gnostics nor the alchemists created symbols for the sake of psychological analysis, but for the sake of magic itself.

Serrano now focuses in on which practices of "alchemy" are at issue, relating directly to the previous citations concerning Jung's patient, and the "Individuation process" they engaged in together, which is also—in an as-yet undefined sense—a "mystic marriage."

> [SERRANO:] In philosophic alchemy, there exists the idea of the *Soror Mystica* ["Mystical Sister"] who works with the alchemist while he mixes his substances in his retorts. She is with him at all times throughout the long process of fusion, and at the end, there occurs a mystic wedding, involving the creation of the Androgyne…In the processes of individuation worked out in the Jungian laboratory between the patient and the analyst, the same fusion takes place…
>
> This psychic union never takes place in ordinary love…The magic wedding is alone capable of closing the gap. Jung said that this psychic union could only take place in a spirit of love, since only then would one be willing to risk everything. Nevertheless, the love of the psychic union is tricky and dangerous; it is a love without love, contrary to the laws of physical creation and history.

In the Jungian literature can be found many similar statements. It is often read as a less technical, more "poetic" way of talking about "transference," the love a patient may develop for an analyst, and "countertransference, the reverse. It is here meant to be just that—building upon Freud's conception of transference—but Serrano goes on to explain how it isn't only that. In Jung's view, these emotional events are not necessarily approached with the usual professional constraints.

> [SERRANO:] It is a forbidden love, which can only be fulfilled outside of matrimony. This love for the Queen of Sheba, then, does not produce a child of flesh, but a child of spirit, or of the imagination.

The "Queen of Sheba" is a favorite figure of the *Soror Mystica* in alchemy, and an important figure in the Grail legends as well. Note that Serrano first mentions her in response to Jung's musings about a union of the "King and Queen," in alchemy, most commonly referred to in that literature as the "coniunctio." Somewhat surprisingly, perhaps, this alchemical "coniunctio"—whatever it is— seems to be equally well symbolized by the union of "Christ and his church" as by King Solomon's illicit liaison with the Queen of Sheba (among other women). These passages therefore hint at a quite distinct "spiritual" or "mystical" perspective, one that is very far indeed from both Jewish and Christian understandings of moral constraint—in fact, its polar opposite. It somehow manages to alter things such that Christianity, alchemy (densely laden with polytheistic and astrological symbolism) and Courtly Love (the Grail tradition) can be seen as but different ways of indicating the same thing. The perspective that accomplishes this synthesis is not that of classical Christian mysticism, but of so-called "esoteric" or "occult" Christianity, that is Gnosticism.

> [SERRANO:] It is a fusion of opposing factors within the psyche of each of the lovers—it is a process of magical individuation.

The "fusion of opposing factors" refers to the central notion of alchemy and occult practice, as of Gnosticism: the *coniunctio oppositorum*, as it is fully called— the "union of opposites." But what, precisely are the opposites to be conjoined? The most important are (a) good and evil, which gives Gnostic morality its distinctively relativistic character: "Six thousand miles beyond good and evil" in the words of Nietzsche's *Übermensch*; and (b) male and female. Together, the abolition of these distinctives sets the stage for the "spiritualized" embracing of an androgynous sexuality, in all its variants, apart from the sacrament of marriage. It is sexuality per se that is the "new" sacrament. Serrano proceeds to make explicit this most delicate, and crucial, point, that the matter under discussion, though highly "symbolic," and spiritual, is not *only* that. :

> [SERRANO:] While it is true that this love does not exclude physical love, the physical becomes transformed into ritual.

Readers familiar with Iraneus' descriptions of Gnostic practices imported from the Indian/Persian basin 2,000 years ago should keep them in mind as the description proceeds. Key passages will be referenced shortly. Serrano continues, filling in the details, making clear that what lies behind the syncretic symbolism is simply *sexual magic*:

> [SERRANO:] The best way of explaining this complicated idea is to consider the Tantric practices of India, in which the Siddha magicians attempted to achieve psychic union. The ritual of the Tantras is complicated and mysterious. The initiate had to be chaste, and the woman would usually be one of the sacred

prostitutes…The man and the woman would go off together into the forest, living like brother and sister, like the alchemist and his sister, exchanging ideas, images and words. They would sleep together in the same bed, but they would not touch each other. Only after months of preparation would the final Tantric Mass take place, in which…Maithuna, or mystical coitus [was] performed. This act was the culmination of the long process of sublimation, during which the flesh was transformed and transfigured, just as in alchemy lead is converted into gold, and the act of coitus was really intended to ignite the mystic fire at the base of the vertebral column.

In the above paragraph, Serrano's language moves fluidly among a variety of symbol systems, since in this view, they are all but variants of each other: Tantra, magicians, "psychic union," sacred prostitution, alchemy, a "Mass" during which "mystical," yet also actual, sexual intercourse takes place. To someone unfamiliar with the unifying theme, all this may well have the sound of a somewhat confused, sentimental, mystical poetasting, meaning essentially nothing. Keep in mind, however, that Serrano is describing—in fact, *pre*scribing—actual practices. (A "Mass" during which sexual intercourse is performed, and which has the purpose of joining, *inter alia*, good and evil, is, of course, a so-called Black Mass.") In the last sentence Serrano explains why, to the symbol systems already introduced, he adds one more: Tantric or Kundalini Yoga. It is, in fact, the root system whence the others emerged. And, Kundalini Yoga was central to Jung's psychological and spiritual constructions. The images of this occult technique are ubiquitous in the Jungian world, whence they have spread widely throughout the West. It's inversion of Judeo-Christian symbolism of life and light (hence, the "Black" mass) is explained, and held up for emulation:

[SERRANO:] This inextinguishable fire is the product of supreme love, but has nothing whatever to do with the ordinary sexual act, in which something physical dies in order to produce a new life of flesh. In this love, the spirit of death is operative and produces a life of spirit. The woman is a priestess of magic love, whose function is to touch and awaken the various life cakras of the Tantric hero, who is thus permitted to reach new levels of consciousness until totality is achieved.

The practices being described are essentially the same as were found in the ancient pagan Temples of Canaan before, during and following the Biblical era— "Temple Prostitution," both heterosexual and homosexual—as well as in other locations around the Mediterranean basin, e.g. Corinth. (The homosexual variant happened to be separately highlighted and criticized by St. Paul, but like his forebears, he was equally opposed to all such practices, and in the name of the same God of Israel.) Symbolized by the "divine union" of Baal[7] and Ashtoreth, these forms of "spirituality," and the sacrifice of the fetuses and infants born from the "worship," are the chief object of prophetic wrath against "idolatry," in both Hebrew and Christian Scripture.

[SERRANO:] In the end, the pleasure that is gained is…the opening of the Third Eye, which represents the fusion of opposites. The man does not ejaculate the semen, but impregnates himself; and thus the process of creation is reversed and time is stopped. The product of this forbidden love is the Androgyne, the Total Man, all of whose cakras, or centres of consciousness, are now awakened. It is an encounter with the Self, that Last Flower of the soul on an Island five thousand years ago.

Serrano thus links this description to Jung's ten-year long, planned, "Individuation process" with his unnamed "patient." The goal is to waken the "god within," aptly named by Jung, the "Self."

[SERRANO:] "Only poets will be able to understand me." I realized now the force of Jung's words; I realized too that Jung, the magician, had almost alone made it possible for us today to take part in those Mysteries which seem capable of taking us back to that legendary land of the Man-God…

That is, these practices will enable the participants to experience godhood, the classic goal of all occult practices and of the condemned mystery religions of the Bible.

The final picture in the series drawn by Jung's "patient" was of the "thousand-petalled lotus," the classic symbol for the eruption of "Kundalini"—the serpent of mystic, "Luciferic," initiation—from the base of the spine into the highest cakra, awakening "cosmic consciousness."

In his case study, Jung presents the series of his patients' paintings as though they had all happened spontaneously. The larger Jungian literature is replete with similar studies that purport to demonstrate how "the psyche" and "the collective unconscious" spontaneously reproduce occult motifs in naive subjects. But there has never been any adequate evidence that the subjects are naive, and I know from my own experience how steeped in this material people swiftly seek to become, pulled in by transference and hero-worship.

Indeed, it is evident that this American "patient" was a member of Jung's Psychological Club (composed of present and former patients, at which he held forth) and most likely a participant in his seminars on Tantra (Kundalini) Yoga held in 1932 for Club members only, the contents of which remain semi-secret to this day (only analysts may purchase the notes from this seminar. They may not reproduce them).

The major text for the seminar was *The Serpent Power*, by Sir John Woodruffe, a book which for occultists is still the classic study of Kundalini Yoga. (Woodruffe published it under the tellingly Grail-evoking pseudonym, "Arthur Avalon.")

The patient was later confirmed to be Kristine Mann, who upon her return to America was to cofound the New York branch of the Psychological Club as well as the C. G. Jung Foundation of New York. Paintings of the Cakras after Woodroffe's plates still hang at the Foundation offices in Manhattan, where is located both the

Club itself and the Kristine Mann Library. Prior to her pilgrimage to Zürich, Mann had been prominent in Swedenborgian circles where she would have gained wide familiarity with occult motifs, specifically including those which in his case study Jung explicitly denies he could have "unintentionally infected her with."

What about the 1932 Club seminars themselves? They were held jointly by Jung and by Wilhelm Hauer, founder of the so-called German Faith Movement which sought to replace traditional Christianity with an Aryanized Christ, to replace worship of the LORD with worship of a Mother Goddess, and to replace the traditional Eucharist with occult initiation (in the spirit of the Grail legend as interpreted by Wagner). It aimed to resurrect the pagan vitality that, in line with the ideas of Nietzsche and others, had supposedly been all but killed by an essentially Jewish Christianity. In Hauer's own words (cited by Noll in an unrelated letter to *First Things*):

> The living world is the womb of the high human mind. The All Mother gives birth to Knowing, Being and Mind. We speak of a truly modern religion when we speak of the Mind-Child God, who lives in the womb of the All Mother. The basic religious feelings are Union, Blessedness and Holiness. The Christian sentiments of Sin, Guilt, and Repentance are not really religious feelings. They are artificially engendered complexes in man.

Within but a few years after this seminar, the German Faith Movement was officially adopted by the ascendant Nazi party as the official religion of Germany. Though Jung then somewhat distanced himself from Hauer's official position, he nonetheless continued to suggest to Hauer in letters that they publish together and hold additional joint seminars on "comparative religion." By this time, *Mein Kampf* had already sold over 200,000 copies.

III. Is the Contemporary Practice of Jungian Psychotherapy All That Bad?

Do modern Jungian analysts, then, consider themselves the inheritors of this "new," Aryan mystery religion? In spite of the striking congruences among late-twentieth-century Jungianism, modern liberal theologies and "spirituality" movements, and the German Faith Movement, the vast majority of Jungian analysts today see themselves simply as mental health professionals like any other, though with a keener than average interest in religion and matters spiritual. Few will recognize either themselves or their patients in the above reconstruction; most view themselves in the same naive light as do those many religious institutions which have adopted Jungian spirituality as but an updated version of their respective faiths. All are unseeing as to what they have been fellow travelers to; only a very small minority have ever been involved in relationships such as the ones Serrano describes above and which Jung himself indulged in on more than one occasion (Antonia Wolf, his mistress of forty years and another Club and Tantric Yoga participant, was his chief extramarital *Soror Mystica*); most would not even dream of seeking such a thing—not a few of those who *have* tried have been thrown out of practice altogether, by the Jungian institutes themselves.

Gnostic and occult notions are the most obvious features of Jungian thought. Nonetheless, most people remain unaware of the fact that occult theory, including Tantrism, lies only-partially-concealed at the heart of Jung's own inner experiences, theory and practice. For the most part this is because these ideas have been presented in the Jungian literature, are explained in Jungian training, and when they appear in patients' dreams will be interpreted almost exclusively in symbolic terms, not literally. So, for example, an alchemical picture of a man and woman coupling in a bath—or a dream of something similar—will be taken solely as a metaphor, of a "union of opposites" e.g., the "androgyne;" the reconciliation of good and evil as much as of masculine and feminine.

Furthermore, few people take the trouble to consult the original sources of these ideas and images, and depend instead on secondary or even tertiary interpretations in the Jungian literature. Someone extensively read in Jung and the Jungian literature does *not* acquire an education in them or their sorrier implications, though may superficially seem to. Hence the uncritical acceptance of certain ideas. On the other hand a solid familiarity with Jung's primary sources leads one to see through him. Likewise, a solid familiarity with clinical psychiatry and psychoanalysis leads one to accept but a limited subset of his work.

More importantly, it can and should be argued that the occult ideas embedded in Jungian theory and practice, even taken symbolically, tend to undermine moral standards. The very concept of a "union of opposites," especially at its supposedly highest level—the reconciliation of good and evil—is the dangerous vision found everywhere in Gnosticism, occultism and, indeed, outright Satanism. And yet even critics of the Jungian scheme have had the evidence before their eyes for decades, but have failed to see that however decent, sincere and relatively conventional may have been (and are) most of Jung's followers, Jung himself (and a small number of his closest disciples) had found a way to live out not only symbolically but explicitly the core practices of occultism.

In spite of Jung's massive and growing popularity today, he and his core circle insisted repeatedly that only a very small elite would succeed in "individuating," the hallmark of which is freedom from "bourgeois," "collective" constraint. The pretense to spiritual elitism has a marked adolescent quality. It forms yet another striking contrast to both Judaism and Christianity and their radical vision of all men as equal before God; it is a pretense further fueled by Jung's exaggerated, yet often unscholarly, erudition.

It is a testimony nonetheless to Jung's genius that he has been able to elevate and promote this particular kind of spiritual and ethical system without rousing nearly so much suspicion as he should have.

Nearly two thousand years ago, Iraneus, student of Polycarp (who in turn was discipled by John, the apostle who preeminently among the first Christian disciples battled the early Gnostics within Christianity) noted the following in his study of the Gnostics of his day:

> And committing many abominations and impieties, they run us down (who from the fear of God guard against sinning even in thought or word) as utterly contemptible and ignorant persons, while they highly exalt themselves, and claim to be perfect, and the elect seed. For they declare that we simply receive grace for use, but they have grace as their own special possession, which has descended from above by means of an unspeakable and indescribable conjunction and on this account more will be given them. They maintain, therefore, that in every way it is always necessary for them to practice the mystery of conjunction. And that they may persuade the thoughtless to believe this, they are in the habit of using these very words, "Whosoever being *in* this world does not so love a woman as to obtain possession of her, is not of the truth, nor shall attain to the truth. But whosoever being *of* this world has intercourse with woman, shall not attain to the truth, because he has so acted under the power of concupiscence." On this account, they tell us that it is necessary for us whom they call *animal* men, and describe as being *of* the world, to practice continence and good works, that by this means we may attain at length to the intermediate habitation, but that to them who are called "*the spiritual and perfect*" such a course of conduct is not at all necessary.[8]

Neither is the moral character of a Gnostic worldview, ancient or contemporary, confined to individual, merely private, action, lacking effect upon the community. Miguel Serrano, quoted above, published his book on Hesse and Jung with Schocken, the Jewish house that specializes in Jewish mysticism and in the works of such great Israeli scholars as Gershom Scholem (who was likewise a sometime colleague of Jung). And yet in 1975, *Life* magazine published a photograph of Serrano—in his capacity as a diplomat—attending the Argentine funeral of a former high-ranking Nazi officer, one of the many who had escaped prosecution after fleeing to South America following the war. Serrano and two compatriots are captured standing at the graveside, all three dressed in long matching black leather coats; all three offering their departed colleague the stiff-armed Nazi salute.

Only now, at a time when Jungian and Jungian-related spirituality, with its emphasis on Gnostic "wisdom," sexual freedom, Eastern mysticism, pantheism, goddess worship and accommodation with evil has infiltrated deeply into the church has the veil at long last begun to be lifted.

Everywhere today people claim that Jung revitalized a moribund "patriarchal" morality—and yet that in newly preaching his ancient gospel they are reinvigorating Christianity, not replacing it with something entirely different. Are they? Here is the opinion of one of the most eminent of American Jungian analysts, author of numerous books and a Yale-educated former man of the cloth himself, a convinced follower of Jung, who now tours the country with Elaine Pagels of Harvard explicitly promoting the superiority of the Gnostic gospels found at Nag Hammadi:

What Jung foresaw as a possible future for Christianity… would in many ways be continuous with Christian tradition, but also be very different from it. Jung's concept of Christianity's transformation is on this order: [that]… Christianity and its authoritative source book, the New Testament, would become for the transformed version of the tradition what Judaism and the Old Testament became for Christianity, a perforation and forerunner of the new revelation.[9]

Jung was not himself a major influence in the outburst of occult-mindedness in prewar, early-to-mid-twentieth-century Europe; he was rather the recipient of this influence from others. But having absorbed, digested, and resynthesized in brilliant (psychological) fashion what he received, he has become its major fount in its postwar, late twentieth-century re-eruption—an eruption confined no longer to predominantly Germanic middle Europe (and to a few English aristocrats and civil servants), but spread out widely across the globe, especially to America. As Jung himself foretold sixty years ago in his essay on "Wotan" and Nazi Germany:

National Socialism [is]…not…the last word. Things must be concealed in the background which we cannot imagine at present, but we may expect them to appear in the course of the next few years or decades. Wotan's reawakening is a stepping back into the past; the stream was dammed up…But the obstruction will not last forever…the water will overleap the obstacle.[10]

Much of what we now see happening in the domains of religion and spirituality and culture can be laid at Jung's doorstep—the modern amalgam of goddess worship and polytheism; the replacement of morality-oriented Jewish and Christian worship with ancient pagan initiation rituals; resurgent pantheism in "environmental" and pseudo-scientific guise; and above all a brutal moral relativism, the result of the reconciliation of good and evil which forms the ever-recurring, always transmuting, heretical heart of Gnosticism in every age .

How salutary is this pagan "new revelation?" Heinrich Heine, the mid-nineteenth century German Jewish-Christian poet peered a century into his own era's future, and saw the end result of that same process of religious transformation, then restricted only to middle Europe. His words should be a caution to us as well:

…should ever that taming talisman break—the Cross—then will come roaring back the wild madness of the ancient warriors, with all their insane, Berserker rage, of whom our Nordic poets speak and sing. That talisman is now already crumbling, and the day is not far off when it shall break apart entirely. On that day, the old stone gods will rise from their long forgotten wreckage and rub from their eyes the dust of a thousand years' sleep. At long last leaping to life, Thor with his giant hammer will crush the gothic cathedrals. And laugh not at my forebodings, the advice of a dreamer who warns you away from the…*Naturphilosophen*. No, laugh not at the visionary who knows that in the realm of phenomena comes soon the revolution that has already taken place in the realm of spirit. For thought goes before deed as lightning before thunder. There will be played in Germany a play compared to which the French revolution was but an innocent idyll.

What Heine rightly saw was that the morality of a culture is intimately bound to religion, and that the behavior of the people who carry that culture are likewise bound. To be moral, it as a whole and they as individuals must be bound to a religion that is (at least sufficiently) *true*—else the consequences will be dire. Paganism is also a religion; it has its own, polyvalent (because polytheistic—in effect, "multicultural" or "multitribal") moralities.

Judaism and Christianity, as well as Islam, the great monotheistic faiths rooted in Judaism, all tie morality to a very specific God who is God of all men, not merely of some—however offensive this claim now seems to many. And He is a God who both loves and judges according to a specific, unitary and unvarying set of transcendent standards. (The similarities among monotheistic moralities are far greater than their differences, when viewed against pagan polytheism.) A psychology which, in the name of neutrality, does not grapple with the demand made by the monotheistic standard, will sooner or later descend into, and become a carrier for, pagan polymorality. Jung has thus only made explicit that which an earlier generation of psychologists would neither have anticipated nor accepted.

The God of Biblical morality offers all men choice—but of a specific kind. He does not hold out an unlimited smorgasbord of moral options free of consequence, but delimits that freedom precisely. He abjures with fierceness all relativization, conduction of good and evil, however subtle and crafty. He makes a simple, binary offer, in which "the opposites" are maintained forever apart, utterly irreconcilable:

"Here are my claims; make of them what you will: I say that *these* standards and none other suit your distinctive natures—your "psychology", as you now call it—because I designed those natures. However implausible it may seem to you in your turning from Me, such standards alone can produce true good, and deep satisfaction, in your lives."

"Other, smaller, truths that, by the power of your own minds, you will surely discover, may indeed assist you in clinging to these standards—and so employed will be beneficent. But as for 'truths' that violate or confute these standards, I claim are no truths; their gods no gods."

"These claims I lay before you. You may accept them, or you may reject them. You may worship Me, or you may worship another god, but knowingly or not, worship you will. And if it seem evil unto you to serve the LORD, choose you this day whom ye will serve....I call heaven and earth to record this day against you, that I have set before you life and death, blessing and cursing: therefore choose life, that both thou and thy seed may live."

Of course, Jungian psychology is merely a vector, one among many—albeit an especially effective one. The affliction it carries is rather the Gnostic and occult ideas and practices which, in varying guise, most often unnamed and unrecognized, are now spreading rapidly through the West as vain slake to our profound spiritual thirst. Via these we turn inward to worship the instincts of man—power, sex, wealth, pleasure in all its guises: gods which are no gods. As prophesied by Heine—as by prophets long before him, again and again—such worship can only spell catastrophe. Consider: there is but a single day between the writing on the wall and the closing act.[11]

NOTES

1. Iraneus. *Iraneus Against Heresies*, Book I. In *The Apostolic Fathers with Justin Martyr and Iraneus*. Ante-Nicene Fathers, Volume 1. Editors: Alexander Roberts and James Donaldson (Peabody, Mass. Hendrickson Publishers, 1994). Cited in Jerome Politzer, *The Counterfeit Prayer Book.* (The Prayer Book Society of the Episcopal Church, 1987).

2. Ibid., p. 41.

3. Ibid., p. 40.

4. Ginette Paris, *The Sacrament of Abortion* (Dallas: Spring Publications, 1992) p. 19, cf.

5. Richard Noll, *The Jung Cult: Origins of a Charismatic Movement.* (Princeton: Princeton University Press, 1995).

6. This case, "A Study in the Process of Individuation," comprises a major portion of Volume 9,1 of Jung's *Collected Works.*

7. Among his many epithets, Baal is known as the "LORD of the Hole."

8. Iraneus. op. cit., p. 325.

9. Jews have long suffered the consequences of the common Christian claim that, having been replaced by the Church, as a people they no longer had any reason to exist. Perhaps a common mortal enemy will bring about the mutual love and dependency that a common God apparently could not.

10. C. G. Jung, "Wotan," *Collected Works* vol. 10, pp. 180, 192.

11. But thou hast lifted up thyself against the Lord of heaven; and…hast praised the gods of silver, and gold, of brass, iron, wood, and stone, which see not, nor hear, nor know: and the God in whose hand thy breath is, and whose are all thy ways, hast thou not glorified:

    Then was the part of the hand sent from him; …And this is the writing that was written, *Mene, Mene, Tekel, Upharsin.* This is the interpretation of the thing: *Mene*; God hath numbered thy kingdom, and finished it. *Tekel*; Thou art weighed in the balances, and art found wanting. *Peres*; Thy kingdom is divided.

    In that night was Belshazzar the king of the Chaldeans slain. [KJV Daniel 5:23-30]

Appendix:
Philosophical Principles of the Institute for Personalist Psychology

In an effort to define its own *personalist* goals, IPP has drawn up a list of ten philosophical principles. IPP intends its conferences and publication efforts to further substantiate the truth of these theses, and to integrate them into psychological research, teaching, and clinical practice.

1. The Nature of Evidence. Because human beings are complex beings, and because each scientific procedure has its limitations, we encourage the use of a wide variety of methods of studying the person. This requires the psychologist to espouse a broad notion of evidence, to view evidence as any way in which a truth reveals itself. Such a notion of evidence will serve to justify supplementing the traditional empirical methods of psychology with the use of philosophical methods of research in psychology, particularly as one approaches peculiarly personal phenomena such as love, freedom, ethical action, and religious practice.

2. Human Beings as Personal Beings. Human beings must not be viewed simply as "higher animals," but must be seen in their specifically personal dimension. In referring to persons, we refer to beings who are ordinarily, and most properly, conscious, rational, free, responsible, related to a world of values, and capable of recognizing themselves as the subject of action. While fully recognizing that intellectual abilities and personality develop and change throughout life, IPP recognizes all human beings as persons.

3. The Spiritual Dimension of Human Persons. Recognizing the personal dimension of human beings entails that we view them as more than physical beings, as spiritual beings who may rise above the chains of causality found in the material world, and preserve a self-identity which goes beyond the identity of their bodies. This is not to deny that persons depend upon their brains and are intimately and mysteriously united to their bodies. We emphasize only that persons are not identical to their bodies or bodily processes.

4. The Objectivity of Value. Human beings are capable of being motivated by goods and values which are objective insofar as they are discovered, rather than subjectively produced. These goods may offer human life meaning and direction, as well as make demands upon human behavior. The moral life consists largely in the conformity of human responses to these goods as they exist in a hierarchy. The task of counseling is not merely to enter the subjective world of the patient, but to help the patient turn to and conform to reality. ,

5. Rationality. Rationality arises from the ability of persons to transcend themselves and respond to reality appropriately. In its fullest sense, rationality presupposes that one apprehend not only what is true, but also what is good and of value. This feature of persons also contributes to the ethical life, in which not only our judgments, but our actions must conform to what is true and good.

6. Human freedom. Without freedom, a variety of personal acts such as taking responsibility, making promises, loving another person for his or her own sake, and many others, would be impossible. It is not denied that some human behaviors arise from compulsions or unconscious causes, but it is evident that some human actions, indeed those of the greatest significance, are free.

7. Moral responsibility. Intimately connected with the abililty to perceive values and to act freely is the responsiblity of the human person. Thus, it is correct to attribute guilt and praise to human persons and their action. Certainly there exist feelings of guilt or obligation which do not correspond to any true guilt or obligation. These must be identified as such, and worked through. However, any counseling activity which seeks to free persons from feelings of guilt must be accompanied by a sensitivity to instances of real guilt and a willingness to pursue themes of forgiveness and reparation.

8. The Religious Dimension. Religious beliefs and practices need not be the product of unhealthy psychological needs, nor a sign of superstitious or underdeveloped patterns of thinking. In fact, it may well be that a nonreligious person cannot find adequate answers to the most fundamental questions concerning the nature and meaning of human life. It is not the business of IPP to promote one religion as true, but only to affirm that religious practice has a healthy and legitimate place in the life of the individual and society.

9. The Limitations of Human Persons. A realistic understanding of the aims of counseling and research entails recognition of the fact that no amount of counseling or social engineering can free human beings of all personal and moral short-comings. Human beings are by nature imperfect, and all human perfections are limited.

10. Society and the Family. Human beings are social by nature, and develop intellectually, spiritually, emotionally and morally within a variety of social settings. IPP holds that the most basic and essential social structure for personal development is the family, including here both mother and father. Cases of death, divorce, unexpected pregnancy, severe abuse and the like, often prevent this ideal from being realized, but the committed relationship of a man and a woman remains the ideal. This assertion is not intended as a political judgment, but rather as a psychological fact, and a consideration for individual and marriage and family counselors.

About the Authors

Marvin Berkowitz, Ph.D., is an associate professor of psychology at Marquette University. He is the associate director of the Center for Ethics Studies as well as of the Center for Addiction and Behavioral Health Research located at Marquette. He is the co-editor of, and a contributor to, *Moral Education: Theory and Application.*

Josef Seifert, Ph.D., is the Rector of, and a professor at, the International Academy of Philosophy in the Principality of Liechtenstein. He is the author of numerous books on the body-soul problem, the theory of knowledge, ethics, and, forthcoming in English, *What is Life?*

Paul Vitz, Ph.D., is a professor of psychology at New York University, a practicing psychologist in Manhattan, and the author of *Psychology as Religion: The Cult of Self-Worship* and *Freud's Christian Unconscious.*

Philip Mango, Ph.D., is a practicing psychotherapist in Manhattan and Bethesda, Maryland. He is a founding member of Human Sciences International.

Robert Kugelmann, Ph.D., is an associate professor and the chair of the department of psychology at the University of Dallas. He is the author of *Stress: The Nature and History of Engineered Grief.*

Howard Kendler, Ph.D., is a professor emeritus at the University of California, Santa Barbara, and author of *Psychology: A Science in Conflict* and *Historical Foundations of Modern Psychology.*

John Crosby, Ph.D., is the chair of the department of philosophy at Franciscan University of Steubenville, and author of a forthcoming book entitled, *The Structure of Personal Selfhood.*

Richard Cross, Ph.D., is an associate professor of psychology at Franciscan University and a co-founder of the psychology and psychiatry sectionof the Society of Catholic Social Scientists. He is the author of articles on psychometrics and the philosophy of psychology.

John White, Ph.D., is the chair of philosophy at St. Mary's College in Michigan, and the author of articles in philosophy and the theory of knowledge.

Jeffrey Burke Satinover, M.D., is a practicing psychiatrist and the former president of the Jungian Society. He has taught at Yale Univerity, and is the author of numerous articles in scienfic journals and of a recent book entitled, *Homosexuality and the Politics of Truth.*

James DuBois, Ph.D., is an assistant professor in the Viktor Frankl chair for philosophy and psychology at the International Academy of Philosopy in Liechtenstein, and the director of the Institute for Personalist Psychology. He is the editor of *The Nature and Tasks of a Personalist Psychology.*